W9-BSZ-505

eBrands

eBrands

BUILDING AN INTERNET BUSINESS ▼
AT BREAKNECK SPEED

Phil Carpenter

WITHDRAWN

HARVARD BUSINESS SCHOOL PRESS

Boston, Massachusetts

Copyright © 2000 President and Fellows of Harvard College

All rights reserved

Printed in the United States of America

04   03   02   01   00   5   4   3   2   1

Library of Congress Cataloging-in-Publication Data

Carpenter, Phil, 1967–
   eBrands : building an Internet business at breakneck speed / Phil Carpenter.
   p. cm.
   Includes index.
   ISBN 0-87584-929-6 (alk. paper)
   1. Business names 2. Brand name products. 3. Electronic commerce.
4. Internet (Computer network) I. Title.
HD69.B7 C37 2000
658.8′4—dc21   99-089360

The paper used in this publication meets the requirements of the American
National Standard for Permanence of Paper for Publications and Documents
in Libraries and Archives Z39.48–1992.

To Carol and Jessica

Contents

Acknowledgments   ix

Introduction   1

CHAPTER 1   **iVillage**   15

CHAPTER 2   **CDNOW**   61

CHAPTER 3   **Barnesandnoble.com**   109

CHAPTER 4   **Yahoo!**   153

CHAPTER 5   **Fogdog Sports**   205

CHAPTER 6   **Onsale**   231

Conclusion   267
Appendix: Coordinates   269
Notes   273
Index   287
About the Author   301

Acknowledgments

I began writing this book in the late fall of 1997. Over the last two years, I have spent numerous mornings here in my study, watching the shorebirds below as I attempt to structure my thoughts on the fluid field of Internet marketing. It is quiet work done solo.

To get to the point of putting thoughts on paper, however, I have relied on the support of many people. Their help goes to show how much the success of a project like this one depends on people beyond the author, and I'd like to take this opportunity to express my thanks.

I'll start with the marketing and executive teams at iVillage, CDNOW, Yahoo!, Barnesandnoble.com, Fogdog Sports, and Onsale. These high-tech professionals opened their "corporate kimonos" for me, enabling me to study their marketing activities in detail. Without their support, this book would not have been possible. I greatly appreciate their willingness to give me an inside look at the way their companies work.

I also drew good insights from conversations with representatives from the ad agencies and PR firms that work with the companies I've featured, as well as the research firms that follow them. Their perspectives as informed outsiders provided valuable input, and I'm thankful for the time they devoted to my background interviews.

A number of my current and former colleagues deserve special mention. Sue Barsamian and Lisa Ramirez have been my fellow marketing provocateurs at RemarQ, and I've enjoyed hashing through challenging Web marketing issues with them. While at PointCast, I learned much about both marketing and management from Ann Shepherd, Lisa Gerould, Bob Sofman, Don Albert, Adam Smithline, Stephanie Gnibus, and Jaleh Bisharat. Their intellectual and moral support for this project—as well as their friendship—has been important to me.

Special thanks should also go to Bill Crandall, Warren Packard, and John Foster. These three friends gave me good advice on my early drafts; I've appreciated their thoughtful counsel.

My agent, Alice Martell, my transcriber, Leslie Dawson, and my editor, Kirsten Sandberg, also offered critical assistance. Alice not only sold the book, but also provided advice on myriad issues along the way to publication. Leslie was patient enough to transcribe the more than forty interviews I taped during my research, providing me with essential raw material. And Kirsten's editorial eye and intellectual guidance were of great help.

Finally, I'd like to say how important the support of my family has been for me during the time it has taken to turn my original ideas into a completed book. My parents, writers themselves, gave me excellent editorial advice. My daughter, Jessica, offered smiles and laughter that were a great spiritual boost. And my wife, Carol, gave me her love, her industry insights, and the gift of time.

Thank you, one and all.

Phil Carpenter
December 1999

eBrands

Introduction

Imagine that you're walking down the aisle of the local grocery store on your weekly shopping run. As you reach for the laundry detergent, you're surprised to see the range of options in front of you suddenly double. You attempt to grab the fabric softener. The number of brands on the shelf doubles—then triples—in about thirty seconds. Choice rapidly becomes overwhelming.

Welcome to the Internet. Although the variety of products available at your local Safeway or Star Market is clearly not increasing at warp speed, the number of sites on the Web is. From its origins as a communications network for the government, military, and academics, the Internet made its commercial debut in 1994. By 1999, there were more than 800 million pages of content on the Web. The most robust search engine covered a mere 16 percent of this content.

Although launching a new consumer product such as a soft drink or shampoo may require tens of millions of dollars, on the Internet, barriers to entry are low—at least on the technical end. Starting yet another yellow pages site, for example, requires little more than basic programming skills and a CD-ROM full of phone numbers. The extraordinary growth in the number of sites to choose from has caused confusion and frustration for the average Internet user.

In an environment characterized by extreme choice, perplexed customers will turn to the familiar. They will establish relationships with specific Internet brands and do business with them repeatedly. This assumption is confirmed by a recent *Business Week*/Harris poll, which found that 57 percent of Internet users go to the same sites again and again, rather than drifting from one site to the next.[1] As the number of companies online multiplies, the increased choice will strengthen customer/company relationships—not weaken them—for those organizations that have built premier Internet brands.

The rewards for those firms that craft major online brands will be impressive. Global consumer ecommerce is projected to generate $1.3 trillion a year by 2003.[2] Business-to-business sales will reach $1.5 trillion that same year.[3] The Internet advertising sector should hit close to $22 billion in annual revenues by 2004.[4] These are large, promising markets. Already, power is flowing to those companies with brand cachet. In the Internet advertising category, for example, 75 percent of all advertising revenues currently goes to the top ten advertising-supported sites.[5] For companies that want to profit from the growth of the Internet, the time to invest in Internet branding is now.

The time to invest in Internet branding is now.

As a high-tech marketing professional, I've struggled with the challenges of Internet marketing and brand development for several years. Along with my industry colleagues, I've observed closely companies that have been successful in developing dynamic Internet brands, as well as companies that have failed. I've written this book to pass along the lessons learned by a number of these firms, a set of companies whose collective experience offers valuable insights for those looking to build Internet brands of their own or to understand the companies that are working to do so.

The Case Studies ▼

eBrands is built on an analysis of the brand-building efforts of six companies. Four of them, which represent the core of the book, are established Internet ventures that rose to the challenge of developing brands distinctly for this new medium. The fifth is a brick-and-mortar company that has brought its brand from the physical world to the Web (such companies are sometimes referred to as *crossover marketers*). The sixth is an Internet start-up, a firm just beginning to develop a brand on the Web at a time when it is becoming increasingly expensive to do so. Each chapter focuses on one of these case study companies.

How did I select these six firms? While none of them is perfect, they've all uncovered key ingredients required to build a robust Internet brand. Some have made innovative use of both traditional and unconventional tools to raise awareness of their products or services. Others have locked in distribution agreements that have brought them competitive advantage, or have developed an intimate knowledge of customer needs. These are companies that have made some smart choices; their successes are worth study.

Equally informative, however, are their flaws. All of the companies I've included in this book have their shortcomings—even a firm such as Yahoo!, which many see as the strongest brand on the Web. The companies I've profiled have made their share of mistakes. And all face substantial short- and long-term challenges. The lessons to be learned from both past gaffes and prospective problems are just as important as the knowledge that can be distilled from the victories of these firms. The companies included here all have multidimensional stories to tell.

Are these organizations profitable? No—with the exception of Yahoo!. But these are the early days of the commercialization of the Internet; we are still in investment mode. Canny companies realize this and are willing to invest in their brands now based on anticipated future returns.

iVillage ▼

iVillage—The Women's Network—is a collection of popular branded Internet communities designed for wired women. The company has crafted destinations for people who want to share information about real-life issues with others who face similar challenges, from how to ask for a raise to how to find a nanny. iVillage sites such as Parent Soup and Better Health are branded virtual spaces that attract and retain a base of highly loyal customers, people who not only visit these sites frequently themselves but also encourage friends and colleagues to do the same.

CDNOW ▼

CDNOW is an online music retailer, one of the top shopping sites on the Web. Customers can select from among hundreds of thousands of titles, from Janis Joplin to Scott Joplin, from Elvis Costello to Elvis Presley. To help people make informed purchasing choices, CDNOW complements commerce with content from sources such as MTV and *Rolling Stone*. And once someone has bought from CDNOW, the company sends him regular emails to keep him posted about new music he might enjoy, one of several loyalty-building strategies that contribute to repeat purchase rates of over 50 percent.

Barnesandnoble.com ▼

Barnes & Noble is the behemoth of the book industry. With over 481 of its own branded bookstores and 520 B. Dalton stores under its management, Barnes & Noble is well known in the "real world." When the company entered the online arena, it was more than a year behind start-up Amazon.com. In a short time, however, Barnesandnoble.com forged a substantial presence online, porting its powerful offline brand to this new medium and initiating a Coke vs. Pepsi–style battle for market dominance. Other old-world companies have had mixed success in their efforts to bring their brands online. Time Warner, for example, saw a poor reception for Pathfinder, its Web-based amalgamation of magazines such as *People* and *Time*. Barnesandnoble.com offers an intriguing case study of an offline firm that has managed the move to the Internet effectively. To supplement the Barnesandnoble.com example, the chapter that covers the company compares and contrasts its Web marketing efforts with those of other organizations with offline roots, such as the Gap and Playboy Enterprises.

Yahoo! ▼

Yahoo! has grown from what was once a distracting pastime for two Stanford grad students to a public company with more than 1700 employees and perhaps the most powerful brand on the Internet. What's more, Yahoo! is an Internet company that actually turns a profit. The firm's comprehensive Net directory is the first stop for millions of surfers every day as they attempt to hunt down valuable information within the labyrinth of data the Internet represents. Yahoo! also provides a host of other services, such as free email and personalized stock portfolios, that have made Yahoo! usage a regular habit for a great many of its customers. To build significant traffic and long-term customer loyalty, management realized that providing a valuable information resource was not enough. Instead, Yahoo! has created a distinct brand personality, a whimsical, approachable character captured in its "Do You Yahoo?" tagline. It is a brand identity that has made a wide audience of Internet users feel at ease with Yahoo!, helping the company to earn its place as the Web's most highly trafficked portal site.

Fogdog Sports ▼

Fogdog Sports is a classic Internet start-up. Founded by a group of young guys from Stanford University, the company sells all manner of sports equipment via the Web—from snowshoes to skateboard wheels. Fogdog is working to build a strong Internet brand; although the service itself is outstanding, the company is facing a variety of challenges as it attempts to make a name for itself in consumer ecommerce. This chapter charts both past accomplishments and prospective problems for the firm as it drives to become the Web's leading sporting goods retailer.

Onsale ▼

The originator of the online auction, Onsale sells computer gear to small business customers both at auction and in a standard, fixed-price retail format. The auction side of the business has been the company's historical focus; more than a million customers have registered to bid on merchandise through Onsale since the service first launched in May 1995. These customers have been extremely loyal, with 77 percent of them returning to make repeat purchases. The company is poised to merge with Egghead.com, the online reincarnation of the former brick-and-mortar retail chain. The new company, which will use the Egghead.com name, will emerge with a stronger fixed-price store to complement its core auction services. The union of the two companies will result in a Web retailer of Amazon.com-like proportions, but with a keen focus on a single category: computer products.

Establishing Common Ground   ▼

Words such as *brand* and *branding* are thrown around loosely in the Internet arena. People frequently have narrowly defined, incomplete, and even incorrect definitions for the words. In talking about "the brand," for example, some focus on things such as logos or taglines, elements that are small parts of a greater whole. But unless the conversation is about a specific marketing communications issue, such as designing a new corporate ID, when marketers refer to *brand*, they are usually using verbal shorthand for a larger concept: brand equity.

To establish some common ground for the analysis of the six companies described earlier, let's begin with some definitions. David Aaker, a marketing professor at the University of California at Berkeley, defines the following terms in his book *Managing Brand Equity:*[6]

> *brand:* a distinguishing name and/or symbol (such as a logo, trademark, or package design) intended to identify the goods or services of either one seller or a group of sellers, and to differentiate those goods or services from those of competitors.

> *brand equity:* a set of brand assets and liabilities linked to a brand, its name and symbol, that add to or subtract from the value provided by a product or service to a firm and/or to that firm's customers.

The more holistic concept of brand equity is at the center of this book. I'm not interested in merely telling you about how Barnesandnoble.com developed its logo. I want to look at subjects such as the techniques the firm has used to generate brand awareness, the ways in which the company has developed brand loyalty, and its approach to securing distribution through strategic partnerships with other Web players. For although creating a great logo may be hard, getting these other things right is much harder. To truly understand why and how a particular company has developed a strong Internet brand, we need to look at a much richer set of issues.

Best Practices ▼

As I looked at the histories of the six companies you'll read about in this book, it became clear that there were key similarities in the way they approached the process of building strong Internet brands. I've captured these concepts here as a set of best practices. Note that not all six firms have adhered to each of these ideas. For example, while Barnesandnoble.com has certainly invested in developing strong distribution and content alliances, it didn't enter the market early, nor has it moved particularly fast when contrasted with other Web players. But each of the six has followed most of these practices. Operating based on these ideas, I would argue, has been a key success driver for these Internet leaders.

Focus on Building Brand Awareness   The Internet players that have set themselves apart from the crowd are those that have made a major commitment to building awareness. To do so means making effective use of a broad range of tools. Offline advertising, for example, is essential because it enables companies to reach and influence large audiences. (Think of Barnesandnoble.com, which has used radio, outdoor advertising, and similar vehicles to tell millions of people about its online store.) Guerrilla marketing ploys can seize customer attention, although on a smaller scale. (If you saw a purple and yellow Yahoo! mobile pass you on the highway, you'd certainly take notice!) And public relations can both generate substantial exposure and enhance credibility. Building brand awareness in the Internet space requires a significant investment of both management time and money. Gone are the "if you build it, they will come" days of the early 1990s. The winners on the Web are proving to be the companies fiercely dedicated to making themselves known names in the markets they serve.

Cultivate Customer Commitment   Much of the focus in the early days of Web marketing has been on acquiring customers. The most successful Internet companies, however, are those that are equally obsessed with keeping the customers they bring through their virtual doors. CDNOW, for example, has repeat customer rates of greater than 50 percent. Sending its customers regular updates by email on the music they care about, tailoring the site to meet shoppers' prefer-

▼
The "Mo Factor"

The strongest Internet brands are like landslides. As they begin to pick up speed, they gain mass, then more speed, then more mass, until soon little can stand in their way. Smart Internet marketers know the power of the "mo factor" (a term frequently used at Excite, the well-known Web portal company, with "mo" being short for momentum). As part of their awareness-building efforts, they do everything in their power to communicate to the market the momentum behind their brands—most frequently through public relations. As soon as they cut a big distribution deal, they're out talking about it. When they hit the "X million customers served" mark, they let the industry analysts know. (Onsale makes such announcements regularly; it has gained particular attention by pointing out the increasingly shorter intervals between one milestone announcement and the next.) Smart online marketers know that with momentum behind them, barriers to business success get pushed out of the way. Strategic partners become more eager to develop alliances. Potential competitors think twice about entering the category. Customers see the company as a winner, which strengthens the perceived quality of the brand. Savvy Internet marketers thus do all they can to communicate momentum, for they know the impact the "mo factor" can have on their success.

ences through its My CDNOW program, rewarding customers with "frequent buyer" points—all of these are initiatives that have kept people loyal to CDNOW. iVillage has developed intense customer commitment by cultivating an online community, a place for women on the Web to seek answers, exchange opinions, and build relationships. Focusing on loyalty has not only meant repeat business, it has transformed customers into disciples, avid supporters who have spread the word about iVillage to friends and colleagues. A dedication to keeping customers—not just getting them—is a practice that unites Web leaders.

Forge Strong Distribution and Content Alliances   Internet companies operate in a highly interdependent environment. Rather than attempt to do too much on their own, the sharper players have focused on building alliances, particularly to secure both content and distribution. For example, instead of developing volumes of information on child-rearing issues itself, iVillage turned to *American Baby* for the content it needed to enrich its site. Rather than focus only on direct appeals to sporting goods buyers, Fogdog Sports teamed up with America Online (AOL) to secure exposure within key departments of Shop@AOL, enabling the start-up to leverage the substantial traffic that AOL had already aggregated. The Internet firms that have made the most headway are those that have realized that on the Web, you can't go it alone.

Move Early, Move Fast   As the title of this book implies, building an Internet business is a frenetic process. Many of those who appear to have gained the lead are the firms that not only entered key markets early, but have maintained a breakneck pace along the way. Yahoo! pioneered the concept of a Web directory. But the company hasn't slowed down since it began, driving the evolution of its category from search to portal by constantly adding content and features to get visitors to spend more time on the site. Fogdog Sports was the first retailer to make a serious attempt to sell sporting goods online. Since it opened its virtual doors, Fogdog has been constantly driving the business forward, adding new merchandise categories, partnering with new suppliers, even looking at how to expand overseas. Winning online not only means recognizing an opportunity early on, but maintaining a torrid pace once you've moved on that opportunity.

Develop an Intimate Knowledge of the Market and Customer   Developing a detailed understanding of customer needs and market dynamics has been core to the success of Web leaders such as those profiled in *eBrands*. iVillage, for example, has leveraged its research into customer needs and attitudes to develop new online discussion forums and to deepen its content offerings in key areas. Barnesandnoble.com has tapped its study of how customers interacted with the site to simplify its order process and thus increase sales. Looking outward, not inward, is a practice that Web leaders share.

Cultivate a Reputation for Excellence Word of mouth is a key driver of success in the Internet space. Savvy Internet marketers have realized that to benefit from the rapid growth that positive word-of-mouth support will provide, they must focus intently on cultivating a reputation for excellence. How have they translated this aim into action? Onsale has worked to make the purchasing process simple, even fun. From the bidding guide it offers to help new users understand how to participate in an auction to its order confirmation emails, the company has dedicated itself to providing an outstanding shopping experience. Yahoo! has pushed not only to deliver a rich array of functionality, but to do so based

Companies that nail the value equation are taking off on the Web.

on a site design that is clear, consistent, and speedy. Their continuous commitment to qual- ity is helping these companies to establish first-rate reputations, which in turn translate into traffic and transactions as the good word spreads.

Deliver Outstanding Value Business school types like to talk about value as a ratio that compares the quality of a product or service to its cost (this ratio is known as the *value equation*). The best Internet brands are those that maximize value according to this definition, as do those featured in this book. Barnesandnoble.com offers a vast array of products that are available for easy purchase at competitive prices. Yahoo! provides its customers with rich content and functionality, ranging from email to scheduling, at no cost whatsoever. The companies that nail the value equation are the ones taking off on the Web.

Crossover Marketers ▼

Crossover marketers are those companies that began their lives offline and have since expanded their businesses to take advantage of the Web. Although the majority of the companies analyzed in this book were born on the Web, I thought it was important to highlight one—Barnesandnoble.com—that had its origins in the real world. As I researched Barnesandnoble.com, I also looked at a number of other crossover marketers (some of which are profiled in chapter sidebars) to see how the company compared with its kin in the move to the Web. And in evaluating these firms, I noticed the following subset of best practices that linked most of the leaders.

Respect Core Brand Elements   The companies that have been most successful in bringing real-world brands to the Internet have a deep understanding of what makes their brands distinctive and bring these brand elements with them when they go online. When you visit Barnesandnoble.com, for example, you'll see the same green color that is found throughout the decor and marketing materials in the retail store. The book readings by well-known authors held in the retail stores have also been brought to the Web, where visitors to the Barnesandnoble.com site have regular opportunities to participate in online chats with writers ranging from Tom Clancy to Tony Hillerman. These are just a few of the basic elements that are at the core of the Barnes & Noble brand. In developing for the Web, Barnesandnoble.com has brought these elements along, maintaining a consistency that makes the customer who is new to the site comfortable, and communicating the character and promise of a brand that millions of people have come to know outside of cyberspace.

One-up Offline Brands   Although smart crossover marketers look to maintain the kind of brand consistency described in the previous section, they also realize that to be successful on the Web, they need to expand the definition of the brand experience to go beyond the kind of interaction that their customers would have with their brands in the real world. Visit the Barnesandnoble.com site and you have instant access to a number of recommended reading lists—a great help when you're looking for a novel to take with you on vacation. To get a sense for what's hot, you can also visit their Books in the News area, which highlights books about current events or books that are getting press themselves, as well as providing the latest reviews from publications such as the *New York Times,* the *Atlantic Monthly,* and *People.* Such features are consistent with the character of the offline brand, yet are above and beyond the kind of information you can find in the Barnes & Noble retail store.

Leverage Key Offline Assets   For organizations looking to bring a real-world brand to the Internet, leveraging the value of offline assets to develop customer familiarity with the Web-based version of that brand is critical. Barnesandnoble.com—the crossover marketer featured in this book—has done some of this cross-promotion, although its efforts have been hampered by legal issues that we'll explore in chapter 3. Some of the comparison companies I researched make much better use of their offline assets. The Gap, for example, has emblazoned the URL for its online store on all of its shopping bags. It even uses the electronic display on the cash registers in its retail stores to flash messages about gap.com to customers as they check out.

On with the Show   ▼

As you review the case studies, you'll see the degree to which the ideas outlined here resonate throughout the book, providing you with a set of core concepts to keep in mind when you are developing Internet brands of your own, coaching others on how to do so, or evaluating the results of companies attempting to build brands online.

Remember that by the time you read this, much will have changed for the companies covered within. New competitors may have arisen; old ones may have died off or been acquired. A firm may be working with a new ad agency or public relations firm. An organization may have entered new markets or exited old ones. So take the profiles for what they are: a snapshot of a set of exciting companies at a particular point in time. Learn from their past victories and failures, from the "present" captured at the time the book was written, and from the analysis of future possibilities based on that present. And realize that although circumstances may have changed, the best practices on which the book is based make up a foundation that will remain constant.

CHAPTER 1

www.iVillage.com

When Bonnie Sakadales's marriage broke up, she turned to the Internet for advice on raising her son and daughter alone. During her search for parenting information, Bonnie found Parent Soup, an online parenting community developed by New York–based iVillage. She began participating in Parent Soup's online chat forums. Within days, she struck up a conversation with Al Oswego, a fellow single parent who was struggling with custody issues. Online exchanges soon became telephone conversations. Eventually, Al drove to Maryland to meet Bonnie. They fell in love and were married on Valentine's Day, 1996. Bonnie continues to voice the highest praise for Parent Soup. "It gave me a world to be in besides work and the kids. I can't imagine what my life would be like without it."[1]

This level of enthusiasm for a product or service represents nirvana for marketers. And although the majority of its customers have not married people that they have met through iVillage, the iVillage network has become a valuable resource for thousands of people every day since the company was founded in 1995.

iVillage was formed by two women with extensive experience in the media industry. Candice Carpenter, chairman and CEO, was president of Q2, Barry Diller's electronic retailing venture, and had also served as president of Time-Life Video and Television, a Time Warner subsidiary. Nancy Evans, president, was the creator of *Family*

Life magazine and had served as president and publisher of Doubleday and vice president and editor in chief of the Book-of-the-Month Club. Both had built successful businesses in the offline world and were intrigued by the possibility of developing an innovative new media venture, one that would take advantage of their past experience but also present them with the intellectual challenges that come with operating in an emerging industry. Their vision was to humanize cyberspace, to develop a home on the Web for people to find and exchange information about some of life's most challenging issues, such as parenting, work, and relationships. As Carpenter described it, "I was really interested in combining the authentic quality of a lot of the communities I saw springing up online—communities that had a powerful influence on people's lives—with a strong commercial model. In addition, I wanted to make cyberspace a really good place for normal people, those outside the CNET crowd. I wanted to build something there that they would find extremely useful."[2]

In its early days, the company had a single online property to its name: Parent Soup, a community available both via AOL and the Web that is dedicated to parenting issues. Over the last three years, however, iVillage has grown substantially, developing additional online communities focused on issues such as health and fitness (Better Health), relationships (the Relationships channel), and personal finance (Armchair Millionaire). The network is now generating more than 73 million page views a month, which makes it the thirty-fifth most heavily trafficked media property on the Web.[3] With 3.9 million visitors each month, iVillage is attracting a healthy number of regular viewers, putting it in the same class as sites such as Ask.com, an emerging search engine, and Sportsline.com, a sports content site.[4] And among its regular customers, more than 1.6 million have registered for the iVillage network, providing the company with valuable demographic data that it can use to generate greater revenues by selling targeted advertising and presenting focused ecommerce offers.

Although such measures cast the company in a positive light, iVillage has its warts as well. It was late in developing an umbrella brand, for example, and focused instead on developing individual

iVillage Snapshot (1999)

URL: www.ivillage.com
Ticker symbol/Exchange: IVIL/Nasdaq   **Headquarters:** New York, NY
Year founded: 1995   **CEO:** Candice Carpenter

Business concept:	Offers online content focused on women's issues. Maintains high repeat usage rate by cultivating community among its customers. Generates the majority of its revenue from the sale of advertising and sponsorships. Beginning to supplement ad revenue with ecommerce.
Brand assets:	Brand awareness; community/customer commitment; distribution and content alliances; early mover advantage; customer and market intimacy; reputation for service excellence
Initial investors:	NBC, Intel, AOL, National Bank of Kuwait, Technology Crossover Ventures, CIBC Capital Partners, Cox Interactive Media, Kleiner Perkins Caufield & Byers, and The Tribune Company
Primary competitors:	Online: CondéNet, Women.com Networks, Oxygen Media Offline: Martha Stewart Living Omnimedia
Major strategic partners:	@ Home, Amazon.com, *American Baby*, AOL, AT&T, Infoseek, Intuit, Lycos, NBC, Simon & Schuster, SportsLine USA

Major milestones:

January 1996	Launches Parent Soup on the Web and AOL
May 1996	Raises $12 million in financing round led by AOL
August 1996	Launches About Work
December 1996	Launches ChatVillage network
February 1997	Forges distribution partnership with Lycos
June 1997	Raises $21.5 million in venture capital round
September 1997	Repositions company as online network for women
October 1997	Forges content partnership with *American Baby*
October 1997	Launches Armchair Millionaire with Intuit
April 1998	Strikes ecommerce agreement with Amazon.com
May 1998	Raises $32.8 million in venture capital round
November 1998	Announces Internet access service co-branded with AT&T
November 1998	Sells minority share to NBC
March 1999	$86.7 million IPO
May 1999	Forges content partnership with ZDNet
August 1999	Acquires Lamaze Publishing Company
August 1999	Acquires FamilyPoint.com

Financial summary (CY 1998):	Revenue: $15 million Net income (loss): ($43.7 million)
Shares outstanding:	23.1 million
Number of employees:	200

Web properties. As a result, it missed out on the marketing efficiencies enjoyed by companies such as Yahoo! that focused on developing an umbrella brand early on. In addition, iVillage has not yet seen financial success. By the end of 1998, the company had lost more than $65 million, and "it is known for having one of the most impressive burn rates in the business."[5] iVillage has also had a fair amount of personnel turnover. Although the company has been successful in cultivating a closely knit online community, it has had much greater difficulty developing a positive work environment.

Its rich mixture of strengths and shortcomings makes iVillage an intriguing case study. What marketing strategies and programs has the firm invested in to get where it is today? How has the company taken advantage of partnerships to enhance the value of its brands? How well is iVillage positioned against the current competition, and what new competitors loom on the horizon? Are the company's personnel problems getting in the way of its brand-building efforts? In this chapter, we'll consider these and other issues in an effort to learn from iVillage's experience as a marketer in the new media sector.

Best of Brand   ▼

We begin this chapter with a look at those things iVillage has done well in its drive to build a major Internet brand. For example, iVillage has made effective use of public relations to build awareness and a sense of marketplace momentum. It has cultivated a rich online community, which in turn has helped iVillage to build a base of loyal customers who frequent the company's sites and evangelize the benefits of the firm's services to their friends. It has developed an intimate understanding of its customers' needs by listening to its users and observing their behavior, and the company has leveraged this knowledge to improve its service and sharpen the focus of its marketing efforts. It has forged a rich network of partnerships with other firms, providing the company with wide-scale distribution across the Internet and thus building both traffic and brand awareness. These are among the notable iVillage successes we'll examine as we come to know the best of the iVillage brand.

Brand Awareness ▼

The efficacy of iVillage's awareness-building efforts stems from the company's strong sense of identity. From the beginning, the company has staked a claim as a place to which people can come for online information and advice on some of life's biggest challenges. Whereas much of the information available on the Web is irrelevant to our day-to-day lives, iVillage concentrates on presenting content that is relevant and useful. I have breast cancer; what are my alternatives to a full mastectomy? I'm pregnant; where can I find more information on the Family Medical Leave Act? What questions should I ask a nanny during an interview? Where should I seek counseling for a child with a drug problem? iVillage is about **iVillage's core brand attributes are utility, relevance, and community.** taking an honest look at tough problems and helping people to develop solutions. iVillage is real, not aspirational, explains vice president of member services and marketing MacDara MacColl. "Part of the essence of our brand is to say, 'This is life. Let's enjoy it and get on with it. Let's not pretend that it would really make our lives great if we gold leafed our ivy.'"[6]

Originally, iVillage focused its attentions on the baby boomer community—a natural for company founders Carpenter and Evans, who are boomers themselves. In the spirit of pragmatism, the company directed its efforts toward the early Web adopters among the boomer audience. But iVillage has always had its eye on the mainstream market. MacColl, the company's sixth employee, explains iVillage's ambitions this way: "From the beginning, we were always building for the time when the Internet became a mass medium. The core mission was to humanize cyberspace, so even in the beginning when the available audience was early adopters, we were not just trying to create a product for them—it's just that that was who [was] there."[7] Carpenter backs her up here. "We were building for an audience that hadn't arrived yet, but we had to have a business in the meantime."[8]

Over time, however, the demographics of the Internet have shifted. In the infancy of the Internet, the average Internet user was a well-educated male cybergeek. Today, 50 percent of adult Internet users are women.[9] And although a typical Internet denizen may be moderately comfortable with technology, the Net is no longer a venue that welcomes propellerheads only. In conjunction with these changes, iVillage has expanded beyond Web pioneers to target a more mainstream audience and has repositioned the company as iVillage: The Women's Network. Despite the shift, however, the core attributes of the brand have remained constant. The basis of iVillage is utility, relevance, and community.

Public Relations   This collection of fundamental qualities serves as the foundation of iVillage's messaging strategy. The company has communicated these ideas via a variety of different marketing channels; among the most effective has been public relations. iVillage manages its public relations programs using a combination of both internal and external resources. The company maintains a small group of PR staffers in house and supplements their efforts with help from Cone Communications, a New York–based communications consultancy that has worked for iVillage since the early days. iVillage's communications work is focused on outcomes. According to Jason Stell, vice president of corporate communications and investor relations at iVillage, "[Our PR] is very results driven, very heavy on the media relations piece as opposed to disciplines that emphasize theory like corporate imaging and crisis planning. Our work is much more tangible."[10] In other words, the mainstay of the PR team's work is communicating the latest news about the company: the announcement of a new distribution deal, for example, or the appointment of a key executive. The focus is on PR pragmatism.

iVillage has modified its PR strategy at multiple points over the past several years to keep pace with the frequent changes of the Internet landscape. In the first year or two, iVillage PR functioned in what the company called "missionary mode." The challenge was to gain credibility with early adopters, because it was essential to secure the support of these online pioneers if the business was going to fly. Not only would the early adopters be the first people to participate in an iVillage online community (at that point, Parent Soup), they would also be the ones who would tell their friends to try the service, write articles about the company, and help it attract advertisers and venture capital. At the center of the company's messaging was the idea of humanizing the Internet. But at this point iVillage also had to serve as an advocate for the concept of online communities, working to convince people that such entities provided value to consumers. iVillage also had to assume the role of spokesperson for a new kind of business model, one based on generating advertising revenues within the context of an online community. As an early mover, iVillage had to use PR to gain credibility for an industry, not just for its own specific business concept.

The firm was certainly not alone in these efforts; indeed, it would have been virtually impossible for a modestly funded start-up to drive such changes in thinking on its own. Companies such as PlanetOut, an online gay community, and Tripod, an Internet-based hangout for the twenty-something crowd, were also working to build credibility for the concept of advertising-supported online communities among key influencers. In 1996 and 1997, these ideas started to gain traction. Mainstream publications such as *Business Week* began writing about the category, publishing articles with titles like "Internet Communities: Forget Surfers—A New Class of Netizen Is Settling Right In." Fellow early movers such as GeoCities, which had created a community of online homesteaders whose free Web pages were grouped into themed "cyberhoods," began showing substantial increases in the size of their customer bases. As the industry began to mature and its own business grew, iVillage was able to modify its PR strategy, shifting away from promoting the business model and the community space as a whole to a new direction.

For starters, iVillage increased the intensity of its consumer PR efforts. As more and more people came online for the first time, the value of consumer-friendly "home bases" in cyberspace was becoming readily apparent. "'To most people, the Internet feels like jumping out into the ocean,' says Douglas Rushkoff, author of *Cyberia,* a book on cyberculture. 'Online communities provide the lifeguards.'"[11] As the interest in participating in online communities gained momentum with an expanded audience, iVillage devoted more money, time, and resources to true consumer PR, cultivating coverage in publications such as *Newsweek* and *Cosmopolitan.* Joe Berwanger, a director at Cone Communications, has said that "what Candice really wants to do is make the iVillage brand a household name, as much as AOL is. She wants every single woman who goes online to know iVillage. com."[12] If iVillage is going to achieve this level of brand ubiquity, these are the kind of magazines on which the company must focus.

Once multiple companies had proven the validity of the concept of advertising-supported online communities, iVillage turned its energies away from defending the merit of the business model to focus instead on publicizing the successes of specific advertisers on the iVillage network. This was a critical decision, in my view, for by communicating the successes of iVillage's early advertisers, the company helped to reduce the perceived risk of advertising on a women-focused community site—not exactly a common ad buy for most media planners several years ago. The iVillage PR team's work to spread the word about sponsorship campaigns run by blue chip companies such as Charles Schwab and Johnson & Johnson on Armchair Millionaire, Better Health, and other iVillage properties secured coverage for the company in key trade publications. For example, pitching news of the three-year, $5 million sponsorship deal that iVillage sold to Charles Schwab for the Armchair Millionaire site, a financial planning site developed with Intuit, led to a positive article in *Ad-Week.* Publicity featuring the success of these advertisers attracted new sponsors to the fold; their positive experiences in turn drew new sponsors to iVillage in the kind of cycle of success required for iVillage to thrive.

Finally, iVillage modified the messages it directed toward the financial community. In the early days, iVillage focused on explaining the core attributes of the brand and how these ideas could serve as the basis for an economically viable business. Later, with more than 1.6 million registered members and tens of millions in capital at its disposal, iVillage concentrated instead on emphasizing its leadership position and the corresponding value of that position. "In addressing the investment community, we have sent a consistent message," explains Jason Stell. "Ours is a business that is going to be around. It's going to be one of the mega-brands in this new economy that everybody is talking about."[13] For Internet companies such as iVillage, communicating with the financial community has a critical effect on the health of the brand. Given the interest of retail investors in Internet stocks, analysts' recommendations travel quickly beyond financial services and influence the opinions of a much wider audience. Nurturing the confidence of such opinion leaders is therefore a company priority.

> **"Momentum is so big in this space."**

In communicating with these various audiences, iVillage has used public relations as one of its most effective tools for cultivating the "mo factor," that feeling of energy behind a company that signifies that it is doing well, that it has market momentum. Each time iVillage signed another distribution deal or secured additional financing, or when one of its advertisers had an extraordinarily successful campaign, the iVillage PR team has been there to tell the story. "We want people to think, 'Those guys are on the move. They are marching. They are knocking down things in their path,'" Candice Carpenter said. "Momentum is so big in this space. On the Internet, you are either gaining market share or losing it—you are never standing still."[14] True, the offline world is also rife with such battles for market share. But on the Internet, the pace of change is substantially greater. In the real world, a cola company might be able to claim the gain of a percentage point of share over the course of six months as a substantial victory. On the Web, however, the introduction of a new competitor or of a technological or marketing innovation might upset an

entire market sector during the same time period. iVillage understands that it needs to provide frequent evidence of its leadership
position in order to maintain that role. Public relations has proven to
be one of the most effective ways the company has found to communicate the momentum required to keep its lead.

Online Marketing   iVillage has also used online marketing to build
both brand awareness and site traffic for the iVillage network. Online
marketing encourages experimentation, for if a campaign isn't working well or a particular medium isn't performing, it is generally easy
to make changes quickly and cheaply (in contrast to traditional media
such as television and print advertising, for which changes require
more lead time and can cost a great deal). iVillage now has several
years of online marketing history behind it, and constant testing and
refining of their ideas has taught the iVillage team to communicate in
a way that produces results.

Some of iVillage's early online marketing efforts fell short of the
mark. For example, the company engaged Cybernautics, an interactive
marketing agency, to seed key search engines and generate interest
within the Internet newsgroups. The search engine work didn't pan
out. "They worked with us for three months," said vice president of
online marketing Hillary Graves. "At the end of that period, we were
roughly the 340th listing that came up in a targeted search on Lycos. I
don't know what they did, but it didn't work."[15] For a search engine
listing to generate much traffic, it needs to be visible within the first
few pages returned for a specific search. (According to Danny Sullivan, editor of *Search Engine Watch,* only 7 percent of searchers look
beyond the third page of results when hunting for information on a
search site such as Lycos or Excite.[16]) If you assume that the average
search engine displays ten results per page, the work that Cybernautics did would have placed the iVillage information more than thirty
pages into the search results, providing little value.

Cybernautics's efforts to interject strategically placed comments
into selective newsgroups also yielded modest dividends. In experimenting with this online marketing technique, iVillage was hoping to

"rent an evangelist," that is, to hire Cybernautics to sing iVillage's praises in online public discussion forums and therefore drive traffic to the iVillage network. Performance was mixed, however. In addition, this was a practice with which Graves never seems to have become fully comfortable. "We haven't mastered the newsgroup thing—it's touchy. We are very conscious of the etiquette on the Internet and want to tread lightly." Today, rather than hire someone to do this work, Graves depends instead on iVillage fans to get the word out in such forums on the company's behalf. "Our community members are the best guerrilla marketers we have."[17]

I think Graves is smart to follow this path, for the Internet's Usenet newsgroups are sensitive territory. With 17 million to 25 million people participating in its online discussion groups each day, Usenet has been around since the beginning of the Internet and is the largest online community in the world. While there are discussion groups within Usenet that are designed purely for business purposes (e.g., alt.business.career-opportunities), many of them (e.g., groups such as misc.kids.breastfeeding and alt.support.alzheimers) were formed as discussion forums for noncommercial issues, and people or companies that post "advertorials" within these groups catch flak for violating Usenet etiquette. As a company that hosts discussion groups itself, the last thing iVillage wants is to be accused of spamming public discussion forums. What's more, as the number of people on the Internet has grown, the amount of frivolous conversation, spam, and other noise within these groups has increased, making it difficult to communicate a message that people will pay attention to and thus decreasing the return on investment (ROI) of such a guerrilla marketing effort. It is better for iVillage to let its customers serve as ad hoc evangelists than to try to spark and control such discussions through a marketing firm.

iVillage has had much greater success with its banner advertising efforts. However, its approach to the management of the program, its messaging, and its media buying strategy have all changed a lot over time. When iVillage first started running banner advertising, it worked with Modem Media, a first-rate agency that has also worked for companies such as AT&T, Intel, Delta Airlines, and Citibank. Modem handled all aspects of iVillage's banner advertising: creative development, media buying, and analysis. Although the two companies worked together successfully, iVillage eventually decided that it wanted to pull the media buying component in house and that it might get more attention from a smaller agency. The company moved on to partner with IN2, a boutique firm that has focused on crafting advertisements and tracking campaign results for iVillage.

In developing its primary messages, iVillage worked with some of the same themes outlined in our discussion of the company's public relations work: community, a home in cyberspace, relevant information, real solutions, and so on. Over time, however, by analyzing the click-through results of its banners, iVillage found that it was the solution-oriented facet of the brand, and not the community elements, that got people to take action and visit Parent Soup, Better Health, or other sites in the iVillage network. Initially, people were more interested in the idea of experimenting with Parent Soup's Baby Name Finder, for example, than they were in the idea of participating in a virtual coffee klatch. "We've used community messages like 'Find Support Here' or 'Women's Support Here,'" explains Hillary Graves, "but these messages just aren't great acquisition drivers. People come to iVillage to find an answer to a question or to find certain information, but what ends up getting them to stay is this sense of community that they find, that emotional release." The idea of "real solutions for busy women . . . is totally core to our brand," Graves states.[18] Given that this message gets viewers to visit the iVillage sites, where they come to know the other attributes of the brand by interacting with the service, iVillage has concentrated on the "solutions" orientation in its more recent banner work.

The company has also put thought into refining its media buying strategy. An early mover in its category, iVillage has had more time than its competitors to experiment, to learn from the results of its trials, and to adjust its course accordingly. iVillage has run advertisements on news sites such as abc.com and nbc.com. It has experimented with online directories such as Big Yellow and InfoSpace. It has tested other women's sites, such as CondeNet; search engines, such as Lycos; and health sites, such as Fitness Online. Over time, the firm has tuned the list of sites it uses based on economic analysis, retaining those that have proven to be most effective, leaving the poor performers behind, and adding new test candidates to the queue. But beyond simply changing the selection of sites on which it advertises, iVillage has changed the nature of the deals it strikes with these sites. Although the company may test new sites using short runs, iVillage has moved toward crafting longer-term alliances with those sites that have proven cost-effective. "We really approach this as a partnership with these sites. We'll make six-month deals to get the best CPMs we can," explains Graves.[19]

With a select group of highly targeted sites, iVillage has gone a step further, striking long-term, integrated deals in which these partners not only run advertising messages for iVillage, but also serve as distribution channels for the company's content. These arrangements are key to building both brand awareness and site traffic. We'll look at such partnerships more closely later in the chapter, but consider briefly the arrangement that iVillage made with Warner Brothers, producers of *The Rosie O'Donnell Show*. Rosie is a high-profile single mom with a large base of fans and a Web site of her own. Warner Brothers and iVillage forged an agreement in which iVillage provides content for Cutie-Patootie Parenting Tips, a section of Rosie's site. When viewers click on the articles in the Tips area, they are taken to the Parent Soup site to get the full text, giving them an opportunity to get to know the brand up close. In addition, Rosie's site features iVillage banners on the home page and in other key sections. This type of joint marketing and business development deal goes beyond the banner to offer iVillage a good opportunity to build its brand among a group of compelling target customers. Such integrated marketing campaigns represent the next generation in online marketing.

Offline Marketing   iVillage has also turned to an assortment of offline marketing initiatives in its drive to build awareness. The company's offline work started in 1998. This was much later than many of the firm's other brand development initiatives, and I believe that iVillage should have started running offline advertising at least a year earlier. But the company eventually recognized that to expand its reach beyond early Internet adopters, offline advertising was a must. For assistance in crafting a multidimensional offline campaign, iVillage teamed up with DDB Needham, the ad agency that has handled advertising for brands such as Yoplait, Bisquick, and the Discover Card. Together, the companies fashioned a two-prong strategy for broadening awareness of iVillage.

The first of these initiatives focused on the business and advertising communities. The campaign had two components. One was a series of print advertisements that iVillage ran in the *Wall Street Journal* heralding the dramatic increase in the number of women online. "More than 42% of all people on the Internet today are women," reads one ad in the series. "By the Year 2000, more than 70 million of them will spend time online. Put another way: in two years, nearly the entire population of the Eastern Seaboard of the United States will be online. And they will all be women." The ad went on to illustrate the purchasing power of female Web users. And, of course, it emphasized that there was one place on the Web that women online call home more often than any other Web destination: iVillage—the Women's Network. This ad was "our mission statement turned into an advertisement," said iVillage brand manager Heather Campbell.[20] By advertising in the *Journal,* iVillage aimed to jolt readers into realizing that a revolution was taking place and that iVillage was there at the forefront. The campaign was not designed to increase traffic or sell ads, but to build brand, to stake out territory. "We felt we really needed to go out and claim this turf early on within the business community," said Paul Ahern, general manager of integrated marketing for DDB Needham. "We wanted to be the first to claim the positioning."[21] iVillage actually was not the first company to adopt such a positioning. Women's Wire, the online community that eventually became Women.com, was in existence before the Web even emerged and took a similar market stance. But iVillage pushed aggressively to own this space in the minds of its key constituents, and offline advertising has certainly helped the firm in its effort to stake out a leadership role in this market.

The second component of the iVillage trade and business communications effort was a campaign the company ran in publications such as *Advertising Age* and *Media Week*. Here, the goal was to talk to the advertising community to contrast the advertising opportunity that iVillage presented with more traditional media buys and to compel readers to contact the company to pursue sponsorships on the iVillage network. This was precisely the kind of footwork that iVillage had to do to expand its base of corporate advertisers. It was an investment in educating prospective ad buyers on the distinctive opportunities that an iVillage sponsorship presented for reaching their target customers. And while it was not an inexpensive effort, it paid off by opening doors to advertisers such as Polaroid and Starbucks.

In addition to utilizing offline marketing to reach the trade and business communities, iVillage has used offline media to reach consumers. The company's management has seen that the market has reached the point at which it makes sense to start investing in more traditional media programs. According to Heather Campbell, "If PCs are going to go from 35 to 45 to 50 percent household penetration, and if the number of women online is going to grow from 22 million to 67 million within the next two years, you are really starting to talk about a mass market now. You are talking about an audience that you can reach effectively via means other than those that have traditionally worked for this industry—namely banner advertising."[22]

The offline consumer campaign that iVillage has developed thus far is "pure image work," said DDB Needham's Paul Ahern—a combination of radio and television designed to make consumers feel that "that company understands women."[23] Both the radio and TV spots featured interviews with real women talking about different issues that had arisen in their lives and how iVillage helped them to grapple with these issues. DDB Needham focused its media buys on those geographic markets in which Internet penetration was already high; iVillage and the agency agreed that in this first radio and TV push, it would be a strategic mistake to attempt to influence women who were not yet online. The campaign raised awareness among "wired women" in these key markets, communicating essential attributes of the brand and "laying the branding groundwork that everything in the future would build on," explained Gregg Greenberg, iVillage account manager for DDB.[24] Sure, this campaign caused some women to fire up their browsers and visit iVillage. More likely, however, is that the messages simply registered a favorable impression. But the next time a woman who saw that TV spot or caught the radio commercial on her way to work saw an iVillage banner on the Web, the probability was higher that she'd click on that banner, for iVillage was then a brand she knew.

With the company's recent deal with NBC, iVillage will build on the foundation established by the campaign just described, increasing its television advertising substantially over the next three years. In return for equity, iVillage has lined up prime-time commercial space on NBC. NBC has a strong presence among 25- to 49-year-old women—the iVillage target market—which makes it an excellent partner. "Women are to NBC what kids are to Disney," said Tom Rogers, president of NBC Cable and executive vice president of NBC. "Women are not only the majority of the population, but they are the majority of the NBC viewing audience."[25] Through this relationship, iVillage will have a chance to gain repeated exposure to the many women watching shows such as *E.R., Friends,* and *Law and Order.* As Patrick Keane of Jupiter Communications put it, "Offline promotional assets are a cherry for any Internet company."[26] Although it did not pay cash for this TV time, iVillage certainly incurred a significant cost for this deal, because the company gave up both a seat on its board of directors and a minority stake that was worth millions. The payback may well be worth it, however, for iVillage will build awareness through this alliance that it could not afford to purchase outright.

Community: The Key to Customer Commitment ▼

Of all the companies profiled in this book, iVillage is the one that has focused most heavily on the development of online communities as a way of forging Internet brands. Indeed, community represents the core of the iVillage business. Co-founder Candice Carpenter describes her company this way: "We strive to help women navigate through increasingly busy lives and maximize their potential in their various roles as parents, friends, spouses, partners, career women, breadwinners, employees, and individuals. We provide the supportive and nurturing environment—a lifespace, if you will, not just another Web site—where women can find sound advice and practical solutions from experts and each other."[27] Her business partner Nancy Evans echoes these sentiments: "We're the virtual 24-hour hotline and community center."[28]

The network of iVillage sites brings together a wide array of individuals with common interests, providing them with communities of peers with whom to share life's experiences. Whether visitors are interested in discussing breast-feeding techniques or postpartum depression, whether they are looking for advice on managing a difficult relationship or just need tips on how to whip up healthy

iVillage acts as a magnet for like minds.

weeknight meals, iVillage acts as a magnet for like minds, drawing people into shared virtual spaces and giving them the chance to exchange their information and insights. As co-founder Nancy Evans explains it, participants in these communities "feel connected—part of something larger. Some of them use it as a reality check with other women. The information we provide informs and the collective support we provide empowers. It's that double whammy that makes us unlike any other medium."[29]

The communal aspects of the iVillage network define the distinct personalities of the company's various brands to a large extent. Visit Parent Soup and it's as if you've dropped in on a neighborhood coffee klatch, with moms trading birthing stories or exchanging tips on what questions to ask when hiring a nanny. Browse Better Health and it's like visiting a local spa, with people discussing workout routines and experts presenting nutritional advice. iVillage has encouraged this neighborhood feeling by listening to its customers and making changes to the service that reflect their needs. As MacDara MacColl describes it, "We tell our customers, 'This place is yours. You create it. You can have an impact. You are respected here.' That's the most compelling thing in the world. They feel ownership and have brand loyalty like nobody else."[30]

This community spirit has helped iVillage to develop brand loyalty. Yes, tools such as the Healthwise Handbook and the Armchair Millionaire Action Planner have been valuable, particularly for drawing people to iVillage sites for the first time. But it is the fact that iVillage has created "destinations of the heart"—communities "where you have an emotional resonance, where you belong"— that has kept customers around.[31] Tom Rielly, CEO of the online gay community PlanetOut, explained this concept as follows: "It's not the content. It's the people, stupid. Content may be why people visit a site. But community is why people stay."[32]

A strong sense of community is a brand asset that is difficult to replicate. It takes substantial time and effort to develop a vibrant community. In the words of Howard Rheingold, author of *The Virtual Community* and founder of an early community venture called Electric Minds, "Any company that thinks they can go out and create a community in 30 days to sell a lot of pantyhose is going to be disappointed."[33] Moreover, once members have made a community a part of their lives, they are unlikely to abandon it and the friends they've made there in favor of another. Switching costs, in other words, are high. In making community a cornerstone of its business, iVillage has developed a brand asset that will help it to fend off intensifying competition (see "The Competitive Threat" later in this chapter for more information on iVillage's fiercest foes). Focusing on community has also helped iVillage generate significant financial value. Building community keeps visitors coming back again and again. The more frequently they visit, the more ads they see and the greater the likelihood that they will purchase products through iVillage as the company ramps up its ecommerce efforts.

Candice Carpenter has said, "We get email notes every day that say, 'I have breast cancer and I came to your site and got help.' Or, 'I'm trying to raise two little kids on my own and ten people came to my aid and gave me books to read, medical questions to ask my pediatrician and ways to talk to my children—your site has changed my life.' The kind of loyalty that those experiences bring is unbelievable—it makes for a different order of relationships."[34] In cultivating loyal customers, iVillage has also developed a set of advocates who spread the word about the network of communities the company has created. Such supporters have been critical to iVillage because this word-of-mouth marketing has helped the company increase site traffic quickly and inexpensively.

Within iVillage's corps of enthusiasts is a subset of people who have been particularly vocal evangelists: the more than 1,000 volunteer discussion leaders who facilitate online conversations on everything from planning for retirement to living with rheumatoid arthritis. These volunteers have strengthened the brand by moderating quality discussions on difficult issues and by "cross-selling" various iVillage resources (for example, the leader of the Preparing for Pregnancy discussion on Parent Soup might encourage participants to experiment with the site's Baby Name Finder). To expand the influence of these volunteers into the offline world, iVillage retained a political organizer to travel to the cities in which the company has run its TV and radio spots and work with local volunteers. Armed with marketing collateral produced by iVillage, these volunteers banded together to meet with local women's groups such as the PTA or Women's League and tell others about iVillage. Although other online companies, such as AOL, have also used volunteers to moderate discussion forums, iVillage is the only company that I have seen take grassroots marketing to this extreme. Through these efforts, iVillage has built brand on a personal level, getting people excited about the service it provides and then tapping this enthusiasm to bring others into the fold. Although such guerrilla marketing efforts are hard to scale, they have the potential to have a significant impact on those people they can reach.

Strong Content and Distribution Alliances ▼

iVillage knows well the value that strategic partnerships can bring to its brands and has invested heavily in a network of alliances. "We are constantly thinking about where the playing field is going, how we get that next deal that lets everyone know that we are on the move, that we are the ones to watch," said Candice Carpenter.[35] Some of these partnerships have been content and commerce focused, engineered to enhance the perceived quality of the company's offerings through partnerships that provide information and services in conjunction with other trusted brands. Others, in contrast, have been distribution focused, designed to extend the visibility of the iVillage family of brands.

Content and Commerce Deals   iVillage has invested in strategic alliances with companies that have helped it to supplement its sites with new content or functionality, or that have enabled specific ecommerce opportunities. By developing such relationships, the company has strengthened its brand in two ways. First, by enhancing the utility of its sites and deepening the richness of the information they provide, the firm has improved the quality of the iVillage network. Second, these enhancements have also served to strengthen customer loyalty, bringing viewers back more frequently and increasing the value of an average iVillage customer (the more often customers visit, the more advertisements they see and the more likely they are to purchase products in one of the company's online stores).

One of iVillage's most important content partnerships is with *American Baby*, America's premier baby magazine. The two companies have worked together to develop a co-branded area on iVillage's flagship Parent Soup site that includes clubs based on due dates (called Pregnancy Circles), an interactive trivia game based on *American Baby* research, and an *American Baby* Roundtable in which Parent Soup members can talk with magazine editors about parenting issues and trends. By partnering with *American Baby*, iVillage has enhanced the strength of its own brand not just by providing excellent content, but by allying itself with a trusted leader in the parenting field.

In addition to partnering to gain access to content, iVillage has also developed relationships that have enabled it to add new functionality to its network of sites. In the Internet space, the "make vs. buy" debate must frequently end in a "buy" decision because the environment is changing too rapidly for a company to make everything itself if it is going to achieve and maintain a leadership position. iVillage understands this. In some situations, the firm has formed partnerships with other vendors to acquire functionality that it thought would add value to the site and thus increase perceived quality. In others, the company has simply bought the technology outright. For example, rather than develop a similar resource itself, iVillage purchased the Interactive Pregnancy Calendar from a programmer in St. Paul, Minnesota, who created it as a "virtual gift" for his wife. Traffic to the original site grew quickly via word of mouth, and iVillage soon heard about Michael Olenick's online calendar. When the Olenicks became overwhelmed by their own success ("Our servers were falling apart, and our telecommunications bills were really high," Olenick said), they called iVillage to propose a sale, and the company jumped on the opportunity.[36]

In the Internet space, the "make vs. buy" debate must frequently end in "buy."

To create the Parent Soup Baby Name Finder, iVillage cooperated with a company called Names & Planes that had developed an offline software package called NAMEASE. The result of this collaboration is a rich, Web-based directory of more than 14,000 names that allows parents to browse names alphabetically or to search for names by origin, popularity, or distinctiveness. In addition to enhancing the overall quality of the site—and thus the power of the iVillage brand—such features bolster the brand by increasing customer loyalty. During the time in which my wife was pregnant with our first child, for example, she would return to the Parent Soup site about once a month to print out an updated, personalized pregnancy calendar. And it was after several visits to the Baby Name Finder that we ultimately decided on the name "Jessica" for our baby girl.

iVillage has also contributed to the richness of its services through the development of a number of ecommerce partnerships. These add-on services have played a dual role for iVillage, increasing the overall utility of the site as well as generating transaction revenues. Based on projections concerning the number of women coming online, potential partners have been interested in teaming with iVillage to tap the purchasing power of its online communities. According to Jupiter Communications, the number of women on the Web will grow fivefold between 1996 and 2000.[37] What's more, *AdAge* research has revealed that women control or influence 80 percent of all purchase decisions. iVillage is well positioned to capitalize on the online influx of this valuable customer set.[38] The strength of its hand has allowed iVillage to forge partnerships with reputable partners, reinforcing the power of the iVillage brand through these relationships with trusted merchants. For example, the firm has allied itself with online retailer Amazon.com to offer book-related features such as reading lists and book reviews across the network of iVillage sites. iVillage has also forged an alliance with RedRocket, Simon & Schuster's online store for children's learning toys. RedRocket is the exclusive partner in this category, and the two companies have worked together to integrate information on RedRocket products and special offers within select locations in iVillage's online communities. "Successfully partnering with a trusted brand like Simon & Schuster is one of iVillage's primary strengths," claims Robert Levitan, iVillage cofounder.[39] To build successful Internet brands, developing such a competency is crucial.

Distribution Deals   On the distribution front, the company has pursued two different types of strategic alliances. The first is the relationship that has offered broad Internet reach, the kind of exposure best delivered by the sites that serve as the starting points for Internet browsing. "One of our goals is to be wherever women might first be online," Carpenter has said. "Wherever they might come through, we want them to look for us."[40] Portal sites fit the bill here, and iVillage has developed relationships with several.

Lycos, for example, is a Web portal that represents one of the top five most frequently visited sites on the Web. Lycos serves as a trusted Internet guide for millions of Web users every month. People can either use Lycos to search the Web for specific information or browse a selection of "Web guides"—thematic directories of particular resources or content. iVillage teamed up with Lycos to create the Women's Channel, a Web guide that covers topics such as female health issues, families, and careers. This Web guide prominently displays the iVillage brand and exposes the company to many target customers who are not familiar with iVillage. In addition to building brand awareness, the Lycos Women's Channel helps to generate trial customers. Clicking on many of the resources within the Women's Channel brings the viewer to one of the iVillage sites, creating an opportunity for iVillage to build a relationship directly with a potential long-term customer.

The second type of distribution partnership iVillage has pursued is one that has connected it with a different target audience. Whereas deals with the portal sites have presented the opportunity to expose the iVillage brands to a broad audience, this second type of partnership has enabled iVillage to build brand awareness among a more tightly defined set of prospects. These prospects are Web users who may be more experienced than those who frequent the portal sites, and who have a specific set of interests indicated by the sites they visit most often. For example, iVillage has partnered with SportsLine USA, producer of *CBS SportsLine*, to produce a co-branded site focused on women's sports. The site presents detailed coverage of five women's sports areas—basketball, golf, tennis, figure skating, and hockey—as well as providing links to the iVillage Fitness and Beauty section. This partnership has built brand awareness in a more directed fashion than have iVillage's portal alliances.

In an agreement that represents a hybrid of these two models, iVillage has teamed up with Intuit, developers of the personal finance site Quicken.com, to create Armchair Millionaire, a site aimed at helping people to invest their money more effectively. Through distribution via Quicken.com, iVillage has built brand awareness among a small but demographically attractive group of prospects. What's more, iVillage has benefited from links to the Armchair Millionaire site that have appeared in Excite's Business and Investing channel (Excite, a popular portal site, is partially owned by Intuit). These links on Excite have provided reach, because Excite exposes the links to large numbers of Web users each day. For a company looking to create a strong Internet brand, building such interconnected webs of alliances is crucial to success. As these examples illustrate, iVillage is developing a network of partnerships that enable it to reach a good mix and volume of potential viewers.

The Early Mover Advantage ▼

iVillage has benefited not only from joining the race early, but by maintaining a fast pace since the day it began. As McKinsey & Company consultants Hagel and Armstrong write in their book *Net Gain: Expanding Markets Through Virtual Communities,* "the race to establish the virtual community belongs to the swift: those who move quickly and aggressively will gain—and likely hold—the advantage."[41] iVillage's track record supports this assertion. The company's early entry and ongoing drive have helped it to secure a leadership position in several ways. For example, iVillage has had more time to invest in building awareness than have companies such as Oxygen Media, which entered the market later. In moving both first and fast, iVillage has established a reputation as an innovator, which has made it easier to cultivate awareness. "When companies get reputations for being thought leaders, the press turns to them constantly," said Candice Carpenter. "No one would ever think of doing a major story on women on the Internet without us being the first people they talk to."[42] What's more, as an early mover and hard driver, iVillage has had the chance to lock in market share and distribution deals while the costs are relatively low. But while iVillage has taken full advantage of its lead, it knows that the only way to maintain this brand asset is to keep running. "We've got to move fast," says Candice Carpenter. "I go to sleep worrying someone is going to leave cleat marks on my face before I wake up."[43]

Customer and Market Intimacy ▼

iVillage has developed a deep knowledge of its customers and market through research. In contrast to other companies profiled in this book, however, iVillage has made little use of usability testing on the product development side. Instead, it has gathered information through analysis of site traffic patterns, review of industry research, and most important, through conversations with its customers and with the leaders of the iVillage online communities. Watching how many viewers spend time in certain areas of an iVillage network site and how they make their way through that site has given the product team a general sense of how attractive specific content is to viewers and how easy or difficult it is for people to find what they're looking for. Reviewing the latest industry reports from firms such as Jupiter Communications or Forrester Research has also sparked ideas about new product directions to explore. The most valuable insights, however, have come from direct communications with customers. As MacDara MacColl explains, "We are engaged in an ongoing conversation with our customers to improve our product and make it what they want it to be. . . . We listen really carefully."[44]

> **The ability to launch a product, gather feedback, and immediately launch it again is distinct to the Internet.**

Exchanges with customers and community leaders, not usability testing or quantitative research, have had the greatest influence on product direction at iVillage. If the company received numerous email notes expressing interest in a new online forum, iVillage opened a new discussion group on the topic—and often invited one of the customers who had expressed an interest in the subject to serve as the discussion moderator. If iVillage received suggestions that the company add information from a specific content source, it was likely to pursue it. Customers, in other words, have had a significant influence over the direction of the iVillage brand as articulated through product. Although this is also the case for other companies in this book, the effect that customer feedback has on the evolution of the brand has been particularly strong at iVillage.

The danger of relying so heavily on this type of qualitative input is that it is subjective: A few vocal customers may create a perception of momentum behind a particular idea that is overblown. I think that iVillage should push for a better balance between qualitative and quantitative research. On the Internet, however, there is less risk in relying on such qualitative research than when developing physical products such as computers. If a computer hardware company decides to alter its keyboard design based on the input of a quick survey or a handful of focus groups, only to learn once the product goes to market that many people are dismayed with the changes, it could be six months to a year before the firm could recover from its mistakes. With Internet services, if something isn't successful, you can change it immediately. "That's the great thing about online," says Chuck Schilling, director of research for iVillage. "You can beef up certain areas of your site, shrink others or fine tune them on the fly. If it doesn't work, you can reverse the changes. It's not like a print run for a magazine where you print it and it's done and gone. You can create and tailor 24 hours a day."[45] The ability to launch a product, gather customer feedback, and immediately launch it again is distinct to the Internet. iVillage can take more risks in making changes than can, say, a packaged software firm, which might perform sophisticated conjoint analysis to help it select the features to include in its annual product release. An Internet-based company can—and should—be less dependent on complex, drawn-out research studies. The market provides better feedback than any such study ever can, and iVillage's less formal approach to research therefore makes sense.

iVillage has also depended on customer input to help it refine the marketing communications programs it has used to build brand and attract new customers. For example, when the company decided to develop an online advertising campaign to bring mothers with teens to the iVillage network, it went to the community leader who moderates a discussion group aimed at this target audience to get her advice on the principal issues that surface in the group. The marketing team then developed banner ads based on these ideas and took them back to the moderator for review. Tapping the community to research issues that resonate most with target customers has provided iVillage with the insights it has needed to develop marketing materials with impact—at a much lower cost than running focus groups or conducting surveys to gather this information.

iVillage has used quantitative research to investigate issues of interest to specific advertisers. This research has enabled iVillage to close advertising sales with some major advertisers, not only providing the company with revenue but also reinforcing the iVillage brand through its association with other quality products and services. For example, iVillage's research work helped it to land an important deal with Glaxo Wellcome, makers of Zyban, a pill that helps people to quit smoking. Glaxo was considering purchasing a sponsorship on Better Health because it believed that this iVillage site would attract the kind of customers it was hoping to reach: white-collar, female "social" smokers who consumed one to two packs of cigarettes per week. But the company was skeptical. Was this the right vehicle for marketing Zyban? Would Better Health viewers be interested in the product? To investigate such issues for Glaxo, iVillage fielded an online survey of its users. Not only was Glaxo impressed by the interest level among Better Health viewers, it was also surprised to get results back so fast—a marked contrast to traditional, offline research, which would have taken much longer to complete. Glaxo bought the sponsorship. And iVillage added a trusted merchant to its list of advertisers, generating ad revenue and building brand through its association with this well-known healthcare products manufacturer.

A Reputation for Excellence ▼

iVillage has worked hard to develop a name as the provider of a quality service; this chapter has touched on many of the ways in which it has cultivated quality. For example, we've discussed how the firm has successfully developed a series of online communities characterized by thoughtful interaction among participants, from medical experts to concerned parents, and have seen how customers' interaction with the iVillage services has led them to become evangelists for the company. In addition, we've examined how iVillage has forged distribution, content, and commerce relationships with premier online and offline brands that extend their halo effect to reinforce the perceived quality of the services iVillage offers.

One additional way in which iVillage has built a reputation for quality has been by providing good customer service. In one sense, iVillage has it easy, for in communities as closely knit as those the company has created, participants provide plenty of support for one another. But if a particular chat session has turned ugly or if a customer cannot find specific information that she is looking for, the iVillage customer service team will help. The company has a group of eight service representatives responding to customer questions. Many Internet companies send cut-and-paste, template-style responses to customer inquiries, while others fend off customer communications altogether with automated help systems. Visit HotMail, for example, and you'll have to wend your way through a series of Frequently Asked Questions (FAQ) documents in your attempt to resolve your problems with Microsoft's free email service. In fact, I challenge you to find an email address within the Hotmail help area that will do anything other than send you an automated FAQ-like response with additional "helpful" hints. iVillage, however, sends its customers individually tailored answers to their inquiries within twenty-four hours—a level of attention that is impressive for a free service. Wrote

> **iVillage has recognized the contribution customer service can make to brand equity.**

one customer in an email note, "Parent Soup is the best thing since Campbell's! Every time I've had a comment or question, I've received personal attention from your staff. No wonder the Soup just keeps growing and growing."[46]

As a community site, iVillage needs to imbue interactions with customer service with the same personal feel that characterizes the other exchanges people have on the site. I think that iVillage has therefore made the right decision in opting for a "high touch" support model. MacDara MacColl explains iVillage's choice this way: "When you are a community-based site, customer support is business development. These are the people who will have a good experience or not and will then talk about that experience. So every time we touch a customer directly—which is every second of the day—it is important to us that we take a lot of care with that interaction."[47]

Many traditional companies have made providing excellent service an integral part of their business strategies. For Nordstrom, American Express, Citicorp, and plenty of other firms, providing outstanding service is a given. It's important to realize, however, that this service orientation has not yet fully percolated through the Internet community. Providing good service can be both expensive and people intensive, and many Internet companies have balked at investing in customer service infrastructure. The iVillage team, however, has recognized the way in which customer service can contribute to brand equity. The company's personalized approach to solving customer problems has reinforced the identity of the brand and further strengthened the relationship between customer and company.

Chinks in the Armor   ▼

As the evidence presented in this chapter demonstrates, iVillage is well on its way to developing a strong Internet brand. It would be wrong, however, to assume that iVillage is fault free. The company has its share of problems, and they are worth a closer look because some of these issues represent significant challenges to the success of the business.

For example, iVillage waited for some time before driving to develop an umbrella brand, concentrating instead on nurturing the brands of individual Web properties such as Parent Soup. The problem with this approach is that the longer a company waits to begin building a network brand, the more difficult and expensive it becomes to do so. As a comparable example, consider the Go Network, a joint effort between Disney and Infoseek, one of the Web portal companies. By the time Disney became serious about developing a substantial Web presence, it was already late to market. To jump-start its online efforts, the company bought a 43 percent stake in Infoseek. Over time, it put a new name and face on the Infoseek portal, rechristened it as GO.com, and cobbled together a collection of Disney's online properties (GO.com, abc.com, espn.com, family.com, and others) into a confederation of sites it called the Go Network. Disney has had to devote significant money and energy to promote its new umbrella brand. The Go Network logo appears throughout programming on ESPN. Its television ads are running on ABC, a member of the Disney keiretsu. Given Disney's marketing knowledge and financial power, I think that the company has a fair chance of turning the Go Network into a competitive Internet brand. But the resources that will be required to do so will be huge.

By focusing on cultivating the individual brands in its portfolio of Web services rather than on developing an umbrella brand, iVillage missed out on the opportunity to leverage the credibility that comes with a strong umbrella brand to help it drive the success of its individual properties. When Yahoo! has launched new services over time—Yahoo! Mail, Yahoo! Pager, and many others—it has been able to tap the strength of the Yahoo! brand name to propel adoption of these additional offerings. iVillage has not had that luxury until more recently, for it has not been until the last year or so that the company has aggressively ramped up its network-oriented marketing efforts. Had iVillage done more to develop the corporate brand earlier on, it would have had an easier time building awareness and usage of follow-on services quickly.

Another key problem for iVillage has been personnel turnover. The company has churned through five CFOs in three years and has lost senior executives in many other functional areas as well, such as sales and business development. The Internet environment is a fluid one, but turnover at iVillage has been uncharacteristically high. The issue is tied closely to the intense nature of the company culture, a culture influenced heavily by the personality of CEO Candice Carpenter. Carpenter is intense. "Ask anyone to describe iVillage chief executive Candice Carpenter," writes *Wired* journalist Craig Bicknell, "and they'll use that word in the first sentence. Some say it with dread, some say it with admiration. But they all say it."[48] This intensity has been hard for many to stomach. "Her hard-charging style has burned out platoons of employees," Bicknell continues. Robert Levitan, an iVillage co-founder who left in January 1999 to start another Internet venture, chooses his words carefully in describing the company culture. "The pace and the pressure helped turn me into a better entrepreneur, but it's not for everybody," Levitan says.[49]

Other former iVillagers have been less diplomatic. In a lawsuit filed against the company by former vice president of business development Todd Kenner (Kenner claims that iVillage fired him unjustly and retracted promised stock options), Kenner describes Carpenter as a "hostile, uncommunicative, and arbitrary" manager who treated executives in "a consistently opportunistic, dishonest, and malevolent manner."[50] Not that he didn't get fair warning before signing on: Before he accepted the job at iVillage, another exec warned him, "'You get lured in, and [Carpenter] sucks all the life out of you, like a black widow. Then you're thrown into the dust pile.'"[51]

It is ironic that a CEO who claims to care so much about crafting an open, homey online community has had such problems building a healthy real-world corporate community. The dysfunctional nature of the iVillage culture and the related turnover are serious issues for the company. The lawsuits filed by people such as Todd Kenner, former CFO Joanne Hindman, and former vice president of sales Steven

Carter have led to negative PR and even jeopardized the company's initial public offering (IPO). Most important, however, such cultural problems are having an impact on the company's ability to attract and retain employees. In the Internet space, the battle for talent is fierce because there simply aren't enough sharp, net-savvy executives to meet the demand of the burgeoning number of new online ventures. For iVillage to be a long-term success, it needs to find and keep the best and brightest. If the company doesn't devote substantial attention to addressing its cultural shortcomings, iVillage could find itself in short supply of one of the Internet economy's most valuable assets: smart people.

In addition to its cultural problems, iVillage has financial worries to contend with. Many Internet companies have run at a loss during these early years of the Web as they spend aggressively to build brand and lock up market share. In the case of iVillage, however, the losses have been much greater than normal. As Greta Mittner reported in *Red Herring Online,* "While iVillage reported revenues of $9.1 million for the nine months ending September 30, 1998, it suffered losses of $32.4 million for the same period. It has a total accumulated deficit of $65.1 million. iVillage attributes some of the loss to acquisitions. This loss is enormous compared to the losses of its community-developing competitors. For instance, Xoom.com reported losses of $6.9 million for the same period, on revenues of $5.2 million."[52]

MSNBC journalist Christopher Byron took iVillage to task for its profligate spending when the company held its initial public offering:

> *Rarely in the short and volatile history of the Internet has a more over-valued and over-hyped stock come to market on a more lurid track record of troubled finances and a weaker product—only to rocket by 300 percent on its very first trade. If iVillage had been in any other business than the Internet, at almost any other time than now, it never would have gotten to market in the first place. In its brief, barely three-and-one-half year history, this boring, unnecessary and fundamentally patronizing 'Web site for women' has managed to blow through*

more than $76 million of startup capital—which works out to
nearly $400,000 of losses for each of the company's 200 em-
ployees.[53]

Such losses are enough to worry even the most bullish Internet investor. "This company is losing a lot of money. Long-term, they are going to have problems," says Tom Taulli, research director at Silicon Investor.[54] But just as Amazon.com has argued, iVillage professes that such losses are required at this stage in the game. For the company to lock in portal distribution deals, build brand awareness, and acquire related companies, iVillage argues, it needs to spend heavily now. Although the argument is logical, the magnitude of the losses is over the top. The stock market has reacted accordingly, sending iVillage's stock price from a high of $130 per share soon after its IPO down into the $20 range. If iVillage does not curb its spending habits soon, it will be forced back to the capital markets in a short time. And with a low stock price, the company will get much less cash than it desires for the equity it will be forced to give up.

The Competitive Threat   ▼

On the competitive front, iVillage faces an immediate challenge from three primary opponents: Women.com Networks, CondeNet, and Oxygen Media. In addition, it must fend off Martha Stewart Living Omnimedia, a women-oriented media company with a strong presence in the offline world and ambitions to grow online. Finally, iVillage will soon begin running into a whole new set of competitors as it moves more aggressively into ecommerce.

Women.com Networks is a joint venture formed by two former rivals, the HomeArts Network and Women.com. The HomeArts Network was originally developed by the Hearst Corporation, publisher of some of the most prominent offline brands in women's media:

magazines such as *Cosmopolitan, Marie Claire, Country Living, Red-book,* and *Town and Country.* HomeArts has made content from these publications an integral part of its network, pulling "best of" articles from twelve different Hearst titles. HomeArts's traffic has been growing at a brisk pace, and the Hearst Corporation has plenty of media space in its print publications that it could allocate toward building awareness and traffic faster.

The second joint venture partner, Women.com, actually came to market earlier with a purer female focus than did iVillage. The company introduced Women's Wire, an online women's community, in 1992—a full two years before the Web had begun to catch on. Since those early days, Women.com has added a series of other sites on women's issues, such as Healthy Ideas, which covers personal health, and StorkSite, a site focused on pregnancy and parenting that Women.com acquired in 1998. The company gained good visibility early through its partnership with Netscape to develop Beatrice's Web Guide, a lively, women-oriented guide to the best of the Web. In those first years, it frequently served in press interviews as a spokesperson for women on the Web, because it was one of the few companies focusing on women online.

The new Women.com Networks has more total traffic than iVillage. And the competition is heated. Says Kate Delhagen of Forrester Research of the rivalry, "They're in a really deep, bitter tooth-and-nails struggle right now."[55] However, the Women.com alliance has plenty of problems to resolve—both at the individual partner level and at the level of the joint venture. Take a closer look at HomeArts, for example. Although brands like *Cosmopolitan* and *Country Living* carry significant power in print, the jury is still out as to whether these brands offer the kind of content that plays best on the Web. *Cosmo,* for example, is not exactly a publication that features "real" women. And *Country Living* does not focus on the kind of difficult life problems that concern the average woman. Given the research indicating that women approach the Web differently than men—that they come to the Web seeking solutions—this core content base does not seem optimized to meet their needs online. Admittedly, HomeArts has recognized the differences between the media and has worked hard to provide a greater feeling of utility within their online properties than you'll find in their print publications. For example, customers can search more than 3,000 recipes in the Eats channel's recipe finder or use the financial calculators in the Money Minded channel to help them plan their retirement savings. But at its core, the HomeArts Network is more aspirational than it is "real." HomeArts will need a stronger solutions orientation if it is going to hold up its end of the joint venture.

Women.com has its individual shortcomings as well. Although the company was the first women's site out of the chute, it has let its early mover advantage slide. How did the firm lose market traction? Women.com may have retained its focus on early adopters of the Web for too long, rather than devoting more energy toward welcoming the large numbers of female newcomers. As Candice Carpenter explains it, "I don't feel they were aggressive enough in reaching out beyond the early adopter audience at a key time when we took a lot of market share from them."[56] Women.com has not been chasing new distribution deals as aggressively as has iVillage; as a result, its brand visibility across the Web has declined relative to that of iVillage. With fewer deals concluded, there is less for the company to talk about, and Women.com's PR impact has correspondingly decreased. Finally, the firm has also done a mediocre job of cultivating community. It has given only modest billing to chat and forums. But the value in these forums and chat rooms comes from the richness of the discussion, the content dynamically created by the participants. With limited support, these interactive discussion areas simply haven't added much value to the Women.com brand.

At the joint venture level, Women.com Networks faces the same challenge that iVillage does: forging a unified umbrella brand. The company can leverage Hearst media properties such as *Redbook* and the A&E cable channel to help build broad awareness. But it is unclear as of yet just how much offline media space Hearst will make available to the new venture. In addition, I question the extent to which Women.com Networks will be able to speak with a common voice that both transcends and unites the myriad individual brands that are part of this consortium. The offline properties are extremely different, and the online properties all have their own tone. Attempting to develop a unified brand voice will be difficult. The joint venture that is Women.com Networks may well have a broader reach than any other Web-based women's network, but based on what I've observed to date, I think that the balkanized brands that are part of Women.com Networks will never be more than a loose confederation of individual players.

Another key iVillage competitor, CondéNet, bears many similarities to Women.com Networks. Like the HomeArts component of that joint venture, CondéNet has its roots in traditional media. Owned by publisher Condé Nast, CondéNet is a network of four sites with a primarily female audience: Epicurious Food, a Web haven for gourmets; Swoon, which focuses on dating and relationships; Epicurious Travel, a Web destination for the ardent traveler; and Phys, a nutrition and health site. While the sites contain plenty of Web-specific content, they also draw liberally on Condé Nast publications such as *Mademoiselle, Glamour, Gourmet,* and *Condé Nast Traveler.* And as you would expect, the problems are parallel. For example, CondéNet, too, is struggling to build awareness for the umbrella brand. In the second half of 1998, the company ran a multimillion dollar ad campaign in publications such as the *New York Times Magazine* and *Yahoo! Internet Life,* as well as in Condé Nast magazines such as *Self* and *House & Garden.* Unlike iVillage and Women.com Networks, however, Condé Nast does not have access to television properties it can leverage to build awareness. And CondéNet's community features are not nearly as robust as those in the various iVillage properties, which means the company misses out on the associated loyalty boost. CondéNet's traffic levels are certainly respectable. But the company plays second fiddle to both iVillage and Women.com Networks.

The third major competitor that iVillage must watch is Oxygen Media, a newcomer with serious ambitions. Oxygen was founded by Geraldine Laybourne, the former head of both Disney/ABC Cable and Nickelodeon and one of the highest-ranking women in television.

Wired magazine has described Laybourne as "the rival from hell," and her celebrity status has already helped Oxygen to secure significant press coverage.[57] I believe that Laybourne and her team are going to cause trouble for iVillage. Laybourne's goal is to create an integrated media company that develops branded content for the Internet, network and cable television, and other media (*Wired* has also dubbed her the "Convergence Queen"). In very little time, Oxygen has attracted a powerful array of partners and investors, including AOL, ABC, Oprah Winfrey's HARPO Entertainment Group, Disney, TCI, and Carsey-Werner-Mandabach, the creative team that developed television hits such as *The Cosby Show, Roseanne,* and *3rd Rock from the Sun.* The money, distribution power, brand strength, and creative talent that these companies bring to the table is significant and threatening.

Oxygen has yet to release any new Web or television content as of this writing. The television content will not launch until January 2000. But the company plans to unveil two original Web properties in the summer of 1999 that focus on relationships and entertainment. At that time, it will also relaunch revised versions of three sites (the set is now known as Oxygen Online) that Oxygen acquired from AOL as part of its equity deal with that company: Electra, an online network for women; Thrive, a site focused on health and lifestyle issues; and Moms Online, a virtual community devoted to supporting, nurturing, and entertaining mothers. These sites boast healthy traffic volumes, and the news that Oxygen had acquired the trio from AOL shocked the iVillage team. "When the deal was announced, 'there was a gasp' in the iVillage office, one executive recalls. 'It was sort of like, There's a giant coming, what do we do?'"[58]

Oxygen Online takes dead aim at iVillage's target market. Not only do its various sites mirror the content available on the iVillage network, it is even sparring with iVillage for the best distribution opportunities on AOL, which is an investor in both companies. Given the amount of traffic iVillage gets from AOL, this is a big concern. The iVillage prospectus, in fact, had a section devoted to this issue titled "Our Dependence on AOL." The text reads "If carriage of our channels on AOL is discontinued, our business, results of operations and financial condition would be materially adversely affected."[59] The contract between AOL and iVillage expires on December 31, 2000. After that, there are no guarantees that Oxygen won't run off with this major iVillage distribution partner.

iVillage is partially protected from Oxygen and other new competitors by the barriers to entry it has developed. The company has done an excellent job in establishing its positioning as *the* home in cyberspace for women. It has forged a web of powerful allies—distribution partners such as Lycos, media partners such as NBC, and content partners such as *American Baby*—that form a network with a combined influence that is difficult to replicate. It has developed a deep knowledge of the kinds of content and services that matter to women after years of listening and responding to the needs of its customers. And most im-

iVillage has developed high barriers to entry. portant, it has cultivated one of the largest and richest communities on the Internet. Its members are women who are unlikely to turn to some new player over iVillage, for the online relationships they've built are with other iVillagers. Not only are these customers going to stick around, but many are going to tell their friends about the benefits of this women's Web haven based on their enthusiasm for iVillage's services. Oxygen and Martha Stewart Living Omnimedia (described next) may give iVillage a run for its money. But the barriers to entry that iVillage has developed will hinder even these major players. Smaller firms that take a run at this market will have virtually no chance of penetrating the defensive battlements iVillage has built.

Martha Stewart's company, Martha Stewart Living Omnimedia, also competes aggressively for the mindshare of the female audience. Of all of the companies covered here, however, Omnimedia is the one that is least entrenched in the online world. Its marketing efforts are also different from those of iVillage, which makes it worth a closer look.

In contrast to iVillage and its fellow "dot-com" competitors, the

Martha Stewart brand is built on the identity of a single person: Martha, the "diva of domesticity," the "nabob of nesting." Stewart and Omnimedia have developed a brand based on an individual, a domestic powerhouse who inspires a combination of envy, admiration, and loathing in women across the country. As Molly O'Neill of the *New York Times Magazine* describes her, "Martha is sexy. Martha is powerful. Martha is rich. . . . She is America's superego. The mother. The lover. The coach. The boss. The woman who can shingle the chicken coop as tastefully as she can cook the petit poulet."[60] It is a brand strategy that has its risks, for those who dislike what the brand stands for can attack it by ridiculing the person who embodies the brand. But in Omnimedia's case, it has been extremely successful. For while most women do not have time to whip up Russian buffet lunches, etch their own glass, or sew their own napkins, there are plenty who yearn to have time to do more around the house than today's microwave/take-out food/lettuce-in-a-bag lifestyle permits.

Another key element of Omnimedia's strategy has been to cast the Martha Stewart brand as a lifestyle. The truly loyal customer—the devotee of the "doyenne of doilies"—should not merely watch Martha's television show or purchase one of her cookbooks. Omnimedia wants that customer to buy pumpkin carving kits and stationery-embossing designs from *Martha By Mail,* the company's catalog outfit. They want her to paint her house with paint co-developed with Sherwin Williams, plant her garden with flowers recommended in *Martha Stewart Living* magazine, and make love between co-branded bedsheets marketed through Kmart. Omnimedia is driving to turn the Martha Stewart brand into an experience, to integrate its brand throughout its customers' lives. And while Omnimedia hasn't yet turned the entire American populace into Martha drones, it has penetrated the lives and minds of its customers to a much greater extent than have iVillage and its online peers.

Building such customer ties to the Martha Stewart brand and the lifestyle it represents has been closely tied to another Omnimedia strategy: the use of multiple media to communicate the "gospel according to Martha." On the print side, Omnimedia publishes two regular magazines—*Martha Stewart Living* and *Martha Stewart Weddings*—and multiple cookbooks, as well as a syndicated newspaper column that appears in 233 different newspapers. On air, the company produces both television and radio shows. It has developed a direct mail business that sells everything from French beach umbrellas to palm-frond "market bags." Its alliance with Kmart gains visibility for Omnimedia within the retail channel. The company even runs occasional gourmet cooking classes. This intensive multimedia strategy provides Omnimedia with an opportunity to communicate with its customers through a mix of channels unmatched by any online player. Even Oxygen Media, once it rolls out its full set of cable properties, will not have the array of links to its customers that Omnimedia has today.

Omnimedia's current Web site does little more than serve as an online brochure, but the company has the potential to develop a significant Web presence. It has volumes of content from its traditional media ventures that could be re-purposed for the Web. Its catalog business could be adapted for ecommerce. It has a broad suite of offline properties that it can use to build awareness for its Web-based business. And its initial public offering has given it the money it needs to grow quickly. Omnimedia may not yet provide day-to-day competition for iVillage and its kin. But the company has developed a unique brand that may soon represent a definite threat to the online players, all of which should be wary of Omnimedia and "the indomitable goddess of the home."[61]

As iVillage invests more heavily in ecommerce, it will begin to encounter a whole new competitive set. Some of these companies, such as BabyCenter, are focused on specific markets that are attractive to iVillage. (iVillage made its initial move into the baby products market through the purchase of iBaby in 1998.) In cases like this, the company will be up against specialists, firms that focus exclusively on particular market niches and have subject expertise that it will be hard for iVillage to match. The company will also face increasing competition from generalists. For example, in a recent visit to eBay, the well-known auction site, a search on "car seat" returned more than forty

```
      #100   12-16-2009 2:53PM
Item(s) checked out to Moser,Steven Dary

TITLE: Sams teach yourself to create Web
BARCODE: 30109010886979
DUE DATE: 01-13-10

TITLE: How to run your own home business
BARCODE: 30109011438366
DUE DATE: 01-13-10

TITLE: The joy of working from home : ma
BARCODE: 30109007563961
DUE DATE: 01-13-10

TITLE: eBrands : building an Internet bu
BARCODE: 30109012811660
DUE DATE: 01-13-10

          NDSU Main Library
            (701) 231-8888
```

6100 12-16-2009 2:53PM
Item(s) checked out to Moser,Steven Dary

DUE DATE: 01-13-10

DUE DATE: 01-13-10

DUE DATE: 01-13-10

DUE DATE: 01-13-10

different infant seats for sale. While Amazon.com has not yet begun selling baby products directly, it is not hard to imagine the company moving in this direction as it increases the scope of goods it offers its customers. And of course, like eBay, Amazon is already running person-to-person online auctions that allow one consumer to sell another an old high chair or baby monitor.

Both types of ecommerce competitors may prove problematic for iVillage. A company like BabyCenter has a reputation as an industry specialist and may well be able to offer a richer selection of products than iVillage can. A firm like Amazon.com has a huge customer base to which it can cross-sell the same kinds of products that iVillage may offer. In the face of daunting competition, the company's best strategy is to position itself as "the village merchant." In a small town, a local grocer, say, will not only know regional food preferences, such as the general affinity that he has observed among the townspeople for a particular kind of bread, but will also be familiar with the specific tastes of individual customers. He'll know, for example, that Mr. Rudoff likes pears but is allergic to bananas. He'll remember that Mrs. Coghlan prefers glazed doughnuts to croissants. And he'll use this knowledge to provide his customers with exactly what they want. He'll also work to integrate himself into the community. Perhaps his store will sponsor a local soccer team. Or he might maintain a store bulletin board that enables locals to post notices about everything from lost dogs to garage sales. By participating in community life this way, the grocer builds trust and good will among the townspeople, increasing the likelihood that they'll do business with him rather than driving off to the Wal-Mart down the way.

eCommerce competitors may prove problematic for iVillage.

iVillage should adopt a similar strategy. Its iBaby store should sponsor iVillage content areas that cover parenting issues. It should leverage the opportunity that it has to talk to its customers via discussion groups to find out more about exactly what they want to buy online. It should provide them with special offers made available only to registered iVillage users. And it should deliver high-quality, personalized service. By following this "village merchant" approach, iVillage may be able to hold its ground against a growing set of ecommerce players eager to nab the online shopping dollars of wired women.

On the Horizon   ▼

In addition to the problems posed by its competitors, iVillage may well face a host of other troublesome issues in the future. One such problem with which the company will likely contend will be pressure to fiddle with the formula. Participants in the iVillage community have a tremendous degree of influence, both over what happens on community sites on a daily basis and over the network's evolution. The extent of its customers' power is unnerving even to the company's management at times; Candice Carpenter has described it as being "like giving the inmates the keys." Some potential advertisers will likely be downright skittish over their lack of control over the message. "Customers can say whatever they want," Carpenter continued. "They can say, 'We hate Tide. We think Chrysler sucks.'" To date, iVillage advertisers have proven themselves to be a wise lot. "Our advertisers are sophisticated," Carpenter said. "They realize that people are going to form opinions about these brands in communities anyway. The closer they are to being able to deliver their message in that environment, the better chance they have."[62]

Although these early adopters of the advertising medium that iVillage offers understand how to work with Internet communities, as the company expands its sales efforts it will encounter plenty of advertising prospects who just don't get it. Some of these organizations will simply be frightened off. Others, however, will argue for increased control, hoping to squelch or at least limit comments that reflect poorly on their products or services. And although they may not fully understand the medium, some of these companies will come to the table with large sums of money to spend.

Therefore, the challenge for iVillage will be to stick to its guns. If community participants feel that their exchanges are being limited in some way by advertisers, that they are losing sway over what happens on their "home on the Web," things would turn nasty quickly. Some community members would raise a ruckus. Others would just leave in disgust.

The company has resisted such pressures to date and has done a good job in evangelizing the nature of the medium to advertisers, helping them to understand how messaging works in cyberspace. Carpenter tells them, "In television, you tell a story and no one is talking back. Online is about people talking back to each other. It's not like television or magazines."[63] But iVillage may encounter advertisers who still don't understand, even after iVillage makes its pitch, and they may be companies with substantial advertising budgets. For iVillage to fiddle with its formula, however, would be to jeopardize its franchise (remember the "New Coke" debacle?). Although the money may be tempting, iVillage must pass on those advertising deals that would lead it to dilute the integrity of the communities it has developed.

iVillage may also see eventual dissension within the ranks of its volunteer network similar to that faced by AOL. AOL has more than 10,000 volunteers who help to moderate the many virtual communities accessible through the popular online service. In return for their time, these volunteers have received free AOL accounts. In April 1999, however, a group of seven disgruntled former volunteers confronted the company, asking the Labor Department to investigate whether the use of volunteer labor by AOL violated the Federal Fair Labor Standards Act. Although the Labor Department has not made any decisions yet, if AOL is eventually found in violation of wage and hour laws, it could be forced to pay double the compensation to which these workers should have been entitled. If the company were found to have made such violations willfully, AOL could be subject to civil penalties and even criminal prosecution.

iVillage has only 1,000 volunteers who work on community-building efforts, a fraction of those associated with AOL. But if AOL is found by the Labor Department to be in violation of federal laws, this precedent could spark unrest within the ranks of the iVillage volunteer corps—particularly if people sense an opportunity to make money through a settlement. iVillage could do a number of things to avoid such problems. The best thing the company can do is to regularly acknowledge its appreciation for the services that these volunteers provide. And it should do so in a public forum. For Candice Carpenter, for example, to post a personal message on a well-managed community message board thanking a volunteer for her hard work would mean a great deal to that person, yet cost the company nothing. iVillage could also consider rewarding its volunteers in some way. GeoCities, another online communities player that relies on volunteer help, offers its 1,800 volunteers Geo-Points that they can use to buy products and services on GeoCities in exchange for their work as community leaders. As iVillage becomes more deeply involved in ecommerce, it will have an increasing array of products available for sale to which such discount points could be applied. Finally, the company could always resort to providing its community leaders with modest cash compensation should the tide turn against online volunteerism. About.com, a guide to the Internet, relies on freelancers to develop its content. The company pays these people a base amount, plus a percentage of the advertising revenues that their specific content areas generate.

Of course, iVillage hopes it does not have to begin paying its community leaders to continue their work. And although the company should definitely reward its volunteers with public praise, I don't think that iVillage will need to do more than that unless the AOL case mucks up the waters. As spokesman Bruce Zanca of GeoCities has noted, "These people are the cyber equivalent of scout leaders and PTA members and the Rotary and Kiwanis clubs. Why do people participate in these programs? It's the same reason I coach Little League on Saturday mornings. It's something people do for their own personal reasons."[64]

Finally, iVillage will face a challenge as it works to integrate ecommerce into the virtual community it has developed in a way that does not offend its members. If iVillage is overly assertive in pitching products to its customers, it could easily anger them. It would be as if a respected physician began hawking phony cure-alls during an office visit. You'd be furious, and for good reason. Instead, iVillage needs to blend its ecommerce efforts into the fabric of the community. If that same respected physician sponsored a bake sale to raise funds for local cancer victims, you certainly wouldn't protest. In fact, you'd probably buy an angel food cake or a raisin nut loaf and feel good about your purchase.

iVillage is fairly low key today about the online shopping opportunities it presents, perhaps because the company is just starting to add such functionality to its network of sites. On the iVillage home page, for example, you might see a small message cross-selling iMaternity.com, "the shopping solution for expectant moms." Or you might encounter in-house banner ads as you browse through sites within the iVillage network that encourage you to visit the iVillage shopping channel. As mentioned earlier, however, iVillage is still operating in the red. As the pressure to produce better financial results increases, so will the drive to market shopping opportunities more aggressively. iVillage will need to proceed carefully as it moves to monetize its customers through ecommerce. If its cross-selling pitch is too blatant, iVillage could be seen as violating the trust it has so carefully cultivated with its community members.

www.CDNOW.com

Jason Olim knew there had to be a better way to buy music. After hearing Miles Davis's album *Kind of Blue*, he had visited a number of different music stores in Boston in an attempt to find other albums by the trumpet virtuoso. The selection these stores had to offer was meager, however, and none of the clerks could advise him as to which of the Davis recordings that they had in stock he might like. Frustrated by the limitations of the traditional music channel, Jason began hatching plans for a Web-based music store in 1994—the earliest days of the commercial Web. He soon roped his twin brother, Matthew, into the venture to help him develop the underlying software needed to make the site work. With several thousand dollars of their own money (Jason had been saving for a new bass guitar) plus a $20,000 loan from their parents, the twins founded CDNOW.

Their original intentions were modest. "I was imagining three people. We were going to manage a computer and eat pizza," said Jason.[1]

But as Web usage grew, Jason and Matthew realized they had stumbled on an unusual opportunity. They focused intensely on building a business and worked on the project seven days a week, with Matthew even brushing his teeth in front of the computer. In 1995, its first year of business, CDNOW sold more than $2 million worth of compact discs. By 1997, sales had risen to $17.4 million. By 1998,

CDNOW had grown to be a public company with hundreds of thousands of items for sale, a 33 percent market share of the online music retailing industry, and a customer base of greater than 300,000 people.

It was in that same year, however, that life began to get complicated for CDNOW. Competition with rival N2K intensified, and both companies were suffering financially from the costs of sustaining expensive marketing campaigns. Then in June, Amazon.com entered the online music market, and the threat posed by N2K was dwarfed by concerns about Seattle's bookish online behemoth. These concerns proved valid when in less than six months, Amazon.com overtook CDNOW to become the market leader. Analysts bemoaned CDNOW's future. The stock swooned.

But the pendulum began to swing the other way in 1999 when CDNOW and N2K merged. Critics started to change their tune. "Now they stand a definite chance to survive or thrive in that specific category," said Kate Delhagen of Forrester Research.[2] Several months later, things got even more interesting when CDNOW merged with Columbia House, the entertainment firm co-owned by Sony and Time Warner. CDNOW brought 2.3 million customers to the table; Columbia House more than 16 million (2 million of whom who had purchased online). Opportunities for future growth look compelling. The number of online households that shop on the Web is projected to quadruple from 9.3 million in 1998 to more than 39.9 million in 2002.[3] By that same year, the online music market is projected to reach $2.8 billion.[4]

There is much to learn from examining both CDNOW's accomplishments and shortcomings, as well as from an analysis of the challenges it is likely to face in the next several years. How has CDNOW effectively leveraged both online and offline marketing to build awareness? How has the company used various forms of research to develop an intimate knowledge of its customers and their specific needs? What difficulties does it face in attempting to migrate N2K customers to the CDNOW brand? What threats and opportunities does the emergence of digital music distribution present to the firm?

CDNOW Snapshot (1999)

URL: www.cdnow.com
Ticker symbol/Exchange: CDNW/Nasdaq   **Headquarters:** New York, NY
Year founded: 1994   **CEO:** Jason Olim

Business concept:	Online music retailer. Improves on the traditional shopping experience by offering substantial selection in a single online location. Provides customers with rich, related content (e.g., reviews) that facilitates informed purchase decisions. Offers limited digital music downloads.
Brand assets:	Brand awareness; customer commitment; distribution and content alliances; early mover advantage; customer and market intimacy; reputation for service excellence
Initial investors:	Grotech Capital and Keystone Venture Capital
Primary competitors:	Online: Amazon.com Offline: Tower Records, Barnes & Noble, Virgin Megastores
Major strategic partners:	Yahoo!, MTV Networks, *Rolling Stone*, SonicNet, Lycos, Excite

Major milestones:

August 1997	Raises $10 million through private placement
August 1997	Forges distribution partnership with Yahoo!
February 1998	$65.6 million IPO
March 1998	Launches integrated Grammy promotion
April 1998	Signs content distribution partnership with *Rolling Stone*
April 1998	Signs three-year, $18.5 million distribution deal with Lycos
May 1998	Signs three-year, $22.5 million advertising deal with MTV
June 1998	Pulls planned secondary offering
June 1998	Enables customers to create custom CDs
July 1998	Launches MTV/VH1 ad campaign
March 1999	Merges with N2K, former archrival
May 1999	Launches merged CDNOW/N2K site
July 1999	Merges with Columbia Records

Financial summary (CY 1998):	**Revenue: $56.4 million** **Net income (loss): ($43.8 million)**
Shares outstanding:	15.7 million
Number of employees:	191

These are among the myriad issues we'll consider in this detailed look at one of the earliest and best known consumer ecommerce players.

Best of Brand   ▼

In its battle for success in its contentious market, CDNOW has performed well in many ways. For example, it has developed innovative, well-targeted marketing programs both online and off that have driven large volumes of traffic and have exposed the brand to millions of potential customers. It has personalized its product offering and its communications with customers in a way that makes them feel that CDNOW is "their store." It has built a capable customer service team that handles customer inquiries from across the globe. It has developed a detailed understanding of its customers' needs that has enabled the company to create both better products and more effective marketing campaigns. And it has established an extensive affiliate network—the online equivalent of a franchise system—that has enabled it to both build awareness and extend its sales reach. We'll begin our analysis of the firm with a close look at these and other brand assets that CDNOW has created since the company debuted in 1995.

Brand Awareness ▼

Key to CDNOW's success has been the clarity and simplicity of its messaging strategy. This platform has had two primary planks. First, CDNOW has emphasized the fact that it has built a better music store, as evidenced by its service orientation and broad product selection (CDNOW offers roughly 500,000 items for sale, whereas a brick-and-mortar music superstore may have tens of thousands of recordings in stock). Second, the company has stressed that CDNOW helps people discover music. It supports this claim by providing its customers with the tools they need for learning more about music that might interest them. The Album Advisor (a home-grown music recommendation service powered by artificial intelligence), a collection of approximately half a million sound clips, and *Rolling Stone* music reviews all aid in the music discovery process. In its efforts to build brand awareness, CDNOW has built the core of its communications efforts around these two simple concepts.

Public Relations   As with many of the other companies featured in this book, CDNOW has made public relations one of the highest-priority tools in its brand-building tool kit. CDNOW formulates the majority of its PR strategy in house; Marlo Zoda, the firm's public relations manager, directs Middleberg Associates, a New York–based agency, in implementation. Public relations is a marketing tool that can generate significant exposure for a company at a low cost per impression, particularly when compared with alternatives such as print and television advertising. And in the high-tech sector, public relations is even more influential than usual

Word of mouth powerfully influences online purchasing decisions.

because word of mouth has a particularly powerful effect on people's purchasing decisions online. Because of these factors, PR has been considered key at CDNOW since the early days of the company.

The story of how CDNOW was founded—the "two twin brothers with little money and lots of guts reinvent the music industry" story—is a compelling one. CDNOW realized the appeal of this story to the "wannabe entrepreneur" in all of us and has had co-founder Jason Olim out on the speaking circuit and interviewing with the press since the company's first year. In addition to serving as an effective way to build general awareness for CDNOW, this story has been a vehicle through which the company has been able to communicate its two major messaging concepts. Jason's failed quest for Miles Davis recordings illustrated the existing need for a music store that not only offered greater breadth and depth in selection, but also helped customers to learn more about music they might like. The founding of CDNOW showed how Jason and Matt delivered on these fundamental customer needs.

The company relied on this story in its early days to deliver its principal messages, securing coverage in publications ranging from the *Financial Times* to *Inc.* And although CDNOW continues to tell the tale of its origins on occasion, it has shifted its efforts to securing stories that emphasize how the company is continuing its work to provide customers with a better music store. This was a wise choice, because CDNOW's mainstream customers are less interested in the origins of the business than in how well it serves them. From strategic partnerships to acquisitions to major new features, the company uses public relations to stress the various ways in which it is providing value to its customers. As one CDNOW manager noted, "You want to make sure that people don't think you've become big and fat, that you've lost your creativity and ingenuity. You have to continue to show people that you are on the edge, that you are still improving the store. It is crucial to the media and to consumers to show them that you are on the move, as they equate that with success."[5]

As we saw with iVillage, CDNOW is driving to show momentum, and public relations can help to do this. Rod Parker, senior vice president of marketing and merchandising, describes his quest for the "mo factor" this way: "Newton's law of brand building states that a brand at rest has a tendency to stay at rest, and a brand in motion has a tendency to stay in motion. What we're trying to do is to create a brand in motion, and it requires outstanding marketing to do that."[6] For CDNOW, recounting its progress through good PR has been almost as important as the actual accomplishments themselves in the effort to create a perception of momentum in the marketplace.

Online Marketing   CDNOW has used online advertising to get the word out for some time now. The company began its marketing efforts with a tight focus on Web enthusiasts. Online advertising was the logical way to reach these early adopters; the firm did not use more traditional marketing tools, such as TV and radio (described later in this chapter), until several years after it first opened its virtual store.

CDNOW views online advertising as a way of both generating traffic and building awareness. Arielle Dorros, account manager at i-traffic (CDNOW's online ad agency) explains the philosophy this way: "It's particularly important online for users to recognize and trust a brand name before they are willing to transact at that site. And so while advertising online is generally seen by online merchants as a direct response vehicle [one that drives the customer to take immediate action], in reality it's a hybrid between awareness generation and direct response advertising."[7] CDNOW's perspective is a logical one, for when compared with traditional advertising media, online advertising resembles a cross between typical direct response advertising, such as direct mail, and the standard awareness-building media, such as print, radio, television, and outdoor advertising. Like the latter forms of advertising, online campaigns can be helpful in generating awareness of a product or service. In addition, however, online advertising presents the prospect with the opportunity to take immediate action: to click on the ad and be transported to another Web site at which she can buy a CD, say, or purchase an airline ticket. In this way, online advertising is closer in spirit to direct mail, which is designed to spark a timely response. But whereas direct mail often requires a prospect to wait patiently to be rewarded for his efforts (fill out that business reply card requesting a subscription to *Time*, for example, and you'll wait several weeks before actually getting a magazine), online advertising promptly engages the prospect in an interaction with the advertiser.

Before it retained i-traffic, CDNOW had experimented with running banner ads on music-related sites such as IUMA, the Internet Underground Music Archive. This strategy made sense; as Rod Parker says, "You fish where the fish are."[8] But once it hired i-traffic, CDNOW and its agency began testing some new ideas. They started with media, trying keyword buys on major search engines (with a keyword buy, the site displays a banner ad when the site visitor searches on a particular word or phrase). What were response rates like based on the purchase of generic words related to the category, such as "CD" or "music"? How did they compare with keywords tied to specific groups, such as "Nirvana" or "Led Zeppelin"?

As CDNOW and i-traffic were learning about the most effective ways to buy advertising on the search engines, these sites were attracting an increasing percentage of Internet traffic, morphing into the portals (the primary gateways to the Internet) they have become today. CDNOW soon became more sophisticated in the way it approached advertising with portal sites, tying ad buys together with the kind of "Web tenancy" deals we discuss later in the chapter. The relationships that CDNOW ultimately developed with the portal sites have given the company a level of exposure beyond that available through simple banner buys, providing the firm both with the opportunity to build awareness among prospects within music-related areas of partners' sites and to generate transactions from people looking to make a purchase.

CDNOW and i-traffic have also tested media buys that were not music related, but would deliver them the same demographic that they would find on the music sites: their target market of twenty-five- to forty-nine-year-old, time-pressed, Internet-connected music lovers. Explains Arielle Dorros, "Our theory was that there were these folks out there—the early adopters—who had been using the Internet for a long time and were more likely to be comfortable using their credit cards online. We wanted to test that thinking."[9] The team's hypothesis was correct, and it led CDNOW to pursue advertising on some unusual sites. Take *The Onion,* for example, a wicked news satire that *Select* magazine has called "the funniest thing on the Internet."[10] With section titles such as "Pathetic Geek Stories" and "Savage Love" and headlines such as "New Wonder Drug Enables Users to Get Higher Than Hell," *The Onion* is an edgy, irreverent online publication that attracts the kind of prospect that CDNOW is looking for— smart and Internet savvy. Another good match has been Spumco.com, a site developed by Ren and Stimpy creator John Kricfalusi that features animated cartoons starring George Liquor and his nephew Jimmy the Idiot Boy. The cartoons are entertaining, raunchy, and feature slick animation—just the kind of thing a true Web-head might enjoy. These sites can't deliver the volume of impressions that a search engine can, but they target an attractive demographic slice for

CDNOW, building brand and generating traffic from highly qualified customers.

i-traffic and CDNOW have also experimented with a wide range of different creative concepts in their joint effort to drive traffic and raise brand visibility. For example, CDNOW did not simply run banners on Spumco.com; rather, i-traffic worked with the Spumco team to secure exposure for its client within the cartoons themselves. At the end of an episode of "The God Damn George Liquor Show," George would indicate that the show had been sponsored by CDNOW. Viewers would then be transported directly to the CDNOW site. This tight integration of marketing message with content is the direction an increasing number of Web marketers are headed (iVillage's success selling sponsorships is a case in point). The more closely the two are intertwined, the more receptive prospects appear to be to marketers' offers.

Although ad units such as the Spumco sponsorship may be more intriguing than banner advertising, banners are and will be a Web marketing staple for some time to come. And although Internet marketers grumble about the limitations of banner advertising, the medium can be effective when it is used thoughtfully. CDNOW, for example, has run "spiff" banners ("the online equivalent of those three-ounce soap samples," quips Rod Parker[11]) that have offered prospects discounts on certain albums, a type of ad that both prompts the viewer to take action and reinforces the value that CDNOW provides to its customers.

The company has also developed banners that allow the viewer to search for albums by a particular artist from within the ad. When the prospect clicks through, he is transferred directly to the list of titles by that artist that are available on CDNOW. Such ads give the viewer first-hand exposure to the wide selection of recordings the company has to offer, enhancing the perceived quality of the service in the eyes of the customer and possibly driving a transaction. CDNOW has run such online ads for several years now—testing, evaluating results, modifying the ads and testing again to continuously improve its marketing at a pace that is only possible on the Web.

Offline Marketing   According to a recent study by the Intermarket Group, 86 percent of the top ecommerce sites now spend marketing dollars on traditional media.[12] CDNOW is one of these firms. The company clearly understands that to build brand and grab share during this time of mass migration to the Web, it has to invest substantially in offline marketing—a change from the early days of the medium. CDNOW has spent tens of millions on offline advertising and will invest even more in the future. The company will augment this spending not only because it has seen increases in both awareness and transactions as a result of its offline advertising, but also because the number of Internet companies using offline media has ballooned since CDNOW first turned to tools such as radio and television. As a result, the firm has been and will be forced to spend more aggressively to rise above the noise created by other Internet companies. What's more, the demand for offline advertising space is resulting in an increase in the price for such media. Once again, CDNOW is going to have to invest ever-greater amounts to secure the media space it needs.

> The number of Internet companies using offline advertising media has ballooned.

CDNOW experimented with limited print advertising early on in publications such as *Rolling Stone, Spin,* and *Variety.* But at the advice of Hampel/Stefanides, CDNOW's ad agency, the company eventually focused on radio and television, media that the agency felt would best help CDNOW achieve the reach it was looking for and would most effectively communicate the CDNOW message. CDNOW has invested in two different types of radio advertising. In the first type, the company has teamed up with Howard Stern, host of the raunchy morning show that has legions of morning drive-time fans—an audience larger than the population of cities such as Philadelphia, Boston, and Dallas. By purchasing sponsorship spots on the show, CDNOW has lined up Stern as a spokesperson for its brand. The ad unit is a sixty-second blurb about CDNOW; but though CDNOW and Hampel/Stefanides have prepared Stern with "speaking notes" galore, when he talks about the brand, he does it his way. "Howard has certain things that you have to understand come with the territory," agency vice president Kevin Perlmutter explained to me. "He definitely has a passion for the brand. He cannot be counted on to talk about everything you want him to say, but then again, you are not buying Howard for his ability to great voice-over according to script. You are buying Howard for his personality and his connection with his audience."[13]

Opting to advertise on the Howard Stern show was a risky decision for CDNOW, for in doing so it was entrusting the communication of the brand message to a spokesperson over whom the company had little control. I believe, however, that the decision was the right one given the make-up of Stern's audience and the influence that the radio personality has over his listeners. These people are serious fans. Perlmutter says, "It's a very distinct following. They love him, they listen to what he says, they use the brands that he advertises."[14] By leveraging Stern as a spokesperson, CDNOW has built awareness and generated sales within an attractive demographic segment (the average Howard Stern fan is a twenty-four- to fifty-four-year-old man with a household income of more than $50,000, a college education, and a white collar job). And given that Stern is into technology and frequently talks about the Internet during his show, the sponsorship has been a natural fit.

Although celebrity endorsements are common in the offline world (think of Mike Meyers—also known as Austin Powers—for Virgin Atlantic, Cindy Crawford for Revlon, Bill Cosby for Jello, and countless others), such endorsements have only recently begun to make their way into Internet marketing. As celebrity endorsements have become more common for Internet companies, some interesting similarities and contrasts have emerged with regard to the use of such endorsements online and off. For example, in the offline world, a company is given more leeway to use a spokesperson who is not connected to its industry. (What does Candice Bergen—who represents Sprint—have to do with telecommunications?) In the Internet arena, aligning with a celebrity who has no affiliation with the online world can draw snickers. Case in point: When Excite signed on Barry Bonds of the San Francisco Giants for a promotional campaign it was running, people found the link to be odd and made fun of Excite as a result. Other issues, however, are common to celebrity endorsements regardless of the industry sector in which they are used. For example, such endorsements always involve risk because a company is linking its brand to a person, and that person may falter. When O.J. Simpson was tried for murder, Hertz—which had not run its "O.J. running through the airport" commercials for years—still felt the heat because its brand was associated with a purported killer. In Excite's case, Barry Bonds has shown himself to be no saint, either; the company took a definite risk in tying its brand to the controversial outfielder.

The Howard Stern sponsorship has had its difficult moments for CDNOW, such as the time when Stern let loose a huge belch in the midst of reading the CDNOW sponsorship blurb. In general, however, the endorsement program has been a good move for the company. As mentioned earlier, the Howard Stern show has not only reached the right target customers for CDNOW, but has also reached large numbers of them. Through the sponsorship, CDNOW has been able to gain access to more than forty different markets, many of which have high Internet penetration rates. And in the majority of these markets, Stern has the highest-rated morning drive-time show.

CDNOW has had to expand beyond Howard Stern, however, in order to get the true reach it needs to build brand on a national level. To do so, Hampel/Stefanides has helped the company to develop a nationwide radio spot program. Unlike the campaign CDNOW developed with Stern, the commercials that run as part of its spot program were prerecorded. These commercials, featuring humorous characters who tout the benefits of CDNOW, have run at high frequency levels in major markets across the country every couple of weeks. CDNOW and Hampel/Stefanides have experimented with different station formats: light rock, easy listening, classic rock, and so on. But in each case, the chosen stations have been among the most popular in their geographic region. By building brand this way, CDNOW has once again been "fishing where the fish are." The campaign has sparked interest in CDNOW among people who have already shown an enthusiasm for music, moving listeners from on-air to online music discovery.

Although radio has been the mainstay of *CDNOW*'s offline efforts to date, television advertising has served as an effective supplement. In its television work, CDNOW has focused on major music events, such as the Grammies and the American Music Awards. When it has run television advertising during these events, CDNOW has complemented the TV campaigns with site changes and public relations support to make them more effective. For example, during the 1998 Grammy Awards, CDNOW ran a series of three TV commercials, plus a fourth on *Late Night with David Letterman,* which followed the Grammies. These humorous spots featured Ian Plimsole, "the world's oldest roadie," a character who knew a lot about music but didn't know about CDNOW and the fact that it could help him to discover new music. The ads used the Ian character to explain the benefits of CDNOW and to offer prospects an incentive to try the service—50 percent off the recordings of all Grammy winners. As the event progressed, CDNOW's engineering staff stood at the ready. As soon as the winners were announced, the engineers updated the site with new pricing information. By the time a winner was half-way down the aisle to accept his or her award, the pricing of all of that artist's recordings had been changed. Soon after, CDNOW posted specific content on the site that highlighted award-winning albums and urged customers to buy them at the newly discounted rates. This close integration between CDNOW's television ads and the content of the site highlights the flexibility of the Web. The ability to make pricing and promotional changes so quickly is something that traditional retailers can't match.

CDNOW's initial television work proved to be effective enough to persuade the company to negotiate a major deal with MTV Networks, paying $22.5 million in cash and stock to secure rights as the exclusive music retailer to be featured on the 1998 MTV Video Music Awards, as well as other MTV and VH1 telecasts. In addition to locking up the advertising opportunity, the deal provided CDNOW with MTV content for use in the CDNOW online store, secured CDNOW a position as the sole online retailer to be featured on the MTV and VH1 sites, and committed the companies to developing a number of co-promotions based on certain MTV and VH1 properties. The alliance "affords CDNOW the opportunity to take its marketing strategy to the next level," said Jason Olim. "These are the only brands that have the true horsepower to move consumers from their televisions to their computers, and that's what marketing convergence is all about."[15]

All of the marketing activities described here have been directed toward building awareness for a sole brand: CDNOW. By focusing on developing a single branded property, CDNOW has avoided spreading itself too thin. In contrast, N2K, the former competitor with which CDNOW merged in 1998, developed a whole series of brands (Music Boulevard, Jazz Central Station, and Rocktropolis), an approach that dilutes the impact of a modest marketing budget and the energies of a medium-sized marketing team. When the two companies merged, the combined firm took the CDNOW name. What's more, the individual genre-specific brands that N2K had developed were eliminated and the content rolled into the main CDNOW site. Point your browser toward www.rocktropolis.com today and you'll simply be redirected to CDNOW instead. The results of this exercise in brand Darwinism support the merit of developing a single, monolithic brand during an Internet company's early years of building brand awareness. Given the challenge of building just one strong Internet brand, attempting to build a series of them from the beginning is likely to leave a firm with a collection of mediocre brands rather than one strong one.

Crafting a monolithic brand makes it far easier and cheaper to eventually develop line extensions of the umbrella brand—as Yahoo! has done with properties such as Yahooligans!, its children's Web directory—or to move into a related business, backed by the power of the strong brand name the company has already developed. After building momentum behind the CDNOW brand, for example, the company might open a site such as Sheet Music Central, an online store with a huge selection of digitized musical scores and charts that customers could order with a credit card and print right then and there. The store could be sub-branded as part of "The CDNOW Network," a collection of smaller, highly targeted sites all thematically tied to CDNOW's main business. By waiting to pursue such expan-

, sion until its primary brand was more established, CDNOW could lend the cachet of its brand to the new sites in its network, enhancing credibility with customers, and could also drive traffic to network sites from its primary site, www.cdnow.com. By concentrating on growing a single brand first, I believe that CDNOW made the right choice, for doing so has created a solid core business and has laid a foundation for later expansion should the company care to pursue such projects.

Customer Commitment ▼

As mentioned earlier, CDNOW has high repeat purchase rates. Forrester Research reports that, on average, 35 to 40 percent of an ecommerce site's sales come from repeat visitors.[16] Repeat customers account for more than 50 percent of CDNOW's sales, bettering this average. This kind of loyalty is one of a brand's most important assets and can have a huge impact on the profitability of the company. In his book *The Loyalty Effect,* Frederick Reichheld, director of Bain & Company's loyalty-retention practice, wrote of a study he and his colleagues performed across a diverse range of industries. They found that raising customer retention rates by 5 percent could increase the value of an average customer by 25 to 100 percent.[17]

CDNOW is a long-time believer in the "loyalty effect" and has constantly looked for ways to keep customers coming back. Such customers not only return to CDNOW, they may well tell their friends about it. How has CDNOW developed loyal, committed customers? We've mentioned many of the contributing factors already. The company has created a better way to shop for music. ("The most important customer loyalty tool is a great store," says Jason Olim.[18]) It delivers a quality service. And though we've covered the ways in which CDNOW communicates to prospective shoppers, we haven't yet looked at how the company communicates with its existing customers—another factor that helps CDNOW reinforce its relationship with its customer base.

When you open an account with CDNOW, you receive an email message from Jason Olim:

> *I started CDNOW with my twin brother Matt because I couldn't find what I was looking for at a conventional record store, and I realized that there must be other unsatisfied music lovers out there. Since then, our goal has been to build a better music store. When you visit CDNOW, we want you to have the best possible experience shopping for music. So if there is anything that we can do for you, please let me know.*

CDNOW reaches out to its customers from the beginning, leveraging the founder as spokesperson to communicate the vision behind the company and encourage dialogue. The note also urges customers to explore the site. "If you want to listen to music before you decide to purchase it, we have hundreds of thousands of sound samples in all musical genres. If you are interested in personalized recommendations based on the kinds of music that you like, visit CDNOW's Album Advisor on our home page." CDNOW knows that by helping new customers discover the information and advice the site offers, it has a greater probability of converting these initiates into long-term customers.

To keep communication with its customers alive after that initial purchase, CDNOW produces an email newsletter. Using email to communicate a marketing message to either customers or prospects is one of the most powerful tools available to an Internet marketer. Email marketing is low cost, direct, and customizable. It can reacquaint a customer with your brand or introduce a prospect to new products or services. It can deliver an educational message or drive a recipient to action. CDNOW is a believer; the company currently sends more than seven million email notes per day to its customers. *CDNOW Update,* the core of CDNOW's email marketing program, is a personalized, bi-monthly "opt-in" newsletter (customers elect to receive it) that helps people to explore music, providing them with information on recordings that might be of interest. The company has enlisted artificial intelligence software from Net Perceptions to analyze customers' prior purchases; the result is a newsletter that is tailored to individuals' musical tastes. If you've shown an interest in trumpet music before, for example, *CDNOW Update* might point you toward the latest album of Mozart recordings by the Canadian Brass. If you've tried Stan Getz, the newsletter may suggest you sample Charlie Parker. *CDNOW Update* will also brief you on sales and contests that may interest you (my personalized edition of the newsletter recently included a blurb on the company's "Million Dollar Music Mania" sweepstakes). In all cases, the newsletter points you back to the store.

The *CDNOW Update* program is an example of *one-to-one marketing*, the marketing concept developed by Don Peppers and Martha Rogers in their book *The One to One Future*. The authors defined their idea this way:

> *The basis for one-to-one marketing is share of customer, not just market share. Instead of selling as many products as possible over the next sales period to whomever will buy them, the goal of the one-to-one marketer is to sell one customer at a time as many products as possible over the lifetime of that customer's patronage.*[19]

This strategy of depth over breadth makes good sense, and the book sparked significant interest. But when *The One to One Future* was first published in 1993, the Internet was still primarily the realm of academics. The environment and tools suitable for one-to-one marketing were not yet ready for prime time. It was not until the emergence of the Web that the stage was set for marketers to begin implementing this concept efficiently. As Rod Parker describes it, "In the early '90s, the big buzzwords were 'one-to-one' and 'relationship marketing.' But these ideas were difficult to put into practice until now. With this technology, we can make these concepts real."[20] *CDNOW Update* provides customers with a regular reminder of the benefits the site has to offer, such as a broad and deep selection and help in discovering new music. By keeping the brand in front of the customer this way, CDNOW is doing everything it can to ensure that the next time that customer buys music, he buys from CDNOW.

CDNOW has also built loyalty by enabling its customers to develop their own personalized view of the store through a feature called My CDNOW. My CDNOW enables each CDNOW customer to customize the store to make it most useful for him. For example, with My CDNOW's Wish List, the music fan can keep track of albums that he finds while browsing the site and wants to buy at some future date. He can maintain a gift registry so that people who are shopping for his birthday gift, for example, will know just what to get him. He can also maintain an address book online, making it easy for him to send music to friends and family members when it's time for him to reciprocate.

Personalization has emerged as one of the big things that Internet marketers need to get right in order to strengthen loyalty and deepen customers' commitment to their brands. With the introduction of its customized storefront, CDNOW has created compelling reasons for its customers to stick around. Providing customers with the opportunity to tailor the store to meet their needs has given them a sense of ownership. It has increased the utility of CDNOW's service. And it has created switching costs, for once someone has filled out a substantial gift registry and has entered numerous addresses into her My CDNOW address book, the last thing she is going to want to do is visit another online store and enter this information all over again. Given such benefits, the development of My CDNOW is something that I think the company should have pursued earlier. CDNOW had seen other ecommerce players launch similar initiatives earlier and knew that it could profit by adding similar functionality. The company did not roll out such a program itself until the fall of 1998. Nonetheless, although CDNOW may have been a bit late to the game in adding such personalization features, the end results of this work have clearly been good.

The creation of its Fast Forward Rewards program is another CDNOW initiative that has reinforced customer loyalty. Taking a page from the playbook of the major airlines, CDNOW has developed an incentive program that rewards customers for doing business with the company. Each time a shopper buys something at CDNOW, he earns Fast Forward Reward points. When he accumulates enough of these points, he can spend them on a variety of different music-related products, from CDs to fold-up concert chairs, from CDNOW T-shirts to travel coolers. Although CDNOW could have turned to a company such as Netcentives to outsource this program and reward customers with frequent flyer miles—the common currency of such loyalty programs—it decided to build its own program because it wanted to offer a reward that was thematically linked to its brand. Such programs have been successful in other offline industries (airlines, rental car companies, and hotels have all put loyalty programs to good use); CDNOW has aimed to replicate that impact with Fast Forward Rewards.

Strong Content and Distribution Alliances ▼

CDNOW knows well that in the Internet space, forging strong strategic partnerships is crucial for a company looking to establish a leading brand. As a result, the company has invested substantial effort in developing these relationships. Like other companies featured in this book, CDNOW has cooked up a mixture of both content and distribution deals, alliances that have bolstered the brand in a variety of ways.

Content Deals   On the content side, CDNOW has focused on securing rights to music reviews, artist biographies, cover art, and other materials that make it easier for customers to explore new music and make informed purchasing decisions. For example, CDNOW has developed a partnership with *Rolling Stone* that enables customers to access thirty years' worth of *Rolling Stone* music coverage, including album reviews, biographies, music news, and audio and video clips. CDNOW has cultivated similar relationships with College Media, publisher of the *CMJ New Music Report* and *CMJ New Music Monthly*, and with MTV (as described earlier). And although it hasn't yet added song lyrics to the range of content it makes available to its customers, one could easily imagine the company working with the record labels to secure and display at least partial lyrics for select songs. By partnering with well-known content providers, CDNOW has leveraged the reputation of their brands to reinforce its own.

Distribution Deals   On the distribution front, CDNOW has focused on two primary types of partnerships in its efforts both to build brand awareness and generate sales. The first is with broad-based, highly trafficked Internet sites—the so-called Internet chokepoints (search engines, Internet access providers, key news and entertainment sites, etc.). The second is with a range of more focused specialist sites.

CDNOW must lock up prime partnerships, because high-value Internet real estate will get more expensive.

One of the most significant examples of the first type of alliance is the relationship that CDNOW struck with Yahoo!. According to Rod Parker, "Marketing is probability theory. We believe the highest probability of acquiring a customer or generating a transaction is where computers and music intersect."[21] To maximize this probability on the leading Internet portal site, CDNOW inked a deal with Yahoo! that secured it a position as "the premier music retailer" on the directory and its network of related properties. Links to CDNOW are featured on all of Yahoo!'s music category pages—from its listing of karaoke sites to its catalog of Barry Manilow fan sites—as well as on all of Yahoo!'s music search results pages. In addition, links to CDNOW are integrated within services such as Yahoo! Mail, the personalized MyYahoo! service, and Yahoo! Chat. The alliance with Yahoo! has generated both traffic and brand visibility for CDNOW and has locked competitors out of valuable online real estate.

Of course, such benefits don't come cheap. CDNOW paid Yahoo! $3.9 million for this exposure in the first year of the partnership—as well as $600,000 for associated advertising. Investors have begun to balk at the amounts that companies such as CDNOW are shelling out for these portal deals, because these pricey partnerships have a major impact on customer acquisition costs (CDNOW pays an average of $45 for every new customer). CDNOW is committed to building brand through such distribution partnerships, however, and its investment is in line with this strategy. And although such an outlay may seem substantial, in my opinion it is important for companies like CDNOW to lock up such prime partnerships now because securing high-value Internet real estate will only get more expensive as time goes by. Patrick Keane, an analyst with Jupiter Communications, also gives CDNOW good reviews for its partnership development efforts:

> *CDNOW understood early on the value of gaining online distribution. There are a lot of brands that have stagnated because they haven't been willing to fork over the cash to get placement on the top online portals. CDNOW has a crucial relationship with Yahoo!, and Yahoo! sees close to 30 million unique visitors a month through their door. That kind of distribution online is crucial for the success of any Internet brand, particularly one where people are executing transactions.*[22]

For another example of the deals CDNOW has struck with the highest-volume Internet sites, consider the strategic alliance that the company developed with GeoCities (recently acquired by Yahoo!). GeoCities provides a place on the Web for the virtual homesteader, offering free Web hosting for anyone who cares to develop and locate a site within the GeoCities community. What's the catch? Homesteaders must put up with GeoCities running banner ads on their pages in exchange for the free online turf. The GeoCities site is broken up into a hierarchically organized series of neighborhoods and suburbs: Business & Money, Shopping, Entertainment, and so on. CDNOW has purchased strategic real estate within key GeoCities suburbs that are related to music. Enter Bourbon Street, GeoCities' jazz area, and you may be enticed to visit CDNOW to purchase *Benny Goodman Live at*

Carnegie Hall. Visit Nashville, the area that features country music Web pages, and you may be extended an offer to buy the latest Garth Brooks album through CDNOW. CDNOW has paid a lot of money for such placement. But in doing so, it has established a key distribution point on one of the ten most heavily trafficked sites on the Web. When GeoCities customers go looking for information on music—whether it be classical or fusion, hip hop or jazz—CDNOW is clearly visible.

In addition to pursuing deals with high-traffic generalists, CDNOW has also teamed up with sites that focus on music. The company has done so in two different ways. The first has been by developing relationships with a small set of high-profile sites dedicated to music issues. The second has been by partnering with a large number of much smaller music-related sites—a microsegmentation strategy that CDNOW has implemented by way of its affiliate marketing program.

Consider the relationship that CDNOW has developed with SonicNet, an online music property that *Advertising Week* has called "the most important rock music site on the Web." SonicNet is focused on a young audience: "college age and just after," according to David Friedensohn, the company's CEO. "When you get out of college, music is a passionate influence on your life," he says. "It's still something you care about, it's something you're interested in and your friends are interested in."[23] To satiate the desire of its target customers for rock-focused content, SonicNet delivers a mix of editorial coverage on the latest bands, chat sessions with popular artists, live Webcasts of major concerts, and backstage tours based on live video feeds. It also provides fans with the opportunities to purchase recordings of the bands they're hearing, reading, and talking about. "We will be connecting [the audience] directly with their artist," says Friedensohn.[24] As the principal retailing partner for SonicNet, CDNOW is there when those connections are made to profit from the passion these music diehards feel for their favorite bands.

To broaden its distribution reach, CDNOW has developed an affiliate marketing program called the Cosmic Credit program. The affiliate network—the online equivalent of a franchise chain—is an idea that has generated substantial momentum on the Web. Through the Cosmic Credit program, CDNOW has extended its distribution reach through a group of more than 230,000 small, music-oriented Web sites that cover the entire musical spectrum—from Green Day to Pat Metheny. Member sites can integrate "buy it" buttons within their content that will enable their viewers to purchase featured albums, T-shirts, videos, and other products through CDNOW. In return for the leads they provide, members of the Cosmic Credit program receive cash and free merchandise. CDNOW's affiliate network has proved to be "our most successful online customer building program," according to Jason Olim.[25] Given the tremendous number of music sites on the Web, there is still plenty of room to expand it. By leveraging the efforts of thousands of other people developing sites dedicated to particular artists or genres, CDNOW has expanded the influence of its brand to a degree that would be prohibitively expensive to accomplish on its own.

The Early Mover Advantage ▼

Like a number of the companies featured in this book, CDNOW identified a market opportunity early and moved quickly to capitalize on the potential it saw. The early mover position is an important asset for any brand, online or offline. But given the rate of change inherent to the Internet space, this asset will lose value quickly unless an Internet company moves aggressively to build on this position. Neil Weintraut, a founding partner of 21st Century Internet Venture Partners, encourages young Web ventures to "get out in front and run like hell." In a recent article in the trade magazine *Business 2.0*, Weintraut writes, "Care to know last week's weather forecast? Like forecasts, innovation loses its value—quickly—with time. As demonstrated all over the Internet, the best thing to do is to get in the marketplace."[26]

By getting to market early, an Internet company benefits from the buzz—and traffic—that comes with innovation. It acquires customers while it's still inexpensive to do so. It locks up important content and distribution partnerships. And it aligns itself with the most influential venture capital sources. Getting to market quickly, in short, can provide an Internet company with a valuable leg up on the competition. Of course, the challenge then lies in keeping up the pace. Mark Hardie, senior analyst with Forrester Research, puts it this way:

"Get out in front and run like hell."

"I liken it to race car driving. You really want to get out of the pit as quickly as possible, get your car up to speed and start lapping, because then all of a sudden it's just a race of fast cars, and if you've got a lead, they can't catch you unless an accident happens."[27]

CDNOW did get to market early, and it has shown in these first crucial years in the marketplace that it understands the need to maintain intensity. As described earlier, the company has continually pushed for new distribution partnerships to widen its sphere of influence. As we've discussed, CDNOW has scaled its investment in awareness-building efforts quickly. And it is constantly adding new functionality to the site, such as the ability for customers to mix and match tracks to create their own custom CDs. According to Olim, "Traditional businesses have multiyear planning cycles. We have multimonth planning cycles. For us, speed is God. For us to survive in the space and continue to thrive, we have to be ready to move faster than the world around us. Sitting around and deliberating for weeks or months means that by the time you come to your conclusion, things will have changed again."[28] The ability to hit the ground running and to keep running is essential for a company that is looking to build a strong Internet brand. The intensity of the competition in this emerging medium has made the race for market leadership a marathon run at full speed.

Customer and Market Intimacy ▼

CDNOW's focus on understanding its customers and market through research has yielded insights that have not only helped the company to build a better service, but also to market that service more effectively. On the product development side, the company has acquired this knowledge through a combination of both formal and informal methods. For example, CDNOW's customer support team has fed bits of "customer intelligence" to the product development group, providing them with information from the front line that has helped them to refine the service. "If we see a trend indicating that customers are having trouble with a certain aspect of the store, we run that right up the flagpole to product management and get them to fix it as soon as possible," explained Bob Trevor, director of customer service. "Our customers are our best friends when it comes to stuff like that."[29] The customer service representatives might notice, for example, that they have recently received a large number of email notes from people who have changed their minds about what they want to buy and have had trouble removing items from their virtual shopping carts. Or they may have processed multiple customer requests to be able to search for recordings by instrument in sections of the site other than the classical music area (the classical section is the only area of the store where you can hunt for music this way). They then pass such information on to the product management group, which determines how and when to fix the problem.

To supplement the information from the customer service team, CDNOW has also performed a fair amount of more structured, product-focused research. It has looked outward to the market, for example, benchmarking the usability and performance of its own site against competitors such as Amazon.com. The company has looked inward as well, analyzing both the performance of its current site and the effectiveness of changes that it has in the works. To help it evaluate the performance of its current service, CDNOW has developed a "digital dashboard"—a series of key metrics that assure management that all systems are go. Customer sessions per day, time spent per session, number of pages viewed, most frequently viewed pages, sales information, and a handful of other indicators are watched closely. Management looks to optimize these factors, and the dashboard readings have helped the company understand how it can improve the service it offers its customers and thus improve the strength of the business itself.

Such sets of key metrics are common to offline businesses as well. A traditional retailer, for example, might look at figures such as sales per square foot. An airline might track numbers such as revenue per passenger mile. One of the major differences, however, between online and offline metrics is that in the offline world there is wider agreement on just which statistics matter. The existence of this numerical lingua franca and the ready availability of the data make it easy for people to compare one company in an industry sector with another and contrast relative performance. On the Internet, however, there is still disagreement on exactly which statistics matter. A variety of different firms are vying to establish their companies, metrics, and calculation methods as the industry standards. In the online audience measurement sector, for example, Media Metrix, Nielsen/NetRatings, and others are all jockeying for position. Even when they do measure the same thing, there are often significant differences between the figures these firms present. Contrast this with the radio industry, in which one firm—Arbitron—leads the way and there is broad agreement on what is worth measuring. The lack of established standards, industry leaders, and universal metrics makes it much harder for an Internet company such as CDNOW to do a detailed comparison of the health of its business with that of others in the field.

Although crunching numbers has provided CDNOW with valuable readings on the state of its business, the company has also done a fair amount of usability testing to evaluate how well its service meets customer needs and how the site could be improved. Observing customers interacting with prototypes of proposed additions or changes to the site has provided product management with input that has helped the team to maximize the impact of these pending features. For example, when CDNOW decided to simplify its order placement process, the company ran usability tests to be sure that it was reducing the number of steps without introducing any confusion for customers. The lessons learned from customers during this research helped CDNOW to cut the number of steps required to place an order in half, a change that improved the customer experience.

CDNOW's penchant for research-based learning has also been

useful in crafting the company's outbound marketing programs. Surveying issues such as brand awareness, usage, customer demographics, and the role the brand plays in people's lives has given CDNOW the knowledge it has needed both to assess the impact its marketing efforts are having and to tune its marketing accordingly. Rod Parker explains the process as follows: "What we've been trying to do here is to understand how much our marketing is creating momentum. We've asked questions like 'Where did you find out about CDNOW?' or 'How did you enter the store?' We've learned how our marketing programs are affecting prospects and what our awareness has been in key local markets and on a national basis."[30]

With this knowledge in hand, CDNOW has adjusted its advertisements to better capture the issues that are most important to its customers. It has also analyzed the effectiveness of its media buying and made changes as necessary. For example, the awareness research that CDNOW has done enabled it to revise its media plan for the spot radio program that I described earlier. When it designed the program, the company had some assumptions as to which geographic markets it should target based on facts such as local Internet usage and the number of Internet service providers in the region. CDNOW conducted awareness research both before the campaign began and several months after launch to assess how awareness levels had changed. The results enabled the company to then focus its buys on those regions that were proving most responsive, maximizing the impact of its advertising dollars. This research/marketing feedback loop is one of several factors that has helped CDNOW to reach 24 percent national awareness within its target audience, a figure greater than any other online music vendor.[31]

A Reputation for Excellence ▼

A reputation for excellence is one of a brand's most fundamental assets—both online and off. This reputation will help engender the trust that prompts customers to do business with a vendor in the first place. This is particularly important on the Internet, where the re-assurance of human contact that is part of a transaction in the physical world is absent. Customers' belief in the quality of the product or service that a vendor offers not only keeps them coming back for more after that initial purchase, but leads them to spread the word among their friends.

CDNOW knows that it must deliver quality if it is going to build a brand that is going to stand up in the face of powerful competitors such as Tower Records and Blockbuster. The company has invested in developing its reputation as a high-quality merchant in a number of ways. For example, CDNOW offers a huge selection of products: over 500,000 CDs, 50,000 movies, and 10,000 music videos, as well as T-shirts, music books, and CD-ROMs. This breadth and depth dwarfs that of a typical music store, which may carry up to 12,000 SKUs (stock keeping units), and even that of a megastore, which may carry up to 50,000 SKUs. At a standard music store, 80 percent of the sales come from 20 percent of the titles on the market. And although more than 66 percent of the new titles released in 1996 came from inde-pendent record producers, the representation these "indies" receive in an average Blockbuster or Borders is slim, because these stores don't have the shelf space to stock such a range of recordings.[32] CDNOW aims to give its customers choice. Whether they're looking for a Char-lie Parker CD or a Metallica T-shirt, a Rachmaninoff recording or a video of Hitchcock's *The Birds*, CDNOW can probably help them track down the products they want. The richness of this range of offerings is attractive to customers and is a key element of perceived quality in the eyes of the company's clientele.

CDNOW supplements this diverse range of offerings with infor-mation that helps customers to make informed purchasing decisions. The site offers more than 155,000 notes, artist interviews, reviews, and related articles that shoppers can peruse as they mull over whether to buy a particular album. Consumers can also listen to song samples from the recordings they're considering (CDNOW offers more than 500,000 of these snippets). The information and assistance they can get from CDNOW to help them evaluate different products presents a substantial contrast to that available at an average retail store (ask the sixteen-year-old behind the counter about Mussorgsky and watch for the blank stare you'll get in return). Providing easy access to such expertise is another factor that has reinforced CDNOW's reputation as a quality online merchant.

Jason Olim has said that "your brand is not just what you say—it's what you do."[33] In this spirit, another factor that has strengthened CDNOW's reputation has been the company's commitment to offering excellent customer service. Providing prompt, courteous answers to customers' questions has made customers feel good about the company with which they are doing business and has enhanced their assessment of CDNOW. According to Bob Trevor, director of customer service, "The two critical aspects to customer service for CDNOW are the timeliness of the response and the quality of that response. We have a commitment to our customers to get back to them within 24 hours; for the most part, we do. And we make sure that our communications are complete, accurate, and helpful. I think getting these two things right has contributed to the CDNOW brand to an extent we have just now begun to realize."[34]

"Your brand is not just what you say—it's what you do."

Handling customer inquiries in a thorough and timely manner is all the more important for CDNOW as a Web-based merchant. If someone shopping at a Virgin Records store has a question or a problem, he can collar a store manager and deal with the issue then and there (although as mentioned earlier, the quality of the response may vary according to the knowledge and service orientation of the store's staff). If a customer is shopping online, however, he does not have the opportunity to have his concerns addressed immediately. If CDNOW is going to position itself effectively as a "better music store," it must respond to customer queries as quickly and in as detailed a manner as possible. Doing so can enable CDNOW to overcome the disadvantage associated with not providing customer assistance in real time.

For CDNOW, nailing customer questions can be tricky. A fair number of them are straightforward issues such as "When will my order arrive?" But handling even these simple questions is made more complex by the fact that almost a third of *CDNOW*'s sales come from overseas. CDNOW's site can be viewed in English, German, Portuguese, Japanese, and four other languages. International interest has been high, so CDNOW has hired a group of multilingual customer service representatives to handle the questions that flow in from everywhere from Tokyo to Milan. Managing the challenge associated with providing international customer support also presents CDNOW with an opportunity. If CDNOW runs international support adeptly, it can make a significant contribution to developing a global Internet brand. For a brick-and-mortar retailer to establish a presence overseas is a significant undertaking. It must secure and develop real estate, hire local staff, obtain and manage inventory, and so on. CDNOW, in contrast, can go a long way toward establishing a beachhead overseas simply by translating its site and providing multilingual customer support. True, it will eventually also want to invest in awareness-building efforts in the most promising overseas markets. But by translating its Web site and supporting customers in their native language, CDNOW can do a significant volume of international business at a fraction of the cost that a traditional retailer would incur to build its business abroad.

Even when the questions come to the CDNOW customer service team in English, they can still pose a challenge. The company frequently receives email notes that read like this: "I'm trying to track down a song from the seventies and can't recall the name of the song or the band that recorded the album. I know that the first line was, 'I met you on somebody's island.' Can you tell me what song this is, what album it's on, and who recorded it? And do you have it in stock?" To handle such inquiries, CDNOW has developed *feedback teams*—groups of customer service representatives with deep knowledge of certain musical subject areas. The feedback teams often surprise customers with their knowledge. The team might write back,

"The song you are looking for is 'Jungle Love' by Steve Miller Band. You can find it on *Greatest Hits (1974–78)*, now on sale at CDNOW for $10.49." The knowledge of different musical genres demonstrated by CDNOW's customer service group is beyond that of your average retail clerk. The feedback teams illustrate a commitment to quality through exemplary service that adds value to the CDNOW brand.

Once a customer has placed his order with CDNOW, he'd clearly like to receive that Steve Miller Band album or Rolling Stones T-shirt as soon as possible. By filling orders promptly, CDNOW has another opportunity to reinforce its image as a merchant that strives to please. The company begins to capitalize on this opportunity by sending an automated order confirmation note via email immediately after the order has been placed. By acting quickly, CDNOW shows the customer that his order is being handled expeditiously and also provides him with an order number and customer support contact information should he have future questions. Through its relationship with Valley Records, a record distributor that handles the majority of CDNOW's fulfillment logistics, CDNOW can then move quickly to deliver the desired product to the customer. Orders are shipped via first-class mail and generally arrive within four to six business days. In today's purchasing environment, customers expect prompt, efficient service; CDNOW meets these expectations.

The company also reinforces its reputation by offering a reasonable returns policy. Customers can return any item within thirty days for a full refund (minus shipping and handling). They can also check on the status of the return transaction in the Order History section of their personalized My CDNOW pages. If a product is damaged or defective, customers can return the merchandise to CDNOW at no cost. Such a policy mirrors that of the average retail music store. I think that CDNOW could do more with its returns policy than it has. It could offer a sixty-day return period, for example, or it could absorb the shipping and handling costs. However, its current approach to returns is a fair one and, administered consistently, contributes to customers' trust in the online merchant.

Chinks in the Armor   ▼

Although the brand assets described in this chapter are significant, there is no guarantee that CDNOW will retain the market position it has fought hard to secure. The company has its challenges, and if we are to develop a holistic understanding of the CDNOW brand, it's essential for us to explore these as well.

For one thing, the firm is feeling the financial pressures associated with rising customer acquisition costs. Margins are mediocre in the offline music business, and the same has been true for Internet-based vendors such as CDNOW. But the growing cost of attracting new buyers is squeezing margins even further, and that doesn't sit well with the investment community. Bob Tedeschi of the *New York Times on the Web* writes that "Internet retailers are being increasingly taken to task by investors for the exorbitant amounts they have spent to acquire customers—typically through advertising deals with portals such as Yahoo and America Online . . . (CDNOW has an estimated $100 million in portal advertising deals alone, according to one analyst.)"[35] In the earlier section on distribution and content alliances, we saw how expensive it is to play the portal distribution game.

Rising customer acquisition costs are squeezing margins.

Factors beyond distribution partnerships are contributing to CDNOW's escalating acquisition costs, however. Television time, for example, has been getting pricey fast. In fact, strong demand for national advertisers interested in buying commercials during the 1999 fall season has boosted the cost of media space by up to 15 percent.[36] As mentioned earlier, CDNOW is already paying an average of $45 per person for each new customer it brings into the fold. There are certainly Internet companies paying more; online brokerages, for example, are paying several hundred dollars per new customer these days. On the other hand, companies such as E-TRADE and Datek will earn much more from a customer over time through selling all manner of financial services than CDNOW will gain from someone buying CDs and music videos.

Given the likelihood that the company's customer acquisition costs will continue to increase, this puts even more pressure on CDNOW to wring greater value from online shoppers by retaining its customers longer and selling them more goods. As detailed in the "Customer Commitment" section, the firm is already doing a fair amount to keep its customers true, from pitching them purchase suggestions via email to rewarding them with frequent buyer points for shopping with CDNOW. If it is going to squeeze greater profits from each buyer, however, the company needs to get even more aggressive. CDNOW could intensify its cross-selling efforts. For example, when you look at a description of a particular recording on CDNOW today, the side bar of the description page tells you to click to get recommendations from the Album Advisor on other, similar albums you might like. But why make the customer take an extra step here? CDNOW should mimic Amazon.com, which presents information on other CDs purchased by customers who have bought this one right at the top of the album summary page. The more tightly integrated the cross-sell appeal within the shopping experience, the more successful it is bound to be.

CDNOW could also launch new services aimed at selling more to its existing customers. For example, the company could take a page from the playbook of its merger partner Columbia and develop an online music club, which could work as follows. A customer interested in a specific genre would sign up for the Jazz Greats Club or the Classical Masters Club. Each month, she would receive an email note with information on the club's selection that month, including reviews of the recording and a biography of the artist. If she liked the album, she need do nothing—it would be shipped to her automatically. If she did not like it, however, she could click through to a Web page on which she could pick one of several other possible selections. By forming such clubs, CDNOW would be gaining permission from its customers to sell to them *automatically* each month. If CDNOW is going to offset the troubles caused by rising customer acquisition costs, it needs to do everything it can to maximize the lifetime value of those customers it does bring through the door.

CDNOW is also grappling with the many complications associated with attempting to fuse three disparate corporate cultures. Things were challenging enough when CDNOW was attempting to absorb N2K. Wrote Janet Stites of the *New York Times on the Web,* "Culturally, the two companies are as diverse as their geography. N2K's management hails from the music industry, as do many of its employees; CDNOW is known more as a storefront rather than as an influence in the music industry, and its young founders are considered e-commerce prodigies. CDNOW has a basketball court; N2K has a house band."[37] The differences were significant, but at least both companies lived in the Internet space and had cultures in which constant change was accepted as a way of life. Adding Columbia House, however, brought into the mix an old-school direct marketer with a decidedly offline orientation. It is unclear just how much effort has been devoted to managing cultural fusion, or how successful that work has been.

Orchestrating the synthesis of the corporate cultures may seem to some like a "touchie-feelie" problem that is less important than resolving changes in the management structure or determining where the customer support group will be located. But managing such culture change is no cakewalk. "You can't just slam companies together and hope they are going to work," explains Craig Marino of Broadview Associates. "You need to spend the same amount of time working with the people as you do working on the valuation."[38] If CDNOW doesn't pay close attention to the cultural details associated with the union of the three companies, the result will be an organizational mess suitable for a business school case study.

In addition to handling the cultural issues tied to the merger adeptly, CDNOW must effectively manage the transition of both Columbia House and N2K customers over to CDNOW. As mentioned previously, one of the best ways to bring Columbia House customers into the fold would be for CDNOW to develop an online record club. Some Columbia House customers will prefer the status quo. But it is in CDNOW's best interest to bring as many of these shoppers into an online club as possible, for such a program would be more flexible and less costly to run than an offline program and would present better cross-sell opportunities. CDNOW has already done a fair amount of work to smooth the way for N2K customers. It has migrated people from N2K's Frequent Buyers Club to the CDNOW Fast Forward Rewards program to help ensure their loyalty, and it has created personalized My CDNOW pages for them based on the information contained in their My Music Boulevard pages.

But could CDNOW be doing even more to ensure that N2K customers don't abandon ship for Amazon.com or another online music vendor? My answer is yes. N2K's customer base was one of the primary reasons that CDNOW pursued the merger. This asset is valuable, and CDNOW should push even harder to maintain it. It could strive to delight previous N2K customers, for example, by surprising them with double the normal number of Fast Forward Rewards points when they complete their first purchase on the combined site to thank them for their continued patronage. In addition, CDNOW could analyze its records to identify former N2K customers whose purchasing volume has dropped off since the merger and send them an email note from Jason Olim urging them to return, along with an electronic coupon they could put toward their next purchase. If CDNOW does not implement more of such creative customer retention programs, much of the value it purchased in the deal it struck with N2K could erode quickly.

CDNOW also suffers from a surplus of bravado, as exemplified by Jason Olim. In contrast to other high-tech executives such as Andy Grove and Bill Gates, who carefully cultivate competitive paranoia, Olim is cocky about CDNOW's market position and flaunts his confidence. He derides the record labels and traditional music retailers, claiming "They're in the stone age."[39] He's particularly critical when commenting on Amazon.com and its move into music retailing and other market sectors. In an article published on *CMPnet*, an online trade publication, Olim declared, "We are certainly far better than Amazon in every regard. There's nothing they do as well as us and it's going to continue that way. We're going to continue to have the best music store, and it shouldn't be a department store. If I were to try to sell different lines of products, I couldn't put this kind of energy and focus and passion behind this one product."[40] And in a recent article in *Business Week* that covered Amazon's expansion, Olim said, "In three or four years, they'll be known for 'big.' Well, whoop-di-do."[41] Rather than drive employees to work harder to beat Jeff Bezos and company, such comments weaken the imperative to win. They also make investors skittish. Ken McCain is a portfolio manager for Wall Street Associates, an investment firm that sold its position in CDNOW last year. "Why get into a pushing war with a gorilla?" asked McCain.[42] Olim could do much for CDNOW by cooling his rhetoric, abandoning bombast in favor of studying and besting his competition in the marketplace.

In addition to struggling to rein in its leader's loose lips, CDNOW is grappling with the question of how it should leverage community to build its brand. With the merger of CDNOW and N2K, Jason Olim claimed, "We're going beyond just being a music store. This is content, commerce and community all coming together."[43] Such a strategy, however, would mark a significant departure from CDNOW's earlier approach to online community. In contrast to iVillage, which has made the idea of building a Web-based community the keystone of its business, CDNOW has rejected the concept of creating its own communities until now, preferring instead to outsource community by participating as a retail partner in communities developed by others.

For example, consider how CDNOW has teamed up with Tripod, an online community aimed at the Generation X demographic. Like iVillage and Women.com Networks, Tripod presents much of its information as a series of channels, covering subjects such as Entertainment, Fun/Games, and Shopping. CDNOW is featured throughout this range of channels. Visit the Entertainment channel, for example, and you can read the latest gossip on Courtney Love, play a Shockwave game featuring washed-up celebrities, or buy music—the latter courtesy of CDNOW. Browse the Shopping channel and you can "learn credit card smarts," get tips on how to get the best thrift shop deals, or, once again, purchase music, with CDNOW as the retailer. In addition to publishing its own content, Tripod encourages its members to become publishers themselves by hosting a large selection of member-created home pages, which are also organized according to the themes mentioned earlier. Throughout the site, Tripod encourages members who are creating home pages to join CDNOW's Cosmic Credit program.

I believe that the approach the company has taken to the "community" issue makes good sense for CDNOW. By partnering with companies such as Tripod, CDNOW has gained exposure within community environments without needing to cultivate community itself. It has instead focused on other ways to build customer loyalty, tapping the community good will and associated loyalty created by others. If CDNOW is going to change its strategy at this point and attempt to build community on its own site, it has a long way to go. There are no online message boards that would enable fans of different artists or genres to exchange ideas and opinions with one another. There are no "ask the expert"–style forums that would let shoppers ask questions of CDNOW-appointed subject experts. There is no opportunity for customers to append their reviews to product listings. In short, there is *no* community feeling at all to CDNOW in its current incarnation. In announcing a new take on community, Olim appears to be ahead of himself. The company's earlier approach was logical, and I question the thinking behind what would be a substantial strategic shift if CDNOW were to try to build a robust community of its own.

The Competitive Threat ▼

CDNOW faces competition on multiple fronts. On the one hand, it must deal with other online merchants—companies that know the

Internet space, understand the market opportunity the music retailing industry represents, and are driving hard to take large chunks of market share. What's more, as technologies such as streaming media become more prevalent, CDNOW will face a challenge from online ventures that never before posed a problem, yet now present an alternative to the purchase of traditional recordings. CDNOW is also threatened by old-school offline players, such as brick-and-mortar music retailers. Although these firms may have been slow to get on the Net, many of them have significant brand awareness in the offline world, along with plenty of capital, extensive merchandising experience, and a rich set of partnerships and contacts. CDNOW's reactions to its opponents' moves will have a definite effect on the long-term strength of its brand, which makes the competitive scene worth a closer look.

Amazon has a customer base larger than the population of Greece.

Now that N2K is no longer a menace, the biggest danger to CDNOW from online vendors is the emergence of Amazon.com as a music retailing gargantuan. Since it opened the doors of its music store in June 1998, Amazon has quickly grown to become one of the Internet's largest music retailers. It offers a deep selection of music across all genres, from jazz to hip hop, from classical to zydeco. It also provides customers with many of the same value-added features that CDNOW has discovered reinforce customer loyalty, such as music reviews, song samples, and personalized recommendations. Amazon has more than thirteen million customers—a customer base larger than the population of Greece. Given the rich information it collects on these customers, it has been easy for Amazon to cross-sell them music products. Based on the strength of the Amazon.com brand, I believe that the company will have great success selling music to those people who are new to the Web. Amazon may not pull scads of current customers away from CDNOW, because CDNOW has done much to cultivate long-term relationships with music fans. But there are many more customers who have yet to buy music online than have bought online to date. Amazon is undoubtedly going to take a healthy chunk of this future business, and CDNOW is going to have to be particularly wily to keep up with Jeff Bezos and the Amazon crew.

Although Amazon.com represents the greatest current danger from an online retailer, CDNOW also must fend off niche-focused Web merchants that attack its flanks. These companies specialize in particular genres, and they are developing depth in different subject areas that CDNOW can never hope to match. Take flamenco-world.com, for example, a site for the flamenco fanatic. In addition to offering the latest CDs from El Viejín and Tomatito, flamenco-world.com markets flamenco books, guitar music, and even professional dance shoes. When a visitor comes to the site to make a purchase, he can also read the latest news and rumors on the flamenco scene, get information on a flamenco course in Seville, or check out a worldwide schedule of live flamenco events. According to Ken Cassar of Jupiter Communications, "There are, and will continue to be, opportunities for retailers that can penetrate specific genres and sub-genres with a breadth of content and services."[44] Players such as flamenco-world.com will keep eroding the edges of CDNOW's market. The firm's best defense is to continue to deepen its genre-specific content and to hope that the market for Carmen Linares CDs doesn't take off soon.

Traditional retailers such as Tower Records and Barnes & Noble (you'll see more of Barnesandnoble.com in the following chapter) could also pose problems for CDNOW as they build their Web-based businesses. These companies have substantial real-world brands that, used properly, could help them to build momentum quickly on the Internet. They also have economies of scale in purchasing that will enable them to compete effectively on price, as well as the deep pockets required to fund the new online side of their businesses during the initial growth period. "If they have a good dual channel strategy, they could kick CDNOW's ass quickly," notes Mark Hardie of Forrester Research.[45]

However, many of these offline music retailers have barely begun to make headway on the Web. For example, Barnesandnoble.com and Virgin Megastores started selling music online in the spring of 1999—

a full five years after Jason Olim began work on CDNOW. Both of these vendors are pushing hard to grow their online businesses, but it feels like they're entering the Indy 500 about five laps into the race. Other traditional retailers appear to consider their Web-based ventures a low priority and have kept their expectations for Web sales to a minimum. Mike Farrace, Tower Record's vice president of publishing and electronic marketing, has been quoted as saying that he would be pleased if Tower's annual online sales equaled that of a successful retail store—$6 to $7 million in revenues per year.[46] I believe, however, that established offline retailers have the potential to do much more. Their brands are extremely well known in the real world, and there is much that these firms could do to leverage the credibility of their offline brands to build awareness of and traffic to their Web-based stores. Some of them seem to be taking a Microsoft-like approach to market development, waiting for others to develop a category beyond the seminal phase before pouncing. But this watch-and-wait strategy has an associated opportunity cost. As Jupiter Communications has described it, "This market is the superstores' to lose, and every day they are not selling aggressively online leaves the window open for start-ups to establish and successfully brand themselves."[47]

The more closely CDNOW can establish its brand in the minds of its target customers as *the* place to buy music online, the more potent a barrier to entry brand becomes—particularly against some of the traditional vendors just described. In addition to building a strong association between online music shopping and its brand, CDNOW has erected a number of other competitive barriers that will help it to protect its franchise. For example, the company has developed long-term contracts with some of the most desirable distribution partners on the Web. In addition to providing large amounts of traffic to CDNOW, securing these alliances has also blocked competitors from the benefits of teaming up with a firm such as Yahoo!. The company has also snared advertising space both on and offline that would be of value to its adversaries. By locking up advertising opportunities that range from desirable search engine keywords (e.g., "music") to television time on MTV, CDNOW has raised awareness and driven site traffic at the same time that it has prevented its antagonists from doing the same. Finally, perhaps the most important competitive advantage CDNOW has developed is its sizeable customer base. Given CDNOW's focus on building customer loyalty, it is unlikely that the firm is going to lose large numbers of these customers to competitors. For rivals to catch up to CDNOW, then, they need to acquire vast numbers of new customers, an expensive proposition that has doubtless made potential opponents think twice about entering this business.

Despite such barriers, however, there are other industry players who may well rush the ramparts. For example, traditional media properties such as *Spin* are undoubtedly eyeing the online transactions sector of the music business. Of the traditionalists that decide to make a go of this market, most will likely develop alliances with Web music retailers rather than try to build this capability themselves. If CDNOW gets the deal, as it has with RollingStone.com, these media companies then become allies, not competitors. But if CDNOW loses the distribution opportunity to a competitor, it then faces a challenging opponent that has both deep music-related content and strong transactional capabilities.

The record labels, too, can be friend or foe. Some, such as Capitol Records, have decided to avoid issues of channel conflict and point prospects toward CDNOW rather than selling direct and irking their traditional retailing partners. Some have teamed up with the competition. For example, although Polygram's primary aim is to drive Web site visitors to purchase its products through regular retailers, it has also developed an agreement with Entertainment Connection to manage some sales online. Others are ignoring channel conflict problems and plunging directly into the market themselves. BMG and Universal Music have announced a new venture, getmusic.com, that will leverage the extensive assets of these two companies to promote their artists and sell their recordings. BMG owns more than 200 record labels in fifty three countries and represents artists ranging from U2 to Herbie Hancock. Universal is the world's largest music company and produces albums for stars such as Elton John and Whitney Houston. Together, these two companies own 44 percent market share in the United States. With aggressive promotional plans that include extensive print and broadcast advertising and the plastering of the getmusic.com URL on all the albums they ship, BMG and Universal pose a long-term threat to CDNOW.

CDNOW could also get sideswiped by a distributor—such as its current partner, Valley Records, which fulfills all of CDNOW's orders. In 1997, payments to Valley accounted for 78 percent of CDNOW's cost of sales. If Valley decides to forward integrate, CDNOW—and the multitude of smaller online retailers that depend on Valley—will be sweating. As one analyst confided to me, "Valley right now is the life line, the oxygen. And Valley will tell you, 'We own those guys. If we decide to sever the contract at the end of its current two-year span, they are going to be in trouble.'"

To make matters worse, CDNOW is also facing competitive pressures from online distribution partners as the portal sites drive to extract as much value as possible from their customers' shopping transactions. Consider the music section of Yahoo! Shopping, for example. CDNOW has secured good visibility in this high-traffic area. Its banner advertisements are prominent, and it also sponsors a Best Sellers section that drives people back to the CDNOW site to complete the purchase of albums from popular groups. But this is where CDNOW's ownership of the Yahoo! customer's shopping experience is curtailed. If a shopper searches for a CD on Yahoo!, he'll see listings from multiple vendors, not just CDNOW. And when he finds a CD he likes and makes his way through the purchasing process, Yahoo! keeps him on its site, rather than passing him off to the retail vendor. The look and feel is therefore Yahoo!'s, and the customer remains on Yahoo! to generate more page views and execute additional transactions. Tim Brady, Yahoo!'s vice president for production, acknowledges the corresponding friction that is growing between portals and merchants, but attempts to dance his way around the issue. "I think it's a healthy tension," Brady says, "and I think that's natural, and there's room for both sides to succeed."[48] The reality of the situation, however, is that some of CDNOW's historical distribution partners are looking more like competitors each day.

As Internet broadcast takes off, CDNOW will begin to face yet another form of competition. At present, the streaming media market is in its nascent stages. For those without a fast Internet connection, listening to music broadcast over the Internet is a painful experience. But with the spread of broadband technologies such as cable modems and DSL (digital subscriber line), the bandwidth limitations that have constrained the growth of the Internet broadcast industry will soon fade. As it becomes easy for consumers to access the music they want in real time via the Internet, one can envision a situation in which customers pay to play the songs they like right when they want them (similar to pay-per-view television). A number of different companies have recognized the potential that the Internet broadcast sector offers and have invested large sums to build their competencies in this area. AOL, for example, recently purchased Spinner.com, a leading In-ternet radio site. Viacom acquired Imagine Radio, another radio site. And Lycos, the popular portal, has launched the Lycos Radio Network. These firms are not yet offering "pay for play" broadcasting of specific tunes, but they will in time. And when they do, remember that with streaming media, the cus-tomer does not actually end up with a copy of the song he likes. As with a traditional jukebox, he plays the tune once, and if he wants to hear it again, he pays a second time. For some music fans, this will be acceptable, and CDNOW will therefore lose at least a modest portion of its business to these Internet broadcast players.

Technological leads are ephemeral; a well-nurtured brand has staying power.

With such a range of current and future competitors, CDNOW is racing to build brand, one of the most important assets a company can develop that yields long-term competitive advantage in the In-ternet space. For whereas technological leads are ephemeral, a well-nurtured brand has huge staying power. Of course, drive as it may for brand strength, CDNOW knows that with so many big-name players involved, it's going to have to share the wealth. And that, according to

Jason Olim, is just fine. "We all recognize this thing as a huge, huge, huge potential pie," he explains. "We're not really jockeying for our slice as much as we're looking to be part of this thing when it builds. As Homer Simpson says, 'When the saints come marchin' in, I want to be part of that rhumba.'"[49]

On the Horizon   ▼

Although many of the competitive concerns just outlined are immediate issues, there are a variety of other challenges CDNOW will face as it looks to the future and strives to further build its brand strength. For example, CDNOW is going to have to deal with an emerging technology that will take a swipe at its value proposition: the bot. *Bots* are intelligent search agents that scour the Web in search of certain products or information. As an example, consider the comparison shopping service developed by MySimon. MySimon has allied itself with a variety of different high-traffic distribution partners; through their partnerships with MySimon, these sites enable their customers to search the Web more efficiently for the best deals on products such as toys, electronics, and, of course, music. Plug in the name of the album that interests you, click the Go Shop! button, and you'll receive a list of various sites that offer the CD and the price at which it is available on each.

As services such as MySimon's spread, they will place even greater buying power in the hands of consumers, making it extremely easy to shop on price. Of course, price is only one aspect of value, but as it becomes easier to run price comparisons across large numbers of Web vendors, customers who previously would have paid less attention to this component of value may give it more heed. The bots, therefore, are a threat to brand for ecommerce companies such as CDNOW. (In fact, CDNOW routinely attempts to block the bots' attempts to crawl its site for information—with limited success.) For

CDNOW to overcome such a threat, it will have to add even more value to its service in other ways—add more personalization features, shorten delivery times, offer products available only on CDNOW, and so forth—so that these incremental benefits counterbalance the effect of pending pricing pressure.

Another technology issue that will be tricky for CDNOW will be dealing with digital music distribution. When CDNOW first began selling music online, the idea of consumers purchasing music as a downloadable digital file—rather than as a disc in a jewel case—was just that: an idea. Today, however, songs and even entire albums encoded in the popular MP3 compression format are being downloaded and redistributed regularly, particularly on college campuses, where large concentrations of music fans have easy access to high-speed Internet connections. CDNOW has publicly committed to making digital distribution a key element of its business in the future. Attracted by the prospects of better margins (imagine: no physical goods, no shipping costs, and no returns!), CDNOW has stated that digital downloading will be at the company's core. The vision of the firm as the ultimate distribution vehicle for digital music was one of the primary factors that enticed Time Warner and Sony to pursue the Columbia House/CDNOW merger. Before CDNOW can recast itself this way, however, the music industry must settle on a format standard for digital music that will prevent listeners from circulating recordings throughout cyberspace without paying for them. Until it does, many entertainment companies—Time Warner and Sony likely among them—will be loath to make their recordings available for distribution in this new way, and CDNOW will therefore have little to sell.

The de facto standard for digital music distribution at present is MP3, and there are now thousands of hours of recordings—most of them illegal copies of popular music—available online as MP3 files. The sound quality of MP3 files is fairly good. And because MP3 files are a digital medium, the quality does not degrade as they are reproduced; the 605th copy sounds as good as the second. This benefit terrifies the music industry, however, because the MP3 format offers no copy protection. A bootleg copy of *Dave Brubeck's Greatest Hits* can be copied by a fan and posted on a Web site for hundreds of others to download with nary a cent paid to Columbia Records. Jon Pareles of the *New York Times on the Web* writes that "The recording business sees MP3 as a Pandora's box of copyright destruction, unleashing anarchy and piracy while robbing musicians of royalties and record labels of capital."[50]

To try to combat the piracy problem, music industry players have formed an international consortium called the Secure Digital Music Initiative (SDMI), a group that represents more than 100 companies from the recording, home electronics, and high-technology industries. Their hope is to supplant MP3 with a new file format that will eventually include anti-piracy technology. The problem, however, is that this copy protection technology is unlikely to be ready until at least 2001. The SDMI has agreed that in the interim, companies should go ahead and release both past and future recordings in SDMI's new file format in order to encourage its adoption by the industry and by consumers. However, many record companies will probably resist this notion. According to Cary Sherman, general counsel for the Recording Industry Association of America, "For some companies we're talking about giving away a musical heritage. Think about Elvis, think about the Beatles—we're talking about giving away the catalog."[51] Despite the fact that SDMI member companies have agreed to follow this direction, I anticipate that there will be plenty of foot-dragging. Jupiter Communications agrees, predicting that by 2002, digital music distribution will account for only $30 million in revenues.[52] Until the record labels have opened their vaults and released a wide range of music in digital format, CDNOW will be stuck hawking a small set of downloadable recordings from minor artists.

Another problem for CDNOW is that its core customer set is aging. Although consumer brand companies from Levi Strauss to Cadillac frequently face such issues, it seems odd that an Internet company would have such a problem given the youth of the medium. But the majority of its customers are thirty- and fortysomething types; CDNOW needs to expand its appeal to the next generation of online shoppers. A big part of the problem here is that just 9 percent of the nation's 30 million teenagers have access to a parent's credit card.[53] As a result, CDNOW has historically paid less attention to this target audience. The company does realize that it needs to do more to reach teens. According to Michael Crotty, CDNOW's vice president of marketing, "We're not selling tons of product to them today. But we need to own the music category for this market, so as they grow and go to college, we'll be part of their vocabulary to start to buy music online."[54]

CDNOW could do a variety of things to court teens. For example, it could start by working with a partner such as RocketCash to enable teens to shop at CDNOW more easily. Parents use their credit cards to establish RocketCash accounts for their children; teens can then spend this virtual scrip with online merchants who honor RocketCash. CDNOW could also devote more of its marketing attention to this audience. The commercials that CDNOW is running on MTV will certainly help to build awareness among teens. But there are many more marketing programs the company could consider to woo teen shoppers, from sponsoring the tour of a group such as the Backstreet Boys to advertising on sites such as MXGonline.com, a fashion and ecommerce site specifically designed for teenaged girls. This would be a long-term investment for CDNOW. But if the company doesn't focus on the issue soon, it will suffer as its traditional customer base ages and shrinks and younger consumers turn elsewhere to buy the music they want.

CDNOW must also find new ways to expand its distribution. As we've already seen, "share of eyeballs" means everything in the Internet space. CDNOW has done a good job of signing up distribution deals with many of the portal sites, the cyberspace equivalent of securing long-term contracts for billboards near high-traffic freeway on-ramps. Securing links to its site from the portals' music sections ("Greatest Hits—All Under $10!" cries one such link) and prominently displaying the CDNOW logo in these areas has done much to build traffic for CDNOW. But the price of such real estate is rising fast. When the well-heeled traditional retailers finally get their acts together and start competing in this space for real, CDNOW may find itself getting outbid for the spots it covets.

As one of the first Internet companies to launch an affiliate program, CDNOW has also been successful in lining up plenty of smaller sites that greatly expand the company's marketing and sales reach. But the affiliate network concept is now well understood; CD Universe, Amazon.com, CDworld, Entertainment Connection, and others all have programs of their own. How will CDNOW differentiate its Cosmic Credit program from other companies' affiliate networks so that as new music-oriented sites come to the Web they gravitate toward CDNOW as their transaction partner? As a public company, CDNOW has the resources to up the ante: It should consider increasing the commission it offers its partners, putting the squeeze on smaller companies such as CDworld and Entertainment Connection. It may also want to improve the level of service it offers affiliate customers, providing them with more frequent reporting, paying commissions faster, showcasing the Cool Cosmic Site of the Week more visibly, and rewarding high-volume producers with music-related gifts such as concert tickets or music memorabilia.

Finally, CDNOW will need to push for totally new distribution opportunities. How can it move beyond the portal sites to secure traffic-driving links on the Yahoo!s of the future? My advice is for CDNOW to take a close look at the emerging Web appliances category. Companies such as WebTV are exploring tools beyond the standard PC that will enable consumers to access the Internet. There will be many more to follow. CDNOW should keep close tabs on this area, striking deals with the most promising of these next-generation Web access providers. These are the companies that will soon deliver a whole new wave of prospects onto the Net. If CDNOW gets in early, it can lock up promising virtual real estate now at a fraction of what it would pay later.

www.**Barnesandnoble**.com

Whereas most of the companies featured in this book were born on the Web, Barnesandnoble.com came to the Internet from the offline world. The online retailer is a subsidiary of Barnes & Noble, Inc., one of the best-known traditional booksellers in the United States. The company's first store, located on lower Fifth Avenue in New York, was founded more than 100 years ago. In 1965, at age twenty-four, entrepreneur Leonard Riggio opened a small bookshop aimed at college students. In 1971, Riggio parlayed the success of his first venture into a $1.2 million bank loan that he used to buy the original Barnes & Noble store.

From those beginnings, Riggio—now the firm's CEO and chairman of the board—developed Barnes & Noble into a retailing phenomenon. With 484 Barnes & Noble superstores across the country (as well as 528 mall-based B. Dalton stores), the company has a substantial physical presence. Over the last several decades, hundreds of millions of people have come to know the Barnes & Noble brand. Some may have only walked by a store or seen an advertisement in a magazine. But many have had much more substantial experiences with the brand. Some have stopped in for a cappuccino or bought a book or a magazine. (Barnes & Noble sells one out of every eight books purchased in the United States.) Others visit repeatedly, attending author chats, buying the latest novels, or dropping by to pick up the local paper. (Barnes & Noble bookstores attract roughly 300 million visits annually.) This is a brand with which more people have had rich, personal interactions than any brand that has existed online.

In May 1997, Barnes & Noble made the move to the Web with the introduction of Barnesandnoble.com. In developing its Internet presence, the firm focused on many of the same issues addressed by other companies we have examined. For example, it invested heavily in both online and offline marketing programs to build awareness and drive trial of the site. It worked to cultivate a sense of community that would keep customers coming back to the site, and it strove to make the site easy to use.

Barnesandnoble.com did many of these things well. But the company was also forced to fight one of the fiercest competitive battles to arise on the Internet. Its nemesis, Amazon.com, had made many of the same moves—several years earlier. By the time Barnesandnoble.com came to market, Amazon had a sizable customer base, significant market momentum, and a well-known Internet brand. The press pilloried Barnesandnoble.com, portraying it as slow and clumsy in comparison with the more nimble Amazon. The company was forced to play a relentless game of catch-up ball, and although it gained ground, Barnesandnoble.com took its lumps along the way.

By the winter of 1998, however, Barnesandnoble.com had narrowed the gap. Although Amazon certainly had many more customers, greater sales, and a much more prominent brand online, Barnesandnoble.com had developed a similar feature set. At that point, the company struck an alliance with Bertelsmann AG (one of the largest publishers in the world) that made it difficult to dismiss Barnesandnoble.com any longer. Bertelsmann paid $200 million for a 50 percent share in the online retailer. And both Bertelsmann and Barnes & Noble, Inc. chipped in $100 million apiece in working capital for the venture. The alliance brought together two of the most substantial players in the traditional publishing and retailing world, companies with content, customers, distribution facilities, purchasing power, and cash. Barnesandnoble.com then went public in early 1999, supplementing its already sizable war chest with an incremental $450

Barnesandnoble.com Snapshot (1999)

URL: www.bn.com
Ticker symbol/Exchange: BNBN/Nasdaq   **Headquarters:** New York, NY
Year founded: 1997   **CEO:** Jonathan Bulkeley

Business concept:	Web retailer spun out of Barnes & Noble, Inc. Markets books, software, music, and magazines online.
Brand assets:	Brand awareness; customer commitment; distribution and content alliances; customer and market intimacy; reputation for service excellence; value
Initial investors:	Initial funding from parent company
Primary competitors:	Online: Amazon.com, CDNOW, Fatbrain, Beyond.com, Buy.com, Egghead.com Offline: Borders, Powell's, Tower Records, Virgin Megastores
Major strategic partners:	AOL, *New York Times,* Microsoft, Lycos

Major milestones:

May 1997	Barnesandnoble.com launches Web store
May 1997	Announces distribution relationship with the *New York Times*
September 1997	Launches Affiliate Network
December 1997	Forges distribution deal with AOL
March 1998	Develops distribution alliance with Wired Digital
May 1998	Launches revamped site, including software store
July 1998	Launches Business Solutions program
October 1998	Sells 50 percent stake to Bertelsmann for $200 million
October 1998	Adds used, rare, and out-of-print books to inventory
November 1998	Attempts to buy Ingram Book Group
May 1999	$450 million IPO
May 1999	Price war erupts with Amazon.com
July 1999	Launches music store
August 1999	Announces plan to develop huge distribution center

Financial summary (CY 1998):	**Revenue: $61.8 million** **Net income (loss): ($83.1 million)**
Shares outstanding:	25 million
Number of employees:	701

million and creating a new currency—Internet stock—that it could use to motivate employees and make acquisitions to further build the business.

Although it is well armed for its bitter competitive contest, Barnesandnoble.com continues to face numerous challenges. Its merger with Bertelsmann has brought significant assets to bear, but has also raised both cultural challenges (mixing two distinct national and corporate cultures within a single entity will be no cakewalk) and competitive issues (Bertelsmann's other Internet venture, BooksOn-line, sells some products that overlap with those marketed by Barnes-andnoble.com). Price competition is increasing, damaging the economics of what is already a low-margin business. And pressures to improve customer service are growing as online shoppers become more demanding. As a crossover marketer—a company bridging the gap between the physical and online worlds—Barnesandnoble.com must also grapple with a set of problems beyond the sort faced by a pure Internet player. To what degree should it maintain consistency with the look and voice of Barnes & Noble, Inc.? How and where should it differ? How should Barnesandnoble.com leverage the Barnes & Noble retail stores to build awareness? This rich mixture of issues and experiences makes Barnes & Noble's push to the Web worth careful review, for it presents lessons not only for companies that are entirely Internet based, but also for traditional companies looking to make their mark on the Web.

Best of Brand   ▼

We begin with a look at those things Barnesandnoble.com has done well in its drive to establish a robust Internet brand. The firm has run extensive and effective online advertising and has tapped the full range of traditional media to build awareness for and spark trial of its online store. It has worked hard to imbue its Web-based shopping venue with a community feeling similar to that of a neighborhood Barnes & Noble store. It has lined up premium distribution deals through partners such as AOL and the *New York Times*. It has come to know its customers' behaviors and preferences in detail and has translated this knowledge into more effective service. It offers an extensive selection of products at competitive prices. It has thoughtfully carried over elements of its real-world brand to the Web, yielding a logical brand consistency between the two environments. And it has made good use of the functionality the Web provides to do more with its brand in this new medium.

Brand Awareness ▼

Barnesandnoble.com began its push for brand awareness with a distinct advantage: the familiarity of its parent brand, Barnes & Noble, Inc., to consumers throughout the United States. The challenge for the online subsidiary has been to leverage this recognition of the parent brand effectively in driving awareness and trial of Barnesandnoble.com. The effort has been complicated by the fact that the company has significant limitations on the marketing programs it can run in its retail stores to support the Web-based store, a conundrum I'll explain in greater detail later in the chapter.

In its awareness-building efforts, Barnes & Noble, Inc. has emphasized themes such as a love for and knowledge of books, the benefits of interacting with authors, and the value of a broad selection and discounted pricing. Barnesandnoble.com has stayed true to many of these ideas in its own awareness messaging. However, it has also worked to establish a slightly different personality. Ben Boyd, the company's director of communications, explains things this way: "The way I try to describe us is if Barnes & Noble is the Chair of the English Department, a tenured professor at Harvard, then we at Barnesandnoble.com are the newest addition to the staff—very intelligent, very articulate, the hip new addition to the team. It's that same credibility, just a different presentation."[1] This attitude is visible in the range of awareness-building programs you'll encounter in the following sections.

Online Marketing   Barnesandnoble.com has experimented widely with online advertising. To produce and field its online ads, the company has worked closely with Organic Online, a well-known interactive agency that also works for clients such as the Gap, Avis, and Toys 'R' Us. The two companies have tested a variety of different messages, media properties, and advertising media in their joint effort to find the best ways to bring people into the store. In evaluating messages, for example, Barnesandnoble.com and Organic have found that some of the most effective have been those that have simply stated core elements of the online retailer's value proposition. Bargain books, fast delivery, millions of books—these themes have all resonated with people who viewed the company's online ads. Another creative direction that has proved to be effective has been an emphasis on specific high-visibility titles. For example, when the Tom Clancy novel *Rainbow Six* was published, Barnesandnoble.com ran ads featuring this particular book.

To deliver these messages to prospective eshoppers, Barnesandnoble.com has tested a variety of online venues. Most successful, it turns out, have been news and information sites such as *USA Today,* the *New York Times on the Web,* the *Los Angeles Times* (latimes.com), and MSNBC.com. It seems natural that people who value the kind of information these sites provide would be book fans as well; testing has proved the hypothesis true. For Barnesandnoble.com, however, these sites have represented low-hanging fruit. The challenge has been to expand beyond this core group of sites, to come up with other advertising opportunities that deliver the same kind of target customers and extend the company's reach. To help Barnesandnoble.com expand its reach, Organic Online has suggested sites that have a focus different from that of the standard news service, yet that provide access to customers with a similar psychographic profile. (The term *psychographic* refers to the way in which a person thinks about the world; among the psychographic attributes of the Barnesandnoble.com customer are an affinity for information and a trust of established brand names.) Through a long history of testing various campaigns, Organic has developed a proprietary database of sites and the psychographic segments they can deliver. The information has proved to be valuable to its customers, and Organic's knowledge and counsel have led Barnesandnoble.com to advertise on sites that it may never have thought to test. For example, at Organic's suggestion, Barnesandnoble.com ran ads on the sites for Internet service providers such as AT&T.

In addition to experimenting with different messages and media properties, Barnesandnoble.com has tried an assortment of media types in an effort to identify online advertising vehicles more sophisticated than simple banner ads. "We investigate every new form of 'rich media' that emerges," says Tony Orelli, account manager at Organic.[2] For example, to persuade target customers to purchase tax preparation books during tax season, Barnesandnoble.com ran thirty-second animated commercials on PointCast, the Internet news and information service. Barnesandnoble.com found the PointCast commercials to be

Results of Web-based marketing efforts are available almost immediately.

distinctive and engaging, offering an effective alternative to the standard banner. The company has also tested Excite@Home's Enliven technology. Using Enliven, Barnesandnoble.com has run ads that have enabled customers to purchase a book from *within* a banner itself. When Clancy's *Rainbow Six* was released, Barnesandnoble.com deployed these commerce-enabled banners with good results.

As more sophisticated advertising formats emerge, Barnesandnoble.com and Organic will continue to test them, winnowing out those that underperform and increasing the use of those that work well. "This is the most accountable medium you can use," says Orelli. "Everything you do, you can test."[3] In contrast to more traditional forms of marketing, the results of these tests are clear quickly. If Barnes & Noble, Inc. launches an in-store promotion or a direct mail campaign, it may have to wait weeks before it can judge the efficacy of its marketing program. For Barnesandnoble.com, however, the results of its Web-based marketing efforts are available almost immediately.

Offline Marketing   Barnesandnoble.com began its offline marketing effort in May 1998 when it essentially relaunched the site. With the relaunch, the company overhauled the interface, the ordering process, and other facets of the site based on research and customer input. It was at this stage that the firm felt that the store was robust enough to trumpet its existence to the world. Barnesandnoble.com turned to offline marketing under the guidance of Weiss, Stagliano and Partners, its original ad agency, as part of its drive to build awareness. The company changed agencies roughly a year later. The successor, TBWA/Chiat/Day, has built on the awareness push begun by Weiss, Stagliano.

To jump-start its awareness-building efforts, Barnesandnoble.com used television. Barnesandnoble.com and Weiss, Stagliano developed and ran a series of four television spots on national television— including during the last episode of *Seinfeld,* a media event watched by millions of people across the United States. Such premium air time is extremely expensive. The company's purchase of these commercial slots exemplified its commitment to bringing powerful resources to bear in order to build mass awareness for Barnesandnoble.com quickly. It also illustrates the benefits that deep pockets bring in the intensifying battle to build prominent Internet brands.

The commercials established the fact that Barnes & Noble had come to the Web via Barnesandnoble.com and played on themes such as speed of delivery, selection, security, and competitive pricing. The commercials were fast paced and colorful, part cartoon and part reality. In one, a pair of menacing Doberman pinschers guarded a shopping cart full of books, emphasizing the security of transactions conducted on Barnesandnoble.com. In another, which focused on the personalized recommendations available on Barnesandnoble.com, a hatchet flew through the air and struck the bull's eye of a dart board. The voice-over on all of the commercials emphasized key benefits— "personal recommendations, deep discounts, millions of books"—

and informed the viewer that "Barnes & Noble is now online at Barnesandnoble.com."

The commercials Barnesandnoble.com crafted in conjunction with TBWA/Chiat/Day were longer: thirty-second creative units as opposed to fifteen seconds. They were also run more broadly, appearing on cable TV channels such as CNN and A&E and on spot TV in fifteen major U.S. markets. The ads featured a virtual bookstore, symbolized by an all-white space. Shoppers plucked from the air the books they'd been looking for, while famous authors such as Stephen King and Tom Clancy served as guides to the wealth of books available through Barnesandnoble.com. The commercials conveyed many core elements of the Barnesandnoble.com shopping experience—it is virtual, it features a huge selection, it showcases leading authors—and communicated the ideas with humor. These segments were wrapped (opened and closed) with footage that displayed the Barnesandnoble.com logo and zoomed in on the "dot-com" portion of the mark: white text on a big red circle. Chiat/Day wants to help Barnesandnoble.com build a brand mark that is simple but bold, one with the resonance of Apple Computer's apple logo or Nike's swoosh. To build this level of familiarity, all of the ads developed under Chiat/Day's direction have prominently featured the "dot-com," whether on television or in print.

Barnesandnoble.com has also made extensive use of radio advertising. Some of its most creative and effective radio commercials were those developed by Weiss, Stagliano and Partners. Barnesandnoble.com and its agency ran these spots in those media markets with the greatest Internet penetration, such as the cities of San Francisco and New York. The ads took a stream-of-consciousness approach and followed along as different customers shopped on Barnesandnoble.com. In one, for example, a man typed in the Barnesandnoble.com URL and browsed his way through the online store, tracking down and purchasing *Barbecue 101* for his father's upcoming birthday and *Bushwalking in Australia* to help him plan a future vacation. In another, a woman looking for books to send to her son—a new college freshman—found and bought copies of *The Col-*

lege Success Book and *Dating for Dummies.* In all of these commercials, the narrators remarked on the aspects of Barnesandnoble.com that made shopping there convenient: one-click checkout, gift wrapping, twenty-four-hour shipping, and so forth. Like the television commercials, these radio ads also emphasized the fact that "Barnes & Noble is now online."

The radio commercials crafted by TBWA/Chiat/Day aim to demonstrate the variety of books and depth of selection that Barnesandnoble.com offers by letting the authors "speak for themselves." In each spot, authors spoke as they typed the manuscripts of their latest books. Audio snippets faded out and neatly bridged from one to the next. In one commercial, for example, a sports writer said, "When a punter kicks, his defensive team depends on him to move the ball deep into the . . . " A cooking writer then picked up the thread: " . . . frying pan, and let it simmer. Next, place the chicken in the preheated oven and cook for . . . " And so it continued. The commercials highlighted the range of book categories available through Barnesandnoble.com, from football to fantasy, from weddings to woodwork. And each commercial ended with a reminder of other Barnesandnoble.com selling points: fast delivery, deep discounts, and one-click ordering. Like the Chiat/Day TV commercials, the radio spots ran on a diverse set of national radio networks, generating broad exposure for Barnesandnoble.com.

The company also turned to print advertising to build brand awareness. As with its television ads, the print ads that Weiss, Stagliano developed for Barnesandnoble.com were colorful and spirited. In one, a zany, smiling character hissed, "Psst . . . ever wish you could run amok in our bookstore at 2 A.M.?" emphasizing the convenience of shopping online with Barnesandnoble.com. In another, Barnesandnoble.com focused on customer service. Below line drawings of six smiling, abstract faces, the headlines read, "The world may not revolve around you. But our Website certainly does." Barnesandnoble.com ran advertisements like these in a wide range of publications, from highbrow magazines such as *Atlantic Monthly,* the *Economist,* and the *New York Times Book Review* to popular magazines such as *Entertainment Weekly* and *People.*

Like the television ads that Chiat/Day developed, the print ads that it created placed emphasis on the "dot-com" logo. One series of ads displayed the red "dot-com" circle in the middle of a page. In some of these ads, the circle contained a single attribute of the Barnesandnoble.com brand, such as speed. Text at the bottom of the page then delivered more explanation; for example, "Our selection will make even speed readers beg for mercy." In others, the "dot-com" circle included a word that described a set of authors—"legends," for example—while the remainder of the copy highlighted key works of these famous writers. The Chiat/Day ads ran in some of the same publications as the Weiss, Stagliano ads, such as the *New York Times Book Review* and *People,* as well as some new ones, such as *Time* and *Utne Reader.*

Under Chiat/Day's guidance, Barnesandnoble.com also initiated its first outdoor advertising campaign. The ads first emerged in New York, one of the country's most wired cities (as well as the company's home town). The outdoor campaign was virtually the same as the print work and used the "dot-com" logo as a device for communicating key attributes of Barnesandnoble.com. These ads appeared in all manner of places—on the sides of city buses, on phone booths, on bus shelters, and on the walls outside the Holland and Lincoln tunnels, generating substantial awareness for Barnesandnoble.com in New York.

Customer Commitment ▼

Many of the elements that drive loyalty for Barnesandnoble.com are described in the "Reputation for Excellence" and "Value" sections later in this chapter. Although the work that the company devotes to promoting brand awareness initiates a customer's relationship with the brand, it is his experience with it over time that builds a long-term commitment to that brand—or drives him into the arms of a competitor. Is he finding the products he is looking for? Are the prices fair? Factors like these will keep a customer faithful to Barnesandnoble.com if the company performs up to snuff.

In this section, however, I'll focus on two other themes: personalization and community. Barnesandnoble.com has launched a number of initiatives to forge more personal relationships with its customers. By developing such one-to-one ties with its customers, the company has looked to build the kind of relationships that the owner of a popular local retail bookstore might develop with his long-time patrons. But, whereas the bookstore owner may store in his mind the reading preferences of sixty or seventy regular clients and talk to them about new books they might enjoy when they stop by his store, Barnesandnoble.com can do this for large numbers of shoppers—and still convey a feeling of individualized service.

The firm's "e-nnouncements" feature is one example of how Barnesandnoble.com has implemented technology-based solutions to the personalization problem. If a customer has been searching for information on books written by a particular author and is interested in keeping abreast of issues related to that writer, e-nnouncements will send email alerts when the author releases a new book or participates in a Barnesandnoble.com online chat session. If a customer enjoys a particular genre of books, such as Horror and Suspense, e-nnouncements will keep him up to date with developments in the category by sending him reviews and articles. This ongoing dialogue reinforces in the customer's mind the fact that Barnesandnoble.com offers information on the kinds of books he likes. And when the customer gets an email that attracts his attention, he may well come back to the Barnesandnoble.com site to buy the book that intrigued him.

Like iVillage, Barnesandnoble.com has built customer loyalty by cultivating a sense of community. One of the most effective ways Barnesandnoble.com has done this is through its author chat series, which connects readers with authors they care about. The company has hosted online dialogues with well-known authors such as Tom Clancy, Paul Theroux, Rita Mae Brown, Joseph Heller, Ray Bradbury, and Garrison Keillor. These author chats have proved to be popular, and Barnesandnoble.com has gone on to develop variations on the theme. Its "First Fiction" chat series, for example, features new novelists. The "New York Times on the Web Writers Series" hosts chats with authors whose books have caught the attention of the newspaper's review staff. Connecting writers and readers in this way is one of the things that has kept customers coming back regularly, leading to repeat purchase rates of close to 50 percent.

Barnesandnoble.com has also enhanced customers' commitment to the company by providing book fans with the opportunity to share ideas and opinions with one another. It has done so in two ways. First, Barnesandnoble.com enables visitors to the site to add their own reviews of specific books they liked or disliked. These customer reviews are included alongside information from the publisher and reviews from third parties, which make Barnesandnoble.com shoppers feel that their opinions carry weight in their virtual community. In addition, Barnesandnoble.com hosts message boards on subjects ranging from children's books to travel, from business to poetry. Community participants can post questions, spark debates, and ask peers for recommendations. These forums provide a communal feeling reminiscent of the cafes found in many of the Barnes & Noble retail stores. Like the author chats and customer reviews, the message boards position Barnesandnoble.com as a company interested in the exchange of ideas about good books, a stance that sits well with book lovers. And by developing a venue to which book fans come to share ideas and opinions, Barnesandnoble.com creates additional sales opportunities. Each time a customer comes back to the Barnesandnoble.com site, the company has the chance to pitch him books he may enjoy.

Strong Content and Distribution Alliances ▼

Like other firms featured in this book, Barnesandnoble.com has crafted a broad range of partnerships that have reinforced the strength of its brand. Some alliances have done so by supplementing the site with branded content, increasing the richness and utility of Barnesandnoble.com. The majority, however, have built awareness and generated sales. This section takes a look at both types of alliances and the ways in which they have contributed to the Barnesandnoble.com brand.

Content and Commerce Deals   Barnesandnoble.com has developed relationships with a variety of different publications that furnish information that enables customers to make informed buying decisions. *Publisher's Weekly, Kirkus Reviews,* and others offer synopses, book reviews, author biographies, and user reviews on over 600,000 titles. A partnership with the *New York Review of Books* gives Barnesandnoble.com customers easy access to The Reader's Catalog, a Web site that includes information on over forty thousand recommended titles, books that have been individually selected and reviewed by an independent editorial board. Alliances with such partners provide rich, useful information that has boosted the utility of the service and thus the value of the Barnesandnoble.com brand in the minds of its customers.

Whereas the relationships just described have been pure content deals, Barnesandnoble.com has forged a hybrid content/distribution partnership with Oprah's Book Club, the book review and discussion forum started by popular talk show host Oprah Winfrey. Millions of people tune into Oprah's televised book discussion every week; being featured on the show has propelled a good number of books onto national best-seller lists. HARPO, Oprah's production company, has taken Oprah's Book Club to the Web; the Book Club site features reviews of the books featured on the show, author biographies, and discussion questions for people interested in reading Oprah's picks in book clubs of their own. Barnesandnoble.com handles order fulfillment for visitors who want to order books found on the site—the distribution side of the relationship. On the content end, Barnesandnoble.com has repurposed much of this content for use on its own site. When you visit Barnesandnoble.com, therefore, you get access to the same content from within the company's online store.

Distribution Deals   One of Barnesandnoble.com's most strategic distribution deals was the alliance it forged with AOL. "Time and again we have seen AOL help companies to develop online brands," says Nicole Vanderbilt, group director at Jupiter Communications. "Their ability to channel their customers and the sheer number of impressions they have to play with allows AOL to lend a lot of branding power to their merchant and content partners."[4] Barnesandnoble.com invested more than $40 million to secure a presence on AOL. The agreement gave Barnesandnoble.com visibility throughout the AOL service, including the popular Find Central area, Entertainment Asylum, Real Fans Love@aol.com, and Digital City. Staking this claim on AOL provided Barnesandnoble.com with the online equivalent of the company's real-world store on New York's Fifth Avenue: premier real estate in the midst of significant customer traffic. "It gives us great positioning, locks out the competition, and gives us the next four years" of exclusive advertising, said Barnes & Noble vice chairman Steve Riggio at the time of the deal.[5] Just like New York real estate, this online placement did not come cheap. But given that Barnesandnoble.com came to the Web late, it has been all the more important for the company to invest in significant distribution deals to gain both brand exposure and large amounts of traffic quickly.

> **Premier online real estate on high-traffic sites is especially important for latecomers to the Web.**

In another high-profile alliance, Barnesandnoble.com teamed up with the online edition of the *New York Times* to provide readers of the *Times*'s well-known "Books" section with the ability to purchase featured books via the Web. Customers browsing the site's best-seller list or reading book reviews can move directly to Barnesand-noble.com to buy books that have captured their interest. The close integration of reviews and the online store has been good for visitors to the *New York Times* site because it has allowed them to immediately buy books that have intrigued them. And it has been a great setup for Barnesandnoble.com, associating the company with a highly respected source of advice on books that has lent credibility to the Barnesandnoble.com brand. It has also immersed commerce in context, catching customers when they have a propensity to buy and providing them with both the information they need to make informed purchases and the ability to make those purchases online.

Barnesandnoble.com also partnered with Wired Digital, the original publisher of *Wired* magazine and developer of the HotBot search engine, in a distribution alliance that leveraged the strength of the Barnes & Noble brand offline as well as on the Web. The two worked together to develop a "mini store" within HotBot's shopping section. The store was co-branded, providing good exposure for Barnesandnoble.com with Wired Digital's technically savvy, affluent customer base. And when a customer wanted to buy one of the books featured in the store, Barnesandnoble.com got a cut of the transaction. Whereas such a deal would have stopped there with a pure online player such as Amazon.com, the fact that Barnes & Noble had a presence in the real world as well as online enabled Barnes & Noble and Wired Digital to develop a richer, more sophisticated alliance. Select Barnes & Noble stores featured special, co-branded in-store displays within the nonfiction section that included a selection of high-tech books from Wired Books and other publishers, as well as the latest issue of *Wired* magazine. The display also encouraged customers to visit the co-branded store online for more titles plus reviews and other supplementary information. This deal exemplified the way in which an offline brand that moves online can leverage its presence in both the real and online worlds to reinforce its strength in each.

Such large syndicated selling arrangements all fall under the auspices of Barnesandnoble.com's Affiliate Network program, a distribution effort akin to the Cosmic Credit program developed by CDNOW that we saw earlier. Affiliate Network partners who refer customers from their Web site to Barnesandnoble.com are rewarded with a cut of the resulting sales. Not only has Barnesandnoble.com recruited a select group of large, high-traffic sites as Affiliate Network members, it has also built an alliance of 160,000 smaller sites that feed it customers. By working with organizations such as *Philanthropy Journal Online* and the National Down Syndrome Society, Barnesandnoble.com has spread its influence throughout a broad cross-section of the Web, building awareness and generating transactional revenue.

Competitors such as Amazon.com have developed similar programs that are further along (the Amazon Associates program—a
mirror image of the Barnesandnoble.com Affiliate Network—has
more than 300,000 members). To accelerate the growth of its own
affiliate network, Barnesandnoble.com has tried to provide its partners with greater value. With deeper pockets than its competitors, for
example, Barnesandnoble.com has offered larger commissions on
sales (such moves have generally been temporary advantages, however, matched within short order by competitors). The company has
also improved the visibility of partner brands. When a visitor clicks
through to Barnesandnoble.com from a partner site, the partner's
logo then graces the upper left corner of every page the visitor sees on
the Barnesandnoble.com site. And Barnesandnoble.com has also offered its partners extensive reporting, helping them to see in detail
how their sites have produced sales. According to Chris Charron, an
analyst with Forrester Research, the Web is "the most diffuse medium
that we have ever seen; because of that diffusion, syndication for
marketing purposes is absolutely key."[6] Jupiter's Nicole Vanderbilt
asserts that "by 2002, over 25% of on-line shopping revenues will be
realized through purchases that originate at affiliate sites."[7] Barnes-
andnoble.com recognizes the power of affiliate distribution and is
doing everything possible to build a sizable set of affiliate partners.

Barnesandnoble.com has also expanded on the standard syndicated selling model through the introduction of its Business Solutions
program. The Business Solutions program has tapped a new type of
distribution channel: corporate intranets. In many big companies today, the corporate intranet is the principal place to which employees
turn for all manner of information from their company, from internal
job listings to performance data for the funds in the company's 401K
plan. In launching the Business Solutions program, Barnesand-
noble.com has teamed up with a number of large corporations to help
them add value to their intranets via customized, online "company
bookstores." These customized bookstores are integrated into the
companies' intranet sites. Participating organizations such as Lucent
Technologies, Arthur Andersen, and Microsoft offer their employees a
selection of recommended business books—as well as access to the

full range of Barnesandnoble.com titles—at prices below the already discounted prices available to the public on the Barnesandnoble.com site.

Through this program, Barnesandnoble.com has gained unusual access to an excellent group of target customers. Moreover, the company has benefited from the "blessing" of its corporate customers, for their benediction increases the credibility of the Barnesandnoble.com brand in the eyes of employees considering book purchases through intranet-based stores. It's worth noting, however, that because of the sales effort and customization work involved, Barnesandnoble.com has developed these "company stores" for only a select group of large companies. So although the program is creative, it has not scaled to the degree that the Affiliate Network has.

Customer and Market Intimacy ▼

Barnesandnoble.com has frequently turned to research in its drive to make informed business decisions. Much of this research has been done with an eye toward making the online retail environment as simple to use as possible, because ease of use has a substantial impact on customers' affinity for and loyalty to a site. When Barnesandnoble.com worked with Roger Black's Interactive Bureau, a Web design firm, to craft the first iteration of the Barnesandnoble.com site, it performed usability testing to determine what elements of the site might confuse customers and made corresponding changes before launch.

When Barnesandnoble.com later hired Organic Online to handle both online advertising and site design, Organic began by conducting a detailed analysis of the site's log files. Just as a beach at low tide shows the footprints of passersby, so do log files reveal where within a site visitors have traveled, including the points from which they left to visit other sites. By reviewing these patterns, Organic was able to determine what areas of the Barnesandnoble.com site were confusing customers (the checkout process in which customers purchased the items they had selected proved particularly perplexing). The firm then proposed a modified design based on this data. And as you might expect, before the launch of the revised site, Organic held detailed usability testing sessions, collecting customer input that helped the firm revise the structure of the new, single-click ordering system it had developed for Barnesandnoble.com.

In addition to helping Barnesandnoble.com improve the usability of its site, market and customer research have been valuable sources of new service ideas. By observing competitor Amazon.com, for example, Barnesandnoble.com has borrowed some of that company's best innovations for its own site. Case in point: Amazon.com introduced a service called Eyes, which notified its customers by email when books matching their interests became available. Barnesandnoble.com followed suit with e-nnouncements. Customer feedback has been the genesis of other new additions to the Barnesandnoble.com site. For example, the

Ease of use has a substantial impact on customer loyalty to a site.

software and magazine sections of the Barnesandnoble.com store both started as customer suggestions that came up during focus group research.

The company also has invested in research that has helped it to better understand issues such as customers' relationships with the Barnesandnoble.com brand and the reasons they shop online. This less quantitative research has played a particularly important role in the development of the company's advertising campaigns. The TBWA/Chiat/Day team, for example, used this qualitative input to help it craft the multifaceted campaign described earlier. "We visited tons of stores as part of the creative process and did our own 'man in the street' interviews," said Fred Rubin, group director at the advertising agency. "We needed to look in the eyes of consumers and get a visceral understanding of what the brand means to them. We asked people questions like, 'Why do they shop in a store vs. why do they go online?' 'When they go online, how do they make a brand choice?'"[8] Customers told the research team that their expectations as to breadth of selection online were higher than when they shopped at a real-world bookstore. They confirmed that the familiarity of the Barnes & Noble offline brand had influence with them when they turned to the Web (this finding was validated by a recent *Newsweek* study in which 82 percent of respondents said they had more trust in Web sites from established brands than from new or unknown brands.[9]) They also told the team that price mattered, online or off. The knowledge Chiat/Day gained through this research into how customers in this market think was integrated into the creative brief—the document that laid out the creative strategy for the entire campaign. By capturing such insights, the agency and Barnesandnoble.com have been able to develop advertising material that has resonated with customers' key concerns.

A Reputation for Excellence ▼

Offering an extensive product selection has been critical to Barnesandnoble.com's efforts to develop a reputation as a quality Web merchant, because as mentioned earlier, breadth of selection is one of the principal reasons people shop online. The company does a good job of fulfilling this customer requirement. Whereas the largest Barnes & Noble retail store may carry 175,000 titles in stock, the online bookstore offers more than eight million. In addition to offering shoppers a broad range of titles, Barnesandnoble.com enables them to purchase the titles they want in a number of different formats: hardcover, paperback, electronic, large print, audio, and rare first editions. The company's aspirations here are a bit grandiose, but laudable. According to Ben Boyd, "Our goal is to be the Web destination where consumers can find the information content they desire in whatever format they could dream possible."[10]

If an e-merchant is going to offer such a broad selection of products, it is imperative to make it easy for customers to find what they're looking for. In its initial incarnation, the Barnesandnoble.com site did not live up to this standard. For although the navigation of the site was not overly difficult, the database of books had problems. Customers searching the site for books of interest all too often received a "no results found" message. As time progressed, however, Barnesandnoble.com refined its search algorithms. The search engine is now sophisticated enough so that if a customer who is looking for John Grisham's *The Partner* accidentally spells the author's last name as "Grishum," the site nonetheless produces a full list of Grisham novels for the customer's review. For prospective buyers who visit Barnesandnoble.com without knowing beforehand what they want to buy, the company does a good job of facilitating browsing. Shoppers looking for guidance can check "Top 10 Bestseller" lists in twenty-seven different categories. They can peruse a set of "Editor's Picks." Or they can review recommendations from Oprah Winfrey's Book Club. eCommerce players such as Barnesandnoble.com must couple a wide selection of products with strong search functionality and a site structure that encourages browsing in order to have a significant impact on customers' perception of quality. If a firm does not do a good job of facilitating searching and browsing, the richness of its product selection is worth much less, because customers will not find the products they're looking for—even if the merchant carries those products.

In addition to helping customers find books they like, Barnesandnoble.com efficiently moves them through the purchasing process when they decide it's time to buy. First-time buyers gather books in a virtual shopping cart and "check out" by providing credit card and shipping information in several short screens. Once you've bought from Barnesandnoble.com, the site "remembers" who you are. A feature called Express Lane then enables customers to buy a book with a single click. This single-click purchasing is certainly not unique to Barnesandnoble.com. Amazon.com implemented this functionality much earlier, and others have done the same. It is, however, a convenience that adds to customers' overall positive impression of Barnesandnoble.com.

Buy a book in a Barnes & Noble store and you can head to the in-store cafe, grab a caffe latte, and read it immediately. But if you buy your book online, you need to sit tight until the book is shipped to you. Barnesandnoble.com has realized that it has an opportunity to bolster its reputation by shipping customers their orders quickly. To take advantage of this opportunity, Barnesandnoble.com (in conjunction with parent company Barnes & Noble, Inc.) stocks roughly 750,000 titles in its distribution centers—the largest standing inventory of any bookseller online. With this selection on hand, the company can please its customers with prompt delivery of the books they order. In an effort to further enhance its distribution capabilities, Barnesandnoble.com attempted in 1999 to buy Ingram Book Group, one of the largest book distributors in the United States. The deal fell through based on federal antitrust concerns (much to Amazon's relief, since Ingram was Amazon's primary distribution partner). Barnesandnoble.com moved on, however, to develop two huge distribution sites of its own, a price the company must pay in order to deliver on customer demands. "The whole [delivery] process has sped up dramatically," said Jed Lyons, president of National Book Network. "In the past, it would take maybe two or three weeks and the book would arrive. Today customers aren't willing to wait two or three weeks. They want it tomorrow."[11]

Given the company's real-world roots, another factor that has enhanced Barnesandnoble.com's reputation in the eyes of its customers is the way in which the firm has respected core attributes of the Barnes & Noble brand in making the move to the Web. For example, author chats have been featured in both the retail and online environments. As marketing manager Matt Kelleher explains it,

> *Barnes and Noble, Inc. prides itself on its relationship with authors and the idea that at any store in the country, we always have different author readings going on. When we launched Barnesandnoble.com, we focused on the live author chats in our virtual auditorium. We still emphasize this, and it has been very successful. The idea was to recreate this impor-*

▼
Maintaining
Central Brand
Attributes

The most successful crossover marketers are those who, like Barnesandnoble.com, have done a good job of maintaining central brand attributes. As a brief aside, consider two other real-world companies that have also made the move to the Web: the Gap and Playboy Enterprises. Visit gap.com and you'll feel the consistency between the online and retail stores. From the blue-and-white color scheme to the rotating 3D Gap bag on the home page, the gap.com site makes many visual references to its offline roots. Michael McCadden, executive vice president of global marketing for the Gap, describes the company's brand personality as "direct and straightforward . . . very easy, very efficient."[12] The gap.com site adheres closely to this spirit, making it simple for customers to find and purchase the products they want, from a pair of corduroy cargo pants to a striped wool cardigan.

Playboy, too, does an excellent job of bringing the brand's core qualities online with Playboy.com. Buford Smith, president of Playboy's New Media division, talks about Playboy's "perceptual franchise." "It's about the good life and beautiful women. It's about sexiness, but not crossing over into something that's harder edged. It's a brand that's associated with fun, sophistication and quality."[13] The Playboy.com site communicates these attributes well through interviews with female celebrities, humor, and music reviews. The prominent display of the Playboy logo and features such as the monthly centerfold align the site closely with the company's well-known offline media properties, such as *Playboy* magazine. Like Barnesandnoble.com, both of these crossover marketers have taken pains to tie their Web brands to their real-world brands. By linking the two, such companies maximize the power of existing brand assets as they extend their presence online.

tant aspect of the store environment, to have people come in, stay, and relax.[14]

By bringing key elements of "Barnes & Nobleness" from the retail world to the Web, Barnesandnoble.com has been able to take advantage of the good impressions that retail shoppers have of the offline brand to build its own credibility.

Although Barnesandnoble.com has worked to leverage the heritage of its parent company for branding advantage, the company has realized that it can't simply recreate its retail stores online. For one thing, the cafe concept won't fly: Virtual espresso doesn't have much appeal. ("As soon as we can pour a cup of coffee through this site, I think we'll have it nailed," Barnesandnoble.com vice chairman Stephen Riggio has quipped.[15]) In addition, Barnesandnoble.com has understood that to create a successful online property, it needs to take full advantage of the capabilities the Web presents.

For example, consider the e-nnouncements and Express Lane features described previously. These elements of Barnesandnoble.com service epitomize the opportunity that the Web presents for a crossover marketer to one-up its real-world brand. It would not be cost-effective for your local Barnes & Noble retail store to maintain a list of subjects or authors that interest you and send you a letter every time it gets something in stock that might appeal to you. The Web, however, makes it easy and inexpensive for Barnesandnoble.com to maintain such a database of interests and to email you with updates. Likewise, providing its retail customers with the ability to purchase books in its stores with an efficiency nearing that offered through Express Lane ordering would require each store to employ an outrageous number of cashiers, guaranteeing that you would never wait in line. On the Web, however, it is simple to implement such a concept. As such features exemplify, crossover marketers can and should use technology to enhance the brand experience online. Those who simply mimic the real-world experience on the Web (as many old-world publishers have done) are destined to disappoint their customers.

▼
**Creating Greater
Brand Intimacy**
The Gap and Playboy Enterprises have understood well the need to develop Web properties that one-up their offline brands. On the gap.com site, for example, customers can sample all of the company's latest shades of fingernail polish without muss or mess (site visitors paint the fingernails of a virtual hand with colors such as Jack Frost or Pink Snow). With gap.com's "virtual style" feature, customers can mix and match possible combinations of clothing significantly faster and easier than they could in the store. Playboy.com enables its viewers to chat with Playboy Playmates, zoom in on images of beautiful women, or even get current stock quotes—all of which are beyond the average customer's usual interaction with the brand. Such incremental experiences—built on a brand's core elements—take the customer to the next level of intimacy with the brand. Wise crossover marketers know this and develop their Web properties with this outcome in mind.

Value ▼

Barnesandnoble.com offers its customers a good value. Think of the value equation we covered in the introduction: a ratio of perceived quality over price. As illustrated earlier, the quality of the service that Barnesandnoble.com provides is high. The selection is mammoth, the purchasing process is easy and efficient, and delivery is fast. Prices, on the other hand, are low. The value equation, therefore, is well in favor of the Barnesandnoble.com customer.

Although we've discussed the elements that make up the numerator of this fraction, we haven't yet touched on price—the denominator. The retail arm of Barnes & Noble, Inc. has long offered steep discounts; this aggressive pricing policy is something customers have come to expect from the company. In moving online, Barnesandnoble.com has not only pushed to be consistent with this pricing philosophy, they've actually striven to offer discounts even deeper than those available through retail. For example, Barnesandnoble.com offers 40 percent off any of the books highlighted on Oprah's Book Club. But if you walk into one of the Barnes & Noble retail stores, you'll find no such discounts on these titles. As we'll see in the next section, pricing issues are becoming troublesome for Barnesandnoble.com. From the customer's perspective, however, the low prices are a good deal and make Barnesandnoble.com feel similar in spirit to its parent company, which launched its original famous discounts (40 percent off *New York Times* best-sellers, 20 percent off paperback best-sellers, and 10 percent off hardcovers) back in 1974 and "forever changed the economics of book selling."[16]

Chinks in the Armor   ▼

One of the more significant problems that Barnesandnoble.com faces is deepening price-based competition. As mentioned previously, the firm's parent company has long been known for offering extraordinary discounts. Barnesandnoble.com has priced aggressively from the start, for it saw such pricing as consistent with the positioning of Barnes & Noble, Inc. and as a valuable weapon in the war for market share. But the discounting mania has increased, and as the Yankee Group's Melissa Bane has put it, "It's getting ugly out there."[17] When Amazon.com changed its discounts on best-sellers (as defined by the *New York Times* best-seller list) from 40 percent to 50 percent, it did so right in the midst of Barnesandnoble.com's IPO roadshow—a true kick in the gut. Barnesandnoble.com—as well as Borders and others—were forced to match the move. Leonard Riggio stated, "We were the first bookseller to offer 40 percent off online, which they matched. They went to 50 percent, so we matched them. It's a competitive market, and we intend to remain competitive."[18] This means, however, that these firms are now losing money on the sale of any book from the best-seller list, which features roughly seventy titles each week. The economics of the business are deteriorating even further in this battle for market share, and it's a state of affairs that has many of the combatants worried. Borders spokesperson Rich Fahle admitted, "I have to tell you that this is not the battlefield that we think we're going to win on in the long run."[19]

How should Barnesandnoble.com respond to this situation? For one thing, it should accept that low margins on these most popular titles are here to stay. The best way to think about such books, then, is as loss leaders. Just as a supermarket may sell steaks at low prices over the Fourth of July weekend in order to bring shoppers into the store, so should Barnesandnoble.com consider best-sellers to be customer magnets. To succeed, Barnesandnoble.com must lure a customer to the site with a fantastic offer on the latest Danielle Steel novel, then cross-sell her a variety of other titles during her visit that are not best-sellers and thus offer higher margins. In addition to selling its customers larger orders that contain back-catalog books as well as popular titles, Barnesandnoble.com must try to sell to them more frequently. For although margins may be falling, if Barnesand-noble.com can get buyers to purchase more regularly, total net revenue can still grow. Finally, the company must chase down all possible distribution efficiencies: The more it can squeeze costs out of its current systems, the more it will regain margin points lost in the great price war.

The company has initiatives under way that address all three opportunities. The e-nnouncements feature mentioned earlier, for example, is a good way for Barnesandnoble.com to entice its customers to come back to the store more regularly. And the giant distribution facilities that the company is building will certainly help it to pare distribution costs. But if Barnesandnoble.com is to weather the price wars without losing its shirt in the process, it must continue to push for innovations in these areas in the quest to regain lost margins.

Another serious issue for Barnesandnoble.com has been its poor marketing coordination with Barnes & Noble, Inc. retail stores. When I recently visited a local Barnes & Noble store here in California, for example, there was not a single reference to the online subsidiary. No free bookmarks with URLs. No mention of Barnesandnoble.com on store signage. No information in the cafe about upcoming online author chats. Nothing.

This is a problem, because one of the most important things a crossover marketer can do when making the move to the Web is to take full advantage of the company's offline assets. In the case of Barnes & Noble, the retail store environment is a key asset and presents a prime opportunity for building awareness for Barnesandnoble.com. So why, you wonder, has Barnesandnoble.com not leveraged this real estate? The answer lies in the law. Federal law requires that any company that has a substantial presence in a particular state charge residents of that state sales tax when they shop online. For example, because the headquarters of Barnes & Noble, Inc. is in New York, Barnesandnoble.com—a subsidiary of the parent company—must charge sales tax on books purchased by New York State residents.

These "nexus laws" get a bit squishy when you begin to test their boundaries. For Barnesandnoble.com, the key issue has been whether the existence of retail stores in a certain state constituted enough of a presence to trigger the nexus laws and force the online retailer to tax sales to customers in that state. The awkward legal compromise that has emerged for crossover marketers such as Barnesandnoble.com is this: If the real-world stores look, smell, and feel like separate entities from the online store, the online shoppers don't have to pay tax in that state. If, however, there is integration—particularly on the marketing end—between the online and offline stores in that state, then online shoppers are stuck paying tax. This issue is moot, of course, in states that charge no sales tax, such as Oregon.

Some online retailers, such as the Gap, have opted to simply pass on the sales tax to their customers. For Barnesandnoble.com, however, this is a difficult choice, for it would put the company at a price disadvantage compared with its adversaries. To stay competitive on price, Barnesandnoble.com has therefore opted to forgo the co-marketing—for the most part. It has done some co-marketing in retail stores located in states that do not charge sales tax. And it took advantage of a loophole in the law that gives crossover marketers a one-time, thirty-day exception to the regulation. As Ben Boyd noted, "When we opened the software store and launched the redesigned site, we went full blast in 500 stores across the country with register signs, window signage, bag inserts, cafe table placards. . . . You name it, we did it so that we could take advantage of that one-time window."[20]

At this point, however, I believe that the company must change its ways, because it is essential for a crossover marketer such as Barnesandnoble.com to leverage its offline assets fully in the drive to build a powerful brand online. I am certainly not the only one to call for a shift in strategy. Some of the people closest to the company share my opinion. According to Fred Rubin of TBWA/Chiat/Day, "In the war for the online book buyer, what is the principal asset that Barnes has that Amazon will never have? Their collection of hundreds and hundreds of retail locations. The opportunity to cross-pollinate and use one as an electronic extension of the other has extraordinary power."[21]

So how should Barnesandnoble.com approach this problem? By passing along the sales tax to its customers, the company would finally have the right to roll out a fully integrated cross-selling campaign. But given the intensity of the price competition described previously, I don't think that this is a realistic solution. The firm is planning to offer those 60 percent of Barnes & Noble retail customers who pay with a credit card a $5 bounty for their email addresses. Barnesandnoble.com can then use email to pitch these customers various offers to get them to do some of their book buying online. The idea is a good one, but even if as many as 10 percent of these credit-card-wielding retail customers hand over their email addresses, that still means that Barnesandnoble.com will have no means to communicate with 94 percent of Barnes & Noble shoppers.

Barnesandnoble.com needs to take the plunge, ramping up co-marketing activities and absorbing the cost of sales tax for products sold online. Doing so would enable the firm to take full advantage of in-store marketing opportunities without ceding price leadership to Amazon.com or another foe. Taking the tax hit would certainly cut into Barnesandnoble.com's sales margins. On the other hand, Barnesandnoble.com already has higher gross margins than many competitors based on the volume purchasing discounts it receives from its suppliers and on distribution efficiencies. Co-marketing would help the company to significantly boost its online business, and if Barnesandnoble.com is serious about making its business a runaway success, it needs to make this change. The time to move is now, however. The longer Barnesandnoble.com waits to make a choice and begin to leverage in-store marketing, the more difficult it will be to close the substantial lead that Amazon.com has developed.

Barnesandnoble.com has also fallen short on the public relations front. The company has been unfavorably compared with Amazon.com for several years now, and try as it may, Barnesandnoble.com simply has not been able to shake its "big company, late to market, copycat" image. Its public relations work has been more defensive than offensive, and the press has seldom given the company a break. The David vs. Goliath angle has been an obvious tack for journalists writing about Barnesandnoble.com, and many writers have taken the easy way out, bashing Barnesandnoble.com without putting much thought into what the company is doing that is interesting in its own right. However, the firm is working to educate journalists concerning its unique role as a successful crossover marketer. "We position ourselves on a daily basis as *the* most notable brick-and-mortar company that has made a substantial push online," Boyd notes.[22]

Leveraging Offline Assets

The Gap and Playboy Enterprises—our benchmark crossover marketers—have done much more than Barnesandnoble.com to leverage offline assets to build awareness. For Playboy, the situation is somewhat different. As a media company, not a retailer, Playboy does not have to wrestle with the implications of the nexus laws. Free of such constraints, the company does a fair amount of cross-selling of Playboy.com in offline venues. For example, the company uses remnant advertising space in Playboy magazine to build awareness of Playboy.com and drive traffic to the site. It also works references to Playboy.com into the print magazine's editorial material. Although the firm does not yet take advantage of Playboy TV to build awareness for Playboy.com, the company intends to do so in the future, according to Playboy's Buford Smith.

Like Barnes & Noble, the Gap is a retailer. Unlike Barnes & Noble, however, the Gap has decided to charge sales tax on sales made in its online store. Doing so frees the company to fully leverage its offline presence to build awareness for gap.com. Visit a Gap retail store and you'll see the gap.com URL in store windows, on counter cards, and even on the cash registers, which display "Shop online at www.gap.com" on their screens between transactions. And when you leave the store with a purchase, you'll carry your new madras shirt or lambswool V-neck home in a bag emblazoned with "www.gap.com." For crossover marketers, such aggressive tactics are a must.

Its alliance with Bertelsmann certainly bought the company a bit of media respect; it doesn't take tremendous imagination to realize the potential that such a union brings. Nevertheless, public relations has been an uphill battle for Barnesandnoble.com and likely will continue to be for some time to come. This will put all the more pressure on the company's marketing team to communicate effectively through advertising the messages that the company is not getting across via the media.

In addition, Barnesandnoble.com faces a variety of cultural challenges that come with the Bertelsmann alliance. As we saw in the CDNOW chapter, the fusion of multiple corporate cultures is difficult enough when the companies involved are from the same country. But in this case, the merger involves an American company and a German firm, which means that the combined entity must deal not only with differences in corporate cultures but in national cultures as well. There are certainly companies that have managed such mergers effectively—the fusion of Daimler Benz and Chrysler, for example, has gone fairly well. But to make an international union a real success will require a serious investment from both sides in getting to know their counterparts as people and as members of organizations with distinct characters. This will be no easy task, and whether Barnesandnoble.com and Bertelsmann will handle it gracefully remains to be seen.

The alliance between Barnesandnoble.com and Bertelsmann also makes for tricky organizational questions. Up until the merger, Barnesandnoble.com was led by Leonard Riggio. But with the deal came new leadership; Riggio soon ceded the role of president to Jonathan Bulkeley, previously the head of AOL Europe (a joint venture between Bertelsmann and America Online). Within four months, Bulkeley replaced the CFO and asked the COO to leave, claiming in an email to employees that "we are duplicating our efforts by having both a CEO and a COO."[23] Bulkeley is not known as a hatchet man, and the rate of organizational change slowed down once he did some initial shuffling. But the changes raise the larger question of how Barnesandnoble.com will structure the leadership of its organization over time. Both partners own an equal share of the company. Each, however, will likely have different ideas about the way things should be done, and there could well be jockeying for organizational power.

Such internal struggling would be destructive, and while it has not been a significant issue for Barnesandnoble.com to date, the company will have to watch this closely. Given the competitive intensity of its target markets, the last thing Barnesandnoble.com needs is to get caught up in internal political squabbling that distracts it from the battle with Amazon.com and its kin.

Finally, the company has a significant problem with executive compensation. The compensation model it has in place now is way out of whack compared with standard Internet industry practices and does not align the interests of management with company shareholders. Jonathan Bulkeley's base pay is $400,000, plus a 25 percent bonus. The senior marketing, operations, and technology managers have an average base pay of $253,000; they, too, make a 25 percent bonus. These executives also have plenty of stock options. They even participate in a company pension plan. Such a setup is the inverse of the compensation plan at most Internet companies, where salaries are kept low and managers are motivated to make their riches from the large amount of stock options they are granted. At Amazon.com, the average compensation of its six executive officers is $117,000. At Yahoo!, CEO Tim Koogle earns an annual salary of $180,000; the other four executive officers make an average of $106,000.

> **"The mindset necessary for competing successfully in the Internet firmament doesn't include gold watch pensions."**

Industry Standard journalist David Simons railed about Barnesandnoble.com's compensation plan in a recent article, noting that "it's a red flag when option-laden officers at second-place Internet outfits that hemorrhage investors' cash rake in pay that can finance Ferraris. And the mindset necessary for competing successfully in the Internet firmament certainly doesn't include gold watch pensions."[24] If Barnesandnoble.com is going to be a successful Internet company, it needs to be run like one, and management compensation must change. At present, the Barnesandnoble.com management team does relatively well no matter how the company fares; this is not the kind of compensation structure that compels management to drive a firm forward with Internet-style intensity.

The Competitive Threat   ▼

Perhaps the most serious competition Barnesandnoble.com faces is from Amazon.com. Amazon launched its service more than two years before Barnes & Noble decided to make the move online, which enabled Amazon to gain a substantial lead. "Amazon.com is the poster child for time to market advantage," says Nicole Vanderbilt of Jupiter Communications.[25] CEO Jeff Bezos has used this time wisely, investing heavily in marketing to create one of the most powerful brands online. To Bezos, crafting a powerful brand is essential for success on the Internet. He notes,

> As important as brands are in the real world, they're even more important in the virtual one, because online, people have so few visual clues. If I'm walking down a street and spot a large bookstore, I don't even need to notice the name to have a pretty good idea of what the experience will be like. But online, all Web sites pretty much look the same. Is it a 40,000-square-foot Web site or a 2,000-square-foot Web site? Without a clear sense of brand, I might never log on.[26]

Amazon.com has launched a wide range of initiatives to develop this showcase Internet brand. To build awareness, for example, the company has made public relations a strategic priority. It has retained Waggener Edstrom, the same public relations firm used by Microsoft; with the affable Bezos as spokesperson, it has generated more press coverage than almost any other Internet company (Yahoo! is a close contender). Amazon has leveraged offline media such as television and radio to raise visibility among the masses. And on the Web, the firm has implemented an aggressive banner advertising program, ensuring that those who are already on the Web are frequently exposed to the Amazon name.

Amazon's guerrilla marketing programs have also contributed greatly to awareness of the brand. For example, the firm drew attention by giving away a full year of tuition to law school in conjunction with the release of *The Street Lawyer,* a John Grisham novel that was featured on the site. Amazon also generated a whirlwind of interest when it teamed up with Pulitzer Prize–winning author John Updike in a unique promotion. Updike provided the first paragraph of a collaborative, Internet-based short story; each day for a forty-six-day period, contest participants squared off to provide the next paragraph of "Murder Makes the Magazine."[27] When the story reached its conclusion, Updike delivered the closing paragraph. The contest led to widespread press coverage and plenty of repeat visits, as people kept coming back to Amazon to see how the story progressed over time.

Amazon has known since the beginning that distribution is critical to building awareness—and generating sales—on the Internet. With its early start, the company has locked in deals with premier partners. Amazon is the featured online book retailer on GeoCities, the popular Web community site. It has a multiyear agreement with Excite@Home, provider of high-speed Internet access, to play a similar role. In the portal arena, Amazon has forged distribution alliances with Yahoo!, Netscape, and AltaVista—some of the most frequently visited sites on the Web. It has even flanked Barnesandnoble.com's relationship with AOL by landing the role of exclusive bookseller on AOL.com, AOL's Web site, and on AOL's NetFind search engine. Of course, such deals are temporary. As CIBC Oppenheimer analyst Henry Boldget notes, "Many of Amazon.com's deals are only for three years. When they come up again, it's going to be war—like the television networks bidding for NFL rights."[28] In the meantime, however, Amazon.com has benefited significantly from its position on these sites. This distribution has helped Amazon to build a business robust enough to win many of these bidding wars when they do eventually arise.

Amazon.com's marketing orientation and strong service offering have enabled the company to develop serious momentum during its early years. It took Amazon twenty-seven months to serve its first million customers and less than six months to serve its second million.[29] But despite such progress, the company is far from complacent. It knows that technological leads are ephemeral, and that price leadership provides only temporary benefits. Building brand equity, Amazon has realized, is what leads to long-term competitive advantage. "There's nothing about our model that can't be copied over time," Bezos acknowledges. "But you know, McDonald's got copied. And it still built a huge, multibillion-dollar company. A lot of it comes down to the brand name."[30] It is this commitment to building an online brand that, in the long term, makes Amazon.com the toughest competitor that Barnesandnoble.com is likely to face.

Borders also represents competition for Barnesandnoble.com, although the firm is a greater threat to parent company Barnes & Noble, Inc. Borders operates approximately 1,200 Borders, Waldenbooks, and Brentanos stores. Although the firm does run an online store, sales have been small: $4.6 million in 1998, as opposed to $70.2 million for Barnesandnoble.com and $610 million for Amazon. Borders has invested little money in marketing support for Borders.com and has been unwilling to shell out the large amounts needed for distribution deals with portal sites and other high-traffic Web destinations. Although the company projects that sales will quintuple to $25 million in 1999 through simple organic growth, this will still represent only roughly 1 percent of its $3.1 billion in expected total revenues. Rather than fight it out with Amazon and Barnesandnoble.com, Borders will let its online business grow via word of mouth and concentrate instead on its retail operations. "We're focusing on our profitable business," says Borders vice chairman George Mrkonic. "Doubling or tripling our Internet sales wouldn't do anything for our profit."[31] For Barnesandnoble.com, Borders represents more of a nuisance than a danger.

The company will also see competition—although limited in scale—from smaller retailers. According to the Computer Science

Corporation's Seventh Annual Retail survey, more than one-third of all retailers selling books and music have an online presence, and nearly two-thirds plan to implement a site within the next two years. Some of these players have already carved out niches for themselves online. Consider Powell's Books, a Portland, Oregon–based retailer that the *Wall Street Journal* has called "one of the finest operations in the country, the most innovative and creative."[32] In developing its online store, Powell's has focused on the used, rare, and out-of-print book market—much as it has done in its retail stores. This emphasis gives it a distinct advantage, and although Barnesandnoble.com also offers such titles through an agreement with Advanced Book Exchange, this is not its focus.

The majority of small retailers, however, have done little online as of yet. For example, although the Tattered Cover, a well-known Denver book store, does have a Web presence, it has not done much to develop the store. Matthew Miller, general manager of the Tattered Cover, admits that "our e-commerce sales are somewhat limited."[33] The Elliot Bay Book Company, a popular haunt for Seattle literati, is even more typical: It accepts orders by phone, but not via the Web. No doubt such retailers will do more to develop Web storefronts in the years to come. But for many it will be much more difficult to differentiate their online bookstores from Barnesandnoble.com than it has been for them to position their physical bookstores as distinct from those of Barnes & Noble, Inc. The competitive threat here is thus minor.

"Category killers" pose a more significant menace to Barnesandnoble.com's position as a leading online book retailer. These players are dedicated to being experts in particular markets and are likely to take a chunk out of Barnesandnoble.com's hide through their fierce focus on specific areas. Fatbrain.com, for example, is an online book retailer committed exclusively to serving technical and business professionals. The company ignores customers looking for the latest Clive Cussler thriller, attending instead to people shopping for *The Derivatives Handbook* or the second edition of *Linux Kernal Internals*. eToys, the Internet toy retailer, has launched a children's bookstore with more than 85,000 titles. For parents interested in children's books such as *Wait for Elmo!* or *Eloise in Paris,* eToys may well be a more attractive destination than Barnesandnoble.com. These specialists are stealing away profitable customers from Barnesandnoble.com, for the margins on a book such as *Inside Visual J++* are much better than those on the paperback thriller *Serpent.* If the company does not defend itself vigorously against these attackers by constantly deepening its selection within key categories, Barnesandnoble.com will see its current narrow margins eroded even further.

The Barnesandnoble.com brand "is about books," according to Ben Boyd. "What we are doing is building the best online bookstore—not pets, not T-shirts, not lingerie."[34] The sale of books represented 98 percent of Barnesandnoble.com's revenues in 1998. But although the primary focus of the company may well be books, Barnesandnoble.com has expanded to cover other product categories as well, such as music and software. And in doing so, it has broadened its competitive scope. By entering the music market, for example, Barnesandnoble.com has taken on the whole cast of characters we saw in the previous chapter: companies such as CDNOW, Tower Records, and Virgin Megastores. By tackling the software category, Barnesandnoble.com has pitted itself against firms such as Beyond.com and Egghead.com. Expanding its mission is also leading the company into competition with Buy.com and Yahoo! Shopping, sites that present customers with a wide variety of different product categories to choose from. The broader Barnesandnoble.com takes it business, the tougher it is for the company to win the multifront war in which it is engaged. Given that Barnesandnoble.com has plenty of ground to make up in its core categories, I question the wisdom of addressing new industry sectors any time soon.

In all of the categories that Barnesandnoble.com covers, the company will certainly face new competitors as the ecommerce field matures. But the barriers to entry that Barnesandnoble.com has established will significantly hinder all but the largest contenders. The ecommerce arena has become crowded quickly, making it difficult for new participants to differentiate themselves. To rise above the din of the marketplace and make themselves known to large numbers of consumers, new entrants will have to invest substantial amounts of money in marketing. Buying television time, outdoor advertising, and the like is an expensive gambit, and the marketing costs associated with supporting a new consumer-oriented online store will keep many interested players on the sidelines.

Barnesandnoble.com has also established logistics capabilities that will serve as a critical competitive advantage. Would-be emerchants in markets such as books or music can gain basic fulfillment capabilities quickly by setting up relationships with big distributors such as Ingram Books or Valley Records. But unless they can set up facilities capable of holding large amounts of standing inventory and can ship orders from these warehouses quickly, the aspiring vendors will never be able to match the fulfillment speeds of Barnesandnoble.com.

The shortage of online distribution partners is the third major factor that will serve to block new entrants. Barnesandnoble.com has lined up partnerships with allies such as AOL and Microsoft and has paid a premium to secure this online real estate. Most of the high-traffic distribution options are already locked up, and for a new contender to compete for such opportunities when they come up for bid would be an expensive proposition. An emerging emerchant might have better luck in building an affiliate program, since the costs for securing this sort of distribution are lower. Nonetheless, it is questionable whether a site would want to join an affiliate program run by a new online vendor rather than Barnesandnoble.com's Affiliate Network, an established program with a large number of participants, excellent online sales reporting, and good commission terms. In short, the barriers to entry that Barnesandnoble.com has established are significant. Companies with existing distribution capabilities and large amounts of capital could pose the greatest threat, and the good news for Barnesandnoble.com is that there are simply not that many such potential adversaries to worry about.

On the Horizon   ▼

Although its focus has been on cultivating a domestic customer base, Barnesandnoble.com has already done a fair amount of business overseas. The 1.7 million customers to whom it has sold since the store opened its virtual doors in 1997 have come from 181 different countries. The potential for international growth is substantial. According to the investment banking firm Veronis Suhler, the size of the U.S. consumer book market was $15.4 billion in 1997; it is expected to grow to $17.9 billion by the year 2000.[35] The worldwide market, however, presents an opportunity several times as large. According to Euromonitor, worldwide book sales were roughly $81 billion in 1998 and are projected to reach $85 billion by 2000.[36] Add to this base the opportunities in categories such as music, software, and magazines, and it is clear that Barnesandnoble.com has the chance to generate substantial revenues from international sales.

If it is going to go after this market aggressively, however, Barnesandnoble.com will need to determine to what extent it wants to compete with Bertelsmann. According to the agreement between the two firms, Bertelsmann's publishing companies may sell the books they print on their corporate Web sites, putting them into competition with Barnesandnoble.com. In addition, Bertelsmann has formed its own, independent online venture, BooksOnline (BOL), and plans to operate online stores in the United Kingdom, France, Germany, Italy, the Netherlands, New Zealand, and Australia. The agreement states that BOL virtual stores in the United Kingdom, Australia, and New Zealand have the right to sell English-language books, which pits them against Barnesandnoble.com. The two companies agreed that BOL stores in non-English-speaking countries would include a link to Barnesandnoble.com and to one English-language-focused BOL store to promote the sale of books in English, so at least Barnesandnoble.com gets some international exposure this way. But BOL has no obligation to promote Barnesandnoble.com as a retailer of music, software, or other information products. In these categories, competition will be head to head.

Needless to say, this arrangement has the potential to be messy. The least controversial course of action is for Barnesandnoble.com to approach international sales conservatively, focusing on its domestic business but serving effectively those overseas customers who come to the Barnesandnoble.com online store via word of mouth or through the links on certain BOL stores. If the company follows this approach, however, it will be leaving a lot of money on the table. It will also be ceding an opportunity to competitors. Amazon, for example, already has online stores in the United Kingdom and Germany and will undoubtedly tackle additional markets in the future. For Barnesandnoble.com to get serious about international sales, it too would need to open localized online stores in its target countries. In doing so, the competition with its "partner" Bertelsmann would become blatant. The decision as to whether to get aggressive about key international markets has the potential to be a political quagmire for Barnesandnoble.com. But for the company to maximize the opportunity presented by overseas sales, it must brave the bog and take action soon, or it will be left behind by faster-moving rivals.

Barnesandnoble.com will also face the challenge of how to improve on its customer service. Consider how Charles Piller, a staff writer with latimes.com, described his experience with the online retailer:

> My recent order for out-of-print books from Barnesand-noble.com gradually assumed (perhaps appropriately) Kafka-esque qualities. Multiple emails with conflicting messages were followed by weeks of silence. Luckily, I found one of the obscure titles on another Web site that shipped it promptly. A few weeks later, Barnesandnoble.com located a copy of the same book and e-mailed me that it had shipped the title and charged my credit card.[37]

Despite this discouraging story, it is not as if Barnesandnoble.com has been ignoring customer service. It has a team of more than 100 customer service representatives available to respond to customer inquiries seven days a week. It also offers a toll-free number for those customers who want support by phone—a rare feature among consumer ecommerce companies. But the level of service still does not equate to what you can get offline, even compared with a Barnes & Noble retail store, where the staffers behind the counter are not necessarily bibliophiles.

This is a problem. According to Jupiter analyst Ken Cassar, customers are now holding Web retailers to the same standards as their offline brethren.[38] And they're being disappointed. If service levels—as well as the design of the stores themselves—were better, emerchants could close substantially more sales. According to a recent study by Forrester Research, about 66 percent of Web shopping carts (the virtual repositories for goods that customers select during online shopping sprees) are abandoned before purchases are made.[39] This is the equivalent of masses of customers leaving shopping baskets full of milk, fruit, and frozen chicken wings in the aisles of their local supermarkets. If Internet merchants can improve the quality of the customer service they provide, they have a much greater chance of ringing up those virtual goods that are being left behind.

> **Customers are holding Web retailers to the same service standards as their offline brethren—and are being disappointed.**

To take its customer service to the next level, Barnesandnoble.com will need to evaluate adding technologies such as text- or voice-based chat that will enable customer service representatives to communicate in real time with shoppers, providing instant answers to their many questions. Whereas phone-based support frequently requires consumers shopping from home to log off before calling in, text- or voice-based chat would allow the customer service rep to help a shopper at the precise point at which he is having a problem, resolving the issue and closing the sale. Offering this kind of support would be expensive for Barnesandnoble.com, but it has the potential to significantly increase the number of sales actually closed. And given peoples' general level of dissatisfaction with customer service among Web vendors, for Barnesandnoble.com to stick with the status quo would be dangerous. As journalist Charles Piller wrote, "Bad service can kill fledgling Web brands, and it may not be a slow, agonizing death. In a recent Forrester study, more than half the consumers who had a bad online buying experience said that they had abandoned the offending merchant, and fully half abandoned e-commerce altogether."[40]

Like CDNOW, Barnesandnoble.com will also be forced to grapple with the issues associated with digital content distribution. We covered many of the problems with online music distribution in chapter 2. But consider the complexities tied to making books available in digital format via the Web. Barnesandnoble.com is experimenting with the idea, but so far it has gained minimal traction. The company sells a product called the Rocket eBook, a handheld hardware device that can hold up to four thousand pages at a time. But only seven hundred titles are available for use with the eBook, and prices for both the device itself and the digital books are still high.

Analysts at Gartner Group, an industry research firm, have called electronic books one of the top ten technologies to watch in 1999, but have also cautioned that "it's too early to tell which growth track e-books will take."[41] Others are entirely skeptical and point fingers at publishing companies for holding back the adoption of such technologies. Writes journalist Jimmy Guterman, "The publishing industry's reluctance to accept even the most rudimentary electronic-publishing infrastructure is nothing new. Many publishers still insist that a manuscript be submitted on paper so the company's production staff can retype it. So it's no surprise that the industry is doing all it can to either make believe the new formats don't exist or bury them."[42]

The promise of distributing books in digital book format is alluring: With no packaging costs and with bandwidth fees as the sole distribution expense, margins would be much greater. But in addition to the issues just raised, copyright protection is as problematic here as in our discussion of digital music distribution. Selling books in digital format is an opportunity that may eventually prove fruitful for Barnesandnoble.com. However, the company will need to resolve a variety of problems before digital book sales emerge as a significant revenue source for the firm.

Most important, Barnesandnoble.com will need to face the question of how far to stretch its brand. Amazon.com has moved far beyond books to become a "Wal-Mart of the Web," offering products ranging from toys to consumer electronics. Barnesandnoble.com already sells magazines and software in addition to books. But should it follow Amazon's lead and significantly enlarge the scope of its product and service offerings? I say no. As mentioned earlier, the competitive situation becomes increasingly complicated the more product categories Barnesandnoble.com takes on. In addition to intensifying competition, taking on an ever-expanding range of markets dilutes the meaning of the Barnesandnoble.com brand. As Ben Boyd has noted, Barnesandnoble.com is all about information content. Whereas selling software and CDs is consistent with this theme, pitching PCs and printers is not.

Moreover, were Barnesandnoble.com to expand its charter in this way, it would clash with the positioning of the parent brand, a brand that consumers equate with books. "It's one thing to be a big brand," notes David Aaker, professor of marketing at the University of California at Berkeley's Haas School of Business. "It's another to be a brand in another category. You can damage your reputation if you stretch it too far."[43] Barnesandnoble.com should be looking to draw strength from the Barnes & Noble, Inc. brand, not to conflict with it. CEO Jonathan Bulkeley has said, "Every e-commerce company wants to become 'the Amazon.com of stereos' or 'the Amazon.com of car parts.' Barnesandnoble.com's goal for the next two years is to become the Amazon.com of books."[44] If Bulkeley truly means for the Barnesandnoble.com brand to stand for books in the minds of online shoppers, he must refrain from the temptation to tackle an ever-increasing array of product categories and focus instead on excelling in the business Barnesandnoble.com has already carved out for itself.

CHAPTER 4

www.Yahoo.com

Yahoo! began as an exercise in procrastination. David Filo and Jerry Yang, then Ph.D. candidates at Stanford, were desperately seeking ways to avoid working on their computer science theses. Whereas other Stanford students found distraction in volleyball and Ultimate Frisbee, Jerry and David sought solace from the academic grind in surfing the Web, which in late 1993 was just emerging as a place worth exploring. As they spent more time on the Web, the two both realized that their lists of favorite Web sites—maintained as bookmarks on Mosaic, an early Web browser—were becoming unmanageable. To make their lives easier, they decided to create a simple, "hot list" of their favorite sites, organize it by category, and post it to the Web for easy access.

What started as a pastime grew to an obsession. The directory became popular quickly, and people began sending Jerry and David digital fan mail to let them know how much they valued the fledgling Web guide. The two students were excited about the response to their initial efforts and decided to ramp up the pace (with their thesis advisor out of the country, Jerry and David had no pressure to do anything "productive"). They tried to visit and categorize one thousand sites a day. Holed up in an old university trailer, David and Jerry worked like fiends. "Dave and I would sleep in the same spot," Jerry recalled. "He would sleep for about four hours, and I would work. And then he would get up and work and I would go to sleep."[1]

The directory grew. People noticed—and not just hard-core Web surfers. Jerry and David soon connected with Michael Moritz, a partner at Sequoia Capital, who, like the two entrepreneurs, thought that there might be a business to be built out of this whimsical, hand-cobbled directory of Web links. The business model was still unclear. What was apparent, however, was that the Web was growing at an outrageous pace. And in order to find their way around, people needed a guide.

In April 1995, Sequoia invested $1 million in Yahoo!, a modest injection of capital (by venture capital standards) that gave the young company the money it needed to move out of its trailer and into the fast lane. Had the Sequoia partners retained their 25 percent of the company, their share would now be worth a fortune, for Yahoo! has one of the most powerful brands on the Internet. With an average of 38 million unique adult users per month, Yahoo! has an audience larger than that of almost any other Web site. It also has greater visibility than many conventional media brands. For example, more people visit Yahoo! each week than watch MTV, CNBC, or Nickelodeon. More people use Yahoo! each month than read *Newsweek, Time,* or *Life.*

But despite its success to date, Yahoo! is no Camelot. The company has numerous challenges it must address if it is to maintain its leadership position. For example, Yahoo! is facing growing pressure from *vertical portals*—sites such as CNET, the leading technology news and information hub, that offer deep content, commerce, and community related to specific subjects. As Web users gain familiarity with the Internet environment, a growing number of them are now going straight to these vertical portals, bypassing Yahoo! on the way. Another problem: Yahoo! is on a collision course with some of its online merchant partners, companies that are eyeing Yahoo!'s aspiration to be an ecommerce destination site with suspicion. And while competitors like Snap have partnered with large media companies,

Yahoo! Snapshot (1999)

URL: www.yahoo.com
Ticker symbol/Exchange: YHOO/Nasdaq **Headquarters:** Santa Clara, CA
Year founded: 1994 **CEO:** Tim Koogle

Business concept:	Offers a detailed Web directory, as well as news, information, communication tools, and online shopping.
Brand assets:	Brand awareness; customer commitment; distribution and content alliances; early mover advantage; customer and market intimacy; reputation for excellence; value
Initial investors:	Sequoia Capital
Primary competitors:	Online: Excite@Home, Go Network, Lycos, AOL/Netscape, Microsoft, CNET, LookSmart Offline: Major traditional media properties, such as CNN, *Time*, MTV, and *Newsweek*
Major strategic partners:	Amazon.com, AT&T, Butterfield & Butterfield, CDNOW, Compaq, Hewlett-Packard, InsWeb, IBM, PageNet

Major milestones:

Early 1994	Site goes live
September 1994	Traffic reaches $1 million hits per day
April 1995	Receives $1 million in venture capital funding
April 1996	$33.8 million IPO
January 1997	Launches Yahoo! Chat
February 1997	Launches Yahoo! Classifieds
October 1997	Secures distribution agreement with Compaq
October 1997	Acquires Four11
October 1997	Secures distribution agreement with Gateway
December 1997	Launches Yahoo! Sports
April 1998	Launches Yahoo! Computers
May 1998	Inks cross-marketing pact with AT&T
June 1998	Acquires Viaweb; Launches Yahoo! Real Estate
July 1998	Announces $250 million private placement
September 1998	Opens Yahoo! Auctions
October 1998	Acquires Yoyodyne
November 1998	Launches Yahoo! Shopping
January 1999	Secures distribution agreement with Hewlett-Packard
January 1999	Signs distribution agreement with IBM
January 1999	Acquires GeoCities
March 1999	Secures distribution on PageNet pagers
April 1999	Acquires Broadcast.com; Launches Yahoo! Radio
June 1999	Acquires Online Anywhere
June 1999	Cuts deal with Phoenix Technologies for distribution on PC motherboards
July 1999	Launches Yahoo! Resumes
August 1999	Introduces free e-greetings; Unveils Yahoo! Digital
September 1999	Introduces bill payment services

Financial summary **(CY 1998):**	Revenue: $203.3 million Net income (loss): ($25.6 million)
Shares outstanding:	200.5 million
Number of employees:	803

giving them substantial offline advertising support, Yahoo! has stood alone and has missed out on the opportunity to increase awareness and traffic through such an alliance.

The Yahoo! story—with both its triumphs and troubles—presents a tremendous learning opportunity. How has the company used guerrilla marketing to build its business? What kinds of distribution deals has Yahoo! focused on, and why? Which firms present the greatest competitive threats to Yahoo!, and how should it respond? What opportunities are emerging for Yahoo! as companies introduce new hardware devices that offer Internet access? This chapter explores these and similar issues in a profile of one of the most influential companies in the Internet space.

Best of Brand   ▼

Yahoo! has done many things right in its drive to forge a major Internet brand, and we'll start the chapter with a look at some of its smartest moves. The firm has invested substantially in public relations, boosting awareness at low cost. Yahoo! was the first major Web player to turn to television to build its brand, gaining attention through its presence in a medium that was new territory for the "dot com" set when Yahoo!'s commercials began in 1996. It ran a variety of guerrilla promotions, zany marketing programs that generated awareness as well as related press coverage. It struck content deals that enhanced the utility of the service and distribution partnerships that extended the company's reach. Yahoo! invested in features such as free email and an Internet-based paging service, additions that encouraged customers to come back to Yahoo! regularly. It acted early and quickly. It made a substantial effort to get to know its customers and their specific needs. And the company has been dedicated to providing a high-quality service at no cost to end users.

Brand Awareness ▼

Based on its interest in appealing to Internet newcomers, Yahoo! has positioned itself as the common man's home on the Internet. In its awareness-building efforts, the company has always communicated the utility of the service, but has done so in a way that has expressed other core brand attributes as well: a sense of irreverence, an approachable nature, an inherent friendliness. "The brand is associated with being very open," says Blaise Simpson, a director at Niehaus Ryan Wong (Yahoo!'s public relations agency). "It's not a luxury brand. It's a brand that can speak to just about anybody."[2] Given the unease with which the average consumer approaches technology, Yahoo! has also avoided characterizing itself as a technology-oriented company. "We want to keep the brand from being frightening in any way," Simpson explains.[3] Since the beginning, Yahoo! has presented a human face to the world, conveying a brand personality that is fun, accessible, and helpful. The characteristics of the Yahoo! brand have resonated

Yahoo! has positioned itself as the common man's home on the Internet.

with consumers and have helped to build awareness and enthusiasm reminiscent of the early days of the Apple Macintosh.

Public Relations   Yahoo! has long placed high strategic value on public relations. Venture capitalist Mike Moritz pointed Yahoo! toward PR agency Niehaus Ryan Wong (NRW) when the company was barely out of its double-wide trailer at Stanford. At that time, Yahoo!'s marketing department consisted of one person: Karen Edwards, a former director of marketing for Twentieth Century Fox who went on to become Yahoo!'s vice president of brand management. Karen and the NRW team worked closely to evangelize the importance of this emerging medium and Yahoo!'s role in it. Blaise Simpson recalls, "The Internet as a whole was so new at that point that we had reporters into our offices, sat them down at computers and said, 'This is the

Internet, and this is a company named Yahoo!."[4] Educating the media gave Yahoo! and NRW the opportunity to present information in a way that reflected well on Yahoo!, as well as earning the good will of journalists who valued the background information on the evolution and workings of the Internet.

As Yahoo! took off, the company was able to expand its marketing and public relations groups. But NRW continued to be an important extension of the Yahoo! communications team. Yahoo! set the business strategy; then it and NRW would work together on developing PR strategy. When it came time to implement, NRW had the resources required to communicate Yahoo!'s messages to the diverse assortment of media members it was interested in reaching.

Yahoo! and NRW have divided the media they target into four categories: consumer press, industry press, business press and financial analysts, and the advertising press. Their communications strategies have varied by segment. With consumers, for example, the Yahoo!/NRW team has played up the "celebrity status" of co-founders Jerry Yang and David Filo. The public has been extremely interested in the story of the two disaffected Stanford students who started an Internet company with a goofy name that soon was worth so much money. "Early on, we decided that Jerry and David were themselves a good story," said Simpson. "The strategy was to personify the Yahoo! brand in these two guys who had started the company and show that Yahoo! was a really youthful, interesting, user-friendly kind of service."[5]

To build Jerry and David into Internet celebrities, NRW drove hard to get them out in front of the public. The firm booked frequent speaking engagements for the young entrepreneurs, and Jerry in particular (the more outspoken of the pair) became a regular on the high-tech conference circuit. NRW also arranged countless press interviews, positioning Jerry and David as icons of the Internet age. The two were spirited. They were honest. And they were refreshingly funny. "I'm having a great time," Jerry told a reporter from *Time*. "This is the best job I've ever had. Actually, it's the only job I've ever had."[6] Although a PR firm can strive to turn the standard Internetdweeb-turned-CEO into a star, it certainly helps if he or she has some charisma. In the case of Jerry and David, their candor and spunk made it much easier for NRW to attract attention to Yahoo!'s two founders.

The strategy worked almost too well: Jerry and David received so much press coverage that Yahoo! and the agency eventually became concerned that the consumer publications were focusing too much on the duo as "two guys who wear cut-offs and go barefoot" and not enough on their role as founders, visionaries, and managers.[7] "Yahoo had to present itself as a grown-up, serious company," noted Karen Edwards.[8] So NRW backed off the celebrity angle, placing more emphasis on the "Yahoo! is a well-run company" message. Nonetheless, just as the public is intrigued by figures such as Bill Gates and Steve Jobs, so are they curious about Jerry and David—the human side of Yahoo!. NRW has continued to judiciously exploit this curiosity. "It's neat to know that at the tender age of 28 you can be so successful at something and create a whole new area," said Simpson. "Consumers are interested in this idea."[9]

In working with the consumer press, Yahoo! and NRW have also focused on the breadth of services the company offers. Different Yahoo! sections or features appeal to specific publications and their readers; the strategy has been to match one with the other. To gain exposure among parents for Yahooligans!, the Yahoo! Web guide for children, NRW might pursue story opportunities with publications such as *Parenting* or *Growing Child.* To build familiarity among travel fans for Yahoo! Travel, the company's travel resource center, NRW might work with magazines such as *Travel & Leisure* or *Sunset.* "Our goal is to focus on these vertical audiences and let them know about the aspects of Yahoo! that are pertinent to them," said Simpson.[10] The plan has worked. In addition to general consumer publications such as *People* and *USA Today,* Yahoo! has been featured in magazines such as *Smart Money* and *Rolling Stone* (visibility in the latter has helped Yahoo! to reach teens, another attractive market segment). Yahoo! has become a rich enough collection of resources that it has made good sense for the company to pursue this type of segmentation strategy.

Such directed communications efforts have gained visibility for the brand among audiences who may have been less familiar with it and have provided readers with a specific reason to try Yahoo! features or content of particular interest to them.

With the high-tech trade press, Yahoo!'s strategy has been to provide journalists with the most current, detailed information possible about what the company is up to. Simpson explains:

> For the consumer press, the messages are pretty simple—Yahoo! is fun, it's easy to use, etc. For the industry press, it's more complicated. These writers have a depth of understanding and are likely to be interested in very specific aspects of Yahoo!. Our goal is to get the news to them as soon as we possibly can and to provide them with the detail they need for their stories by linking them to the producers at Yahoo! who are in charge of specific areas of the site.[11]

The high-tech trade press has reported on Yahoo! in a level of detail way beyond what has appeared in *Esquire* or the *New York Times.* Yahoo!'s approach to this group has been straightforward: Keep the journalists constantly informed, and help them to be successful by enabling them to work with company spokespeople and dig deep into relevant issues. It's a strategy that has worked well for the company and has generated exposure for the brand in *Interactive Week, Internet World,* and myriad other industry publications.

In working with the business and financial press, Yahoo!'s aim has been to convey the idea that it is a stable, well-managed company, one that is gracefully managing fast growth in a turbulent industry. Given the huge increase in both the number of users of the service and in the company's stock price over a short period of time, it has been particularly important for Yahoo! to communicate that it is in control and that it is not a temporary phenomenon, but instead is a successful company that is in this business for the long haul. Yahoo! does not use an outside investor relations firm. Instead, company representatives speak directly with financial analysts, and Yahoo! and NRW work together on communications with business and financial journalists.

Although Yahoo! has had a challenge reconciling the fun, youthful image of the company with concepts such as "stability" and "seasoned management" in the minds of some journalists, the firm has the proof it needs to support its claims. Yahoo! has been one of the few Internet companies to turn a profit early in the development of this new medium. Although Jerry Yang, David Filo, and many other Yahoos are certainly young, the company is under the "adult supervision" of capable, experienced managers. CEO Tim Koogle, for example, is the former president of Intermec (a data communications equipment manufacturer) and spent nine years working for Motorola's operations and venture capital groups. COO and president Jeff Mallet helped launch Reference Software, a spelling and grammar checking software developer that was acquired by WordPerfect, which was in turn acquired by Novell. Mallet rose through the ranks to become the vice president and general manager of Novell's Consumer Division.

"When people see us in the advertising trades, I want our competitors to weep."

Strong management has helped to keep the Yahoo! work environment stable and employee turnover low, even though the Internet space as a whole is fluid and chaotic. True, the large increases in the company's stock price have raised questions about whether the company is fairly valued, but this is an issue in the hands of the market, not under the direct control of Yahoo! management.

In talking to the business and financial press, therefore, Yahoo! has generally been successful in communicating the kinds of values this audience likes to see. The PR team has worked closely with its key contacts to keep them informed and to help them communicate to their constituencies information about Yahoo!'s business direction. The successes of the company have been magnified by its communications efforts, and Yahoo! has frequently been featured in business publications such as the *Wall Street Journal, Forbes,* and *Business Week.*

Yahoo! has been conservative when talking to the business and financial press. "Our press releases for that audience are boring," says Karen Edwards. "We are not trying to be funny. We never put anything there we can't substantiate."[12] When talking to advertising trade publications, Yahoo!'s strategy is the inverse. "Then, we sell, sell, sell," says Edwards. "We are talking about Yahoo! as the site on which companies have to advertise. We present all the numbers, make a strong case for why we are the biggest. As the head of our sales group says, 'When people see us in the advertising trades, I want our competitors to weep.'"[13] The voice with which Yahoo! communicates to the advertising trade press represents Yahoo! at its most outspoken. Yahoo! has facts at hand to support the hype, however. And the strategy has worked well: Yahoo! has been written up regularly in *Advertising Week, Advertising Age, Brand Week,* and the other advertising industry journals.

Yahoo! understands the importance of the "mo factor." As the leader in the portal sector, Yahoo! needs to illustrate that it is driving the industry forward. The celebrity marketing of David and Jerry described earlier has certainly been helpful in building momentum, providing a colorful spokesperson—usually Jerry—who has talked regularly about all that Yahoo! is doing. Probably most important for encouraging the momentum, however, has been Yahoo!'s continuous drive to educate the press about the company's latest developments. Yahoo! has plenty of news to communicate: updates on distribution deals, quarterly earnings, strategic investments, and product enhancements. And the firm could issue many more releases than it does. (Yahoo! issued an average of eleven press releases per month in the first half of 1999; in contrast, Lycos issued an average of twenty per month—a much greater volume of news for writers and analysts to process.) According to Karen Edwards, "We try hard to manage the amount of news, to really focus on the things that we believe are newsworthy as opposed to trying to create something to say. I wouldn't ever want us to just try to *look* like we are being innovative."[14] This approach has gained respect among journalists, many of whom now see the news that comes from Yahoo! as "a way to gauge the velocity of the growth of the Internet."[15]

Offline Marketing   Yahoo!'s primary target has been "near surfers": those people who are not yet online, but are likely to begin using the Web in the near future. As Karen Edwards describes it, the near surfers are a large and fast-growing group of people who have a basic understanding of what the Internet is and what it might do for them, but "what they don't know is how do I get on, how do I sign up, where would I start? If you're the brand name that people know, [your site] is where they're going to go first."[16]

To build awareness within this group, Yahoo! has invested in offline marketing. In 1996, for example, Yahoo! launched the first sizable television advertising campaign for an Internet company. Edwards's goal was to make Yahoo! a household name, "a thing of popular culture."[17] She has made good progress: By 1998, 42 percent of U.S. households knew of Yahoo!, according to NFO Research.[18] But back in 1996 this goal seemed a long way off. "In a survey conducted before the first ad, the company asked a cross section of Americans, 'What is Yahoo!?' Only 8% correctly identified the company. A sizable percentage thought it was a chocolate drink."[19]

Yahoo! spent $5 million to develop and air a series of irreverent TV commercials that showed how everyday people might use Yahoo! to help them solve problems in their lives. John Yost, co-founder of Black Rocket, Yahoo!'s ad agency, got the inspiration for these ads by talking to a typical Yahoo! user during consumer research that the company was conducting:

> *This was a woman who had never done much with comput-*
> *ers, as she didn't see that they were very relevant to her life.*
> *She was an orchid grower, however, and when she discovered*
> *that through Yahoo!, she could track down all sorts of infor-*
> *mation about the flowers and exchange ideas with orchid*
> *growers throughout the world, she was ecstatic. This whole*

new world opened up to her. We began to refer to this experi-
ence as a 'magic moment,' and the campaign grew from this
idea.[20]

After hearing the story of this woman's epiphany, Yahoo! and Black
Rocket developed a series of commercials that played on the idea of
Yahoo! as a service that enables everyday people to tap the Internet for
solutions to life's dilemmas. In one such ad, a stymied fisherman
visited Yahoo! to research bait, returning to his fishing hole to haul
out a pile of leviathan-sized tuna. In another, a balding slickster in
1970s-style lounge wear consulted Yahoo! for hair loss help. Later, we
saw him sauntering down a crowded city sidewalk crowned with a
giant afro. Both ended with Yahoo!'s well-known tagline, "Do You
Yahoo!?" (One of Edwards's initial projects for Yahoo! was to develop
this "Big Idea" tagline, which she describes as "the one idea that really
encompasses, or makes a statement about a company."[21]) The sign-off
also included a hillbilly-esque Yahoo! yodel, a distinctive sound bite
that reinforced the brand audibly and resembled the "Intel Inside"
chime that Intel and its partners include in their commercials. Fun
and disarming, the commercials made the Internet feel accessible. The
ads ran in television programming designed just for that average
person—primetime sports, early morning and late night news, *Late*
Night with David Letterman, Saturday Night Live, and other such
shows.

The message resonated with prospects, rousing chuckles and
raising awareness. Yahoo! has kept running a healthy amount of television advertising since the original campaign began, because the
near-surfer audience has continued to expand. The efficacy of the
message that Yahoo! began communicating to prospective users back
in 1996 is validated by the fact that the company has long used many
of these original commercials. "Think about how this industry has
changed, how quickly our business has changed," said Edwards. "We
are in a dramatically different business today, but the messages are
still the same."[22] Yahoo!'s investment in television advertising illustrates the importance that offline marketing has assumed for compa-

nies looking to build a strong Internet brand. "It's pretty much one of the new rules of the game," notes John Yost of Black Rocket.[23]

Yahoo! has also used radio advertising to reach its target audience. "Radio works a little bit harder to tell more about Yahoo! and the things you can do on it," explains John Yost.[24] In the spirit of its television commercials, Yahoo!'s radio ads were a bit wacky. The spots highlighted the full range of content one might find on the Web using Yahoo!, from "lots of maps" to "a recipe for crawfish gumbo," from "a fairly decent urologist" to "topless backgammon in Monte Carlo." Like Yahoo!'s TV ads, these radio commercials ended with the company tagline and the funky Yahoo! yodel. The company experimented with all sorts of different station formats in urban areas with significant Internet penetration. Like TV, these ads provided a great medium for reaching out to near surfers. Listeners might encounter Yahoo! commercials during a drive-time morning show, while checking up on the score of a baseball game, or while listening to a local rock station. The awareness these spots built among near surfers has helped to ensure that when they eventually make it online, they head toward a brand they've come to know through a familiar medium.

TV and radio have been particularly effective in helping Yahoo! build its umbrella brand. By concentrating on creating this strong parent brand first, it has been that much easier for the company to develop line extensions that have built on the equity established in its primary brand. Yahoo! Chat, Yahoo! Travel, Yahoo! Finance . . . these and a growing number of other Yahoo! properties have all piggy-backed on the parent brand. Karen Edwards notes:

> We do have quite a few line extensions, but I think that if you do a good job building the core brand, then that's like an umbrella that protects anything else you do. Take Yahoo! Finance. Yahoo! Finance represents a huge portion of our traffic. We could have called it "FinanceXYZ" or something. But by calling it "Yahoo! Finance," the site benefits from the trust that is associated with the core brand. People come to assume that if it's a Yahoo! site, that means that the pages are going to load

quickly, that it will be easy to use, and that it will have best-of-breed content. These are the things that Yahoo! has become known for and thus, Yahoo! Finance gets the same associations.[25]

Yahoo! has also invested in print advertising, although its print campaigns have been designed primarily to support the sub-brands mentioned above. Consistent with its radio and television ads, Yahoo!'s print ads were spirited and offbeat. Running in publications that ranged from *Money Magazine* to *Sports Illustrated,* the ads built awareness for Yahoo! properties beyond the main directory. The print advertising also extended the definition of the core brand. As Edwards notes, advertising for properties such as Yahoo! Finance "helps people to understand that Yahoo! stands for much more than just a directory or a gateway to the Internet."[26] And given that Yahoo! obtained much of the space for these ads through barter advertising deals with other media companies, it has been able to build its brand via print advertising without spending much cash.

In addition to this traditional awareness-building work, Yahoo! has also pursued all manner of guerrilla marketing campaigns. The aim has been similar to that of the other offline marketing Yahoo! has done: build awareness and convey a strong sense of the brand personality. The implementation, however, has been brilliantly zany, exhibiting a spirit and degree of marketing creativity that has outshone the company's other offline marketing programs. For example, Yahoo! sponsored a series of concerts by the Backstreet Boys, the latest teenybopper wonder band. The group's fans—love-struck girls aged twelve to seventeen—flocked to Yahoo! to participate in online chats with their idols. The company also convinced some of its employees to wrap their cars in purple plastic festooned with the Yahoo! logo. As they commuted up and down Highway 101—the busiest freeway in Silicon Valley—these violet vehicles drew serious attention. As Edwards

> **Guerrilla marketing has positioned Yahoo! as vivacious and approachable.**

points out, "'It's one thing to see a Yahoo! ad on TV; it's another to say, 'I saw the Yahoomobile on the highway.' We have people who write in and say, 'Wow, that's cool!' Now that person has a much stronger relationship with our brand than one who experienced it from a couch.'"[27]

Yahoo! has sponsored a weekly poll on *Marketplace,* the popular National Public Radio show. It has licensed its brand to a snowboard manufacturer. It has even plastered its logo on the Zamboni (an ice cleaning machine) used during the San Jose Sharks' hockey games. For Edwards, who spent several years in the entertainment industry, such "stunt marketing" has been a natural. These guerrilla marketing hijinks haven't gained Yahoo! the kind of brand exposure that a commercial on *David Letterman* would buy, and their effects have often been difficult to measure except through anecdotes that have filtered back to the company from employees, Yahoo! users, and friends of the company. But they've been inexpensive and distinctive. With the exception of AOL, none of the other major portal players have done much on the guerrilla marketing front (and AOL's programs have been tepid by comparison). These antics have also done a great job of positioning Yahoo! as vivacious and approachable—the antithesis of a standard high-tech product. Says Edwards, "The guerrilla marketing helps Yahoo! look creative. It also shows people that we haven't forgotten where we came from. We still don't take ourselves too seriously. Forget all the stuff you are reading about our founders being billionaires. We are still fun people, we believe in what we are doing and we are doing this for you, the customer."[28]

Customer Commitment ▼

Yahoo! has managed to cultivate higher loyalty levels than any other player in its market. According to a recent study by the NPD group, a firm that specializes in Internet-related market research and analysis, 92 percent of Yahoo! users rated the service "excellent" or "very good," and 76 percent turned to Yahoo! before visiting another search or navigational site. The study also found that 73 percent of Yahoo! users bookmarked the service within their Internet browsers—significantly more than bookmarked competitive offerings.[29]

Where has this loyalty come from? As described in the "Reputation for Excellence" and "Value" sections later in this chapter, much of the passion that customers feel for the Yahoo! brand stems from the richness and utility of the underlying service. As you'll read in these sections, Yahoo! has built a Web resource that is sophisticated but simple, and customers are grateful for the assistance that it has given them in their efforts to make the most of the Web. In this section, however, I want to highlight three Yahoo! product initiatives that have enhanced loyalty. The first was the development of MyYahoo!, which gives Yahoo! customers the ability to personalize the site to meet their specific needs. The second was the rollout of a series of supplementary services particularly designed to keep customers coming back for more. The third was the development of virtual online communities called Yahoo! Clubs.

MyYahoo! enables users to craft their own personalized view of Yahoo! through a Web page that delivers stock prices, scores for favorite sports teams, local weather, air fares for cities of interest, and other information. It's a bit like a custom-tailored daily newspaper. By tuning the information it offers based on users' preferences, Yahoo! boosts customer loyalty. Plenty of others in this market have figured out the personalization game; Excite@Home, Lycos, and the rest of the bunch all offer similar capabilities. According to Excite co-founder Joe Kraus, people who personalize return five times more frequently than those who don't. What's more, once someone has taken the time to create a personal page, not only does he come back more frequently, but he is also less likely to use competitive services. "'MyYahoo is getting 6.9 million unique visitors a month, and MyExcite is getting 4.4 million," says Jeff Levy, CEO of RelevantKnowledge, a Web traffic measurement firm. "And there's virtually no overlap."[30] MyYahoo! is having a significant impact on the company's customer retention rates. This is a key contribution, for as Barry Parr, director of Internet and electronic commerce strategies for the research firm IDC

(International Data Corp.), has noted, "With portals, the battle is now about customer retention, and it's a defensive battle. As a result, we'll see fewer changes in market share in the future. It's like World War I trench warfare, where every hundred yards will be very expensive."[31]

On the product side, another way in which Yahoo! has built loyalty is by developing a set of specific features—many of them communications oriented—that encourage repeat usage. Email, for example, is the kind of feature that keeps people coming back to Yahoo! frequently—sometimes several times a day. Chat is another such feature. The stock hound may return to Yahoo! multiple times a week to trade tips about hot companies with others in the Tech Stocks chat room, while his daughter may visit regularly to get the inside scoop on Hanson or to chat directly with stars such as Josie Bissett of *Melrose Place.* By focusing on adding such functionality, Yahoo! has increased *stickiness,* which is Webspeak for a user's propensity to return to a site often.

As with MyYahoo!, these sticky features give Yahoo! the opportunity to ask customers to register in order to use them. The registration process represents a trade: Customers give Yahoo! background information (age, geographic location, interests, etc.) in return for access to Yahoo! services. Yahoo!, in turn, can use this registration data both to develop better content for its users and to direct more targeted advertising to them. The company is driving hard to increase registration, because it knows that by doing so it strengthens the relationship between Yahoo! and the consumer and reduces the chance of losing him or her to the competition. According to Karen Edwards, "This is a really critical time in our evolution, because if we don't get these people to register now and they go register somewhere else, they may never come back to us."[32]

Yahoo! has also leveraged the functionality of communications features such as those just described to enable its users to develop customizable Web communities called Yahoo! Clubs. Through Yahoo! Clubs, groups of people with shared interests can turn to the Web as a virtual gathering place, communicating with one another through chat, message boards, email, and other tools. An extended family might develop a Yahoo! Club to post the latest baby pictures, correspond with relatives across the country, and plan a family reunion. An investment group could post hot stock tips for members and coordinate arrangements for in-person meetings. A number of different public organizations have developed clubs designed to strengthen the value of their brands by cultivating community. The Oakland A's, for example, have designed a Yahoo! Club that allows fans to chat online about last night's game or swap opinions about the likelihood that the team will make the World Series. Through Yahoo! Clubs, the company enables its users to develop a rich network of online communities, shared virtual spaces to which customers return again and again.

On the marketing side, Karen Edwards's team has devoted substantial effort to increasing loyalty. "We spend probably 90 percent of our money against 'near surfers.' We spend probably 90 percent of our time reaching current users and getting them to be more loyal," she notes.[33] Much of this marketing work has been feature or content oriented, however, with an emphasis on those facets of the service that increase retention. The company has made liberal use of remnant banner inventory, for example, to cross-sell properties such as Yahoo! Mail, Yahoo! Messenger (another communications tool), and Yahoo! Finance. Yahoo! has also implemented campaigns to persuade users to bookmark the site, or even better, to make it their home page. In contrast to many offline businesses, Yahoo! has not played up the emotional connection between its brand and its customers in its loyalty-building efforts. Compare Yahoo!'s customer-focused marketing efforts with those of companies such as Volvo or Coca Cola: These latter organizations play up the visceral connection between their brands and the customer to a much greater extent. As John Yost of Black Rocket describes it, "It's not the same relationship as with a product like a soft drink. I think the emotion probably plays a stronger role initially in terms of building awareness and getting people to consider Yahoo!."[34] Yahoo!, like almost all players in the Internet arena, has not communicated with its existing customers at a gut level. Instead, it has emphasized new aspects of the service that customers might find useful.

Strong Content and Distribution Alliances ▼

Yahoo!'s skill in developing strategic business partnerships has been a key contributor to its success. The company has woven itself into the fabric of the Web, intertwining its interests and services with those of numerous different partners. This propensity for partnering has brought Yahoo! content and features that it has needed to generate frequent usage. These relationships have also enabled the company to expand the number of ways it reaches new Internet users as they make their way onto the Web.

Content and Commerce Deals Yahoo! has pursued a broad range of deals with content or commerce companies that have provided the company with resources to supplement its core directory. Such partnerships have helped Yahoo! to become the place to track down a particular Web site, check tomorrow's weather, or get directions to a business meeting. This strategy of concentrating valuable information and resources in one location has been the heart of the portal site movement. By enhancing the utility of its site this way, Yahoo! has increased the value of its brand in the eyes of its customers, who have appreciated the convenience of one-stop shopping.

Consider the deal that Yahoo! struck with InsWeb, a comprehensive, Internet-based insurance marketplace. With content from InsWeb as the core, the two collaborated to develop the Yahoo! Insurance Center, a repository of insurance information and tools. In the market for auto insurance? Use the Insurance Center's Auto Coverage Analyzer to determine how much insurance you need. Looking for life insurance? Rather than pull out the yellow pages and call brokers, you can get term life quotes online. Insurance is not Yahoo!'s core business; it wouldn't make sense for the company to develop this functionality on its own. But by teaming up with InsWeb, Yahoo! has secured good content, InsWeb has gained visibility, and the two of them have probably shared the advertising revenue. This basic arrangement—"you give us content, we give you distribution"—has been the core of most of Yahoo!'s content/commerce deals. It is an arrangement that has often satisfied all parties: Yahoo!, the partner, and most important, the end user.

Another good example of such a partnership has been the joint effort between Yahoo! and Peterson's Education Center to develop Yahoo! College Search, a resource for researching information about hundreds of U.S. colleges and universities. Again, this is not a subject area that is a Yahoo! forte; therefore, partnering with a content expert to develop this resource made good sense. Through Yahoo! College Search, prospective students can read up on schools that interest them, request applications, and even take virtual campus tours. For college applicants (and their eager parents) who are attempting to make sense of the wide range of educational options in front of them, having a convenient, online source of information on college choices is a resource that bolsters their opinion of the Yahoo! brand overall. While Yahoo! has benefited from increased traffic and brand building through the deal, Peterson's has gained good visibility as well as the chance to cross-sell other Peterson's products, such as books and software.

Distribution Deals   Yahoo! has also pursued a selection of key distribution deals, although in contrast to other firms profiled in this book, Yahoo! has focused more on partnerships with hardware manufacturers than with other Web sites. The company has pursued such relationships because it has already achieved broad Web-based distribution organically. More than 900,000 sites on the Web point to Yahoo!. They do so not as a result of deals they struck with Yahoo!, but because they believe the company provides a valuable service from which visitors to their own site will benefit. With distribution like this emerging naturally, Yahoo! has focused instead on developing relationships with hardware providers, the companies that create the products that bring people to the Web. Yahoo! has seen such deals as presenting the best opportunities for extending its reach, and it has forged distribution alliances with a variety of interesting partners.

For example, Yahoo! has struck an agreement with Compaq whereby a co-branded version of MyYahoo! serves as the browser's default start page on Compaq's line of Presario Internet PCs. In addition to offering Compaq customers the standard features available on MyYahoo!, such as national news, sports and financial information, and weather, this custom-developed start page also provides users with information about and support for their computers. With this agreement, Yahoo! has secured an effective, efficient way to get its service in front of large numbers of new Internet users. Rather than having to drive trial user by user, this sort of bundling deal makes trial automatic. When these Compaq customers set up their computers and get online, they'll find Yahoo! as their gateway to the Web. Given the quality of the service, it's likely that once these Internet newbies have come to know Yahoo!, a good number will stick with the service as long-term customers.

Yahoo! has also developed an innovative distribution partnership with Phoenix Technologies, the company that develops the system software in more than 70 percent of the PCs sold. System software, which is embedded in the motherboard of a computer, is what gets a PC up and running before the operating system begins to load. Through its deal with Phoenix, Yahoo! has secured the opportunity to expose the users of millions of "white box" (nonbranded) PCs to Yahoo! services when these machines first boot up. Building access to its portal into the guts of PCs was an innovative move for Yahoo!, providing the company with access to large numbers of new users as they make their initial choices about the Web resources they will use.

Yahoo! has attempted to move beyond the PC in a program called "Yahoo! Everywhere." With this campaign, Yahoo! has pushed to offer access to its service through alternative hardware devices. For example, the company partnered with PageNet, a wireless messaging and information services provider, to offer access to Yahoo! content and functionality via PageNet pagers. Through this alliance, PageNet customers can get personalized news, stock quotes, sports scores, email, and other information from Yahoo! while on the go. In the same vein, Yahoo! struck a deal with Online Anywhere, a company that Yahoo! ultimately acquired for $80 million in stock. Online Anywhere's technology automatically reformats Web pages to work on non-PC devices such as personal digital assistants (PDAs), cellular phones, and television set-top boxes. Yahoo! has long believed that attempts to lock users into using proprietary gateways to the Web will fail. The company's purchase of Online Anywhere was an articulation of its "Yahoo! Everywhere" strategy, a distribution play designed to make Yahoo! a key resource available to all Web users, regardless of platform.

The Early Mover Advantage ▼

Yahoo! was an early mover in its market and has benefited from this position in numerous ways. Providing a distinctive service early on helped Yahoo! gain valuable distribution at low cost. For example, in 1995 Yahoo! forged an agreement with Netscape whereby its directory became the resource behind the Internet Directory button on the Netscape Navigator Web browser. This was, according to Mark Mooradian, "the ultimate gift horse."[35] For much of that year, Yahoo! received a healthy chunk of its traffic through this relationship—as high as 20 percent at times—and paid nothing for it. Netscape eventually realized the value of this real estate and began charging money for it, ending Yahoo!'s free ride. But by the time this change had been made, Yahoo! already had established market traction at no cost. Out early (by comparison, Lycos launched in June 1995, HotBot in May 1996, and Disney's Go Network in January 1999), Yahoo! had made a name for itself and had received a helpful boost from a company that, with the introduction of Netscape Netcenter in September 1997, would ultimately become a competitor.

Providing a distinctive service early on helped Yahoo! gain valuable distribution at low cost.

In the same early mover spirit, Yahoo! also benefited from being one of the first companies to invest significantly in building brand awareness among consumers. As we saw earlier in this chapter, Yahoo! has pursued a variety of different creative tactics to generate such awareness, from showing goofy TV commercials on *David Letterman* to running radio spots on drive-time news shows and from plastering cars with the Yahoo! logo to sponsoring sports events. What is important to remember here is just how nascent the consumer Internet market was when the company began these marketing initiatives. Yahoo! took substantial risk by assuming a leadership role in the development of this market. When the company ponied up $5 million for its initial television commercials, it was "the biggest check Yahoo! had written to date," Karen Edwards explained.[36]

To maintain its lead, Yahoo! has invested relentlessly in new services and marketing programs that have set it apart from the pack. "They have never been complacent," as one Forrester Research analyst put it.[37] On the marketing front, for example, Yahoo! was the first (and only) portal player to sponsor a Championship Auto Racing team. The Yahoo! Sports logo appeared both on driver Scott Pruett's uniform and on his car, gaining widespread visibility for Yahoo! on ABC and ESPN, which televised the races. On the product side, Yahoo! was one of the first destination sites to offer users free email, a move that many have mimicked since. It also was the first portal site to enable merchants to set up basic online stores under its virtual awning; Yahoo! Shopping sells everything from drill presses to shark cartilage supplements, all through merchants who have chosen Yahoo! as their online commerce partner. Yahoo! has been pressured to keep up the flow of new marketing and product ideas, for many competitors consider it to be the one to beat. "The Internet is like the ocean," Yahoo! COO Jeff Mallet tells his employees. "If you turn your back on it, it can crush you in a heartbeat."[38]

Customer and Market Intimacy ▼

Yahoo! has kept close tabs on the evolution of the market and the interests of its customers in an attempt to preserve the distance between it and the many contenders who are so anxious to overtake the company. Yahoo!'s customer and market knowledge has come from a number of different sources. The company has derived some of its most essential insights through regular analysis of who is searching for what through the Yahoo! directory. In his book *Architects of the Web,* author Robert Reid likens Yahoo! to "the Web's seismograph":

> *By executing more searches than anyone else, the company is uniquely well-positioned to listen to the Web and to learn about its users' interests and fancies, and this helps it to develop new sites and services that cater to emerging trends and interests long before they become widely evident. [For example,] Yahoo!'s proprietary view on the Web's evolution has prompted it to launch several affiliated sites targeted at specific groups and geographies.*[39]

Yahoo! has also learned about customer needs and interests by analyzing the input it has received through its customer service organization. When Karen Edwards first joined Yahoo!, she read hundreds of customer email notes every day to get a feeling for the issues of greatest concern to Yahoo! users. She found this experience provided her with valuable insights; Yahoo! staffers have continued the practice as the firm has grown. "Working from the bottom up and keeping focused on the consumer are what make for a successful company," Edwards notes.[40]

Analyzing search trends and customer support queries has given Yahoo! valuable input for the product design process. Once the company has used this knowledge to fashion a new service, it hasn't generally done much additional research before putting that service in front of the public. On occasion, the firm has done some qualitative research to gather feedback before launching a substantial new initiative or a redesign. In general, however, the Yahoo! marketing team has found that the best input it can get comes straight from the market. "This will sound unsophisticated," says Edwards, "but our best form of product research is to actually put the product up and see how it works. It's like a living database. We can see what people are clicking on and what they don't click on, what they use and what they don't use, and we can tailor the product based on that feedback."[41]

In addition to conducting product-oriented research, Yahoo! has gathered a fair amount of data on issues such as customers' perception of and relationship with the brand, customer demographics, and customer retention, as well as comparing its own statistics with those of competitors. Scrutinizing such subjects not only has enabled Yahoo! to gauge the efficacy of its own marketing efforts, but has also helped it to position advertising opportunities and distribution deals most favorably to potential partners.

To assess some of the more subjective elements, such as customers' relationship with the brand, Yahoo! has frequently relied on focus groups or one-on-one interviews. Such qualitative feedback has given the Yahoo! marketing team good verbatim input that has been particularly useful in the creative process; as mentioned previously, it was an interview with an orchid enthusiast in Concord, California, that led the company to develop its "magic moments" series of television commercials. Yahoo! also runs an ongoing tracking study that has enabled it to monitor awareness levels and the degree to which its messages have been understood by its target audience. "What we are looking to see is whether what we are doing is effective," said Karen Edwards. "Are people aware of Yahoo!? Are they playing back the personality attributes we want them to perceive?"[42] If the right values are not being echoed by target customers, Yahoo! can then strategize about the attributes of its marketing mix that it must adjust.

> **"Our best form of product research is to . . . put the product up and see how it works."**

To gather the more quantitative information it needs for its advertisers and content/commerce partners and to make more informed marketing decisions, Yahoo! has relied primarily on a number of third-party sources. Companies such as Media Metrix and @Plan provide Yahoo! with a bevy of statistics; the fact that these numbers come from third parties gives the figures the stamp of legitimacy that is particularly important to advertisers and prospective business part-ners. Information such as the number of people who have book-marked the site or have made Yahoo! their home page has helped the company to analyze customer loyalty. (Yahoo! is the second most popular default home page, second only to AOL.com.) Information on reach, traffic, and demographics is the data the Yahoo! salesforce has needed to sell ad space to clients such as Charles Schwab and Sony. This data has also enabled the business development group to sell tenancy deals to organizations such as Visa and Amazon.com.

A Reputation for Excellence ▼

Yahoo! has cultivated a reputation for excellence in a number of ways. Key to the company's success has been the way it has structured and displayed information. Yahoo! made the decision early on that, in contrast to competitors such as Infoseek (later reborn as the Go Network) and Excite, it would not organize Web listings based on sophisticated computer algorithms. David Filo in particular believed that the human touch was essential in gathering and structuring information. Whereas competitors employ complex computer pro-grams called *spiders* to systematically explore and index the Web, Yahoo! is compiled by hand. In the early days Jerry and David browsed the Web themselves and classified their findings. Over time, Yahoo! has grown to employ more than 100 surfers (under the gui-dance of a chief "Ontological Yahoo") who cruise the Web looking for valuable content and help structure the listings in an intuitive fashion. The goal has not been to list everything under the sun, but instead to be selective and to display the best the Web has to offer in a hierarchi-cal framework that makes good sense to customers. "If you've got 13 Madonna sites, then you probably don't need a 14th," explains Jerry Yang.[43]

Yahoo! has also won fans for keeping the design of its site simple. As Steve Harmon, senior investment analyst with Mecklermedia Corp., describes it, "Their Web pages are fast and clean. That's a point a lot of folks miss. Ninety-nine percent of the people designing for the Internet don't get that you're really building the creative use of white space."[44] What graphics do appear on Yahoo!'s site are modest. Advertisers must limit the file size of their banners to 10K and are forbidden from using Java, Shockwave, or other high-falutin' technologies. As a result of these policies, Yahoo! performance is fast. Given the range of customers using Yahoo!—from the high school student dialing in from home on a 28.8K modem to the marketing executive accessing Yahoo! from the office on a T1 line—Yahoo! *has* to keep its design lean if it is going to satisfy this diverse audience. By optimizing for the lowest common denominator, Yahoo! has made the site fast for everyone. Such speedy performance has had a significant impact on users' opinions of Yahoo!. In fact, it has been a "delighter" in the eyes of many customers, because people have grown tired of wasting time on Web sites that choke their browsers with large, low-value graphics.

Customers also appreciate Yahoo! for its openness, an attribute that the company expresses in several ways. For example, Yahoo! makes finding the answer to your information needs its top priority. If you are not turning up what you're looking for, Yahoo! points you to its competitors by including links to AltaVista, HotBot, GoTo.com, and other search engines at the bottom of its search results pages. What's more, Yahoo! will pass your search term directly to the new site if you visit one of these search engines from Yahoo!. Thus, when you arrive at your new destination, your search will already have been completed; you just see the results. This willingness to point people toward other sites to help with their queries—even if those other sites are direct competitors—typifies the spirit of open information exchange on the Internet. Yahoo! respects this spirit; customers value this.

Yahoo! has also been open in the way it has handled occasional quality problems, an approach that interestingly enough has reinforced its reputation as the provider of a quality service. We've seen similar scenarios play out many times in the consumer products world. Take the well-known Tylenol scare, for example, in which poisoned Tylenol capsules turned up in a number of grocery stores.

Johnson & Johnson acted quickly, pulling the product from shelves in stores across the nation to squelch the scare and fix the problem. In acting this way, Johnson & Johnson not only saved, but bolstered, its brand in the eyes of consumers.

Yahoo!, too, has been decisive and forthcoming in managing quality concerns. For example, in December 1997, some Yahoo! users were temporarily greeted with the following threat: "For the past month, anyone who viewed Yahoo's page and used their search engine now has a logic bomb, a worm implanted deep within their computer. On Christmas Day, 1998, the logic bomb part of this 'virus' will become active, wreaking havoc upon the entire planet's networks."[45] The warning sounded ominous, but it was completely false—mere bombast posted by a hacker looking to alarm Yahoo!'s customers. Although the hacked message was only visible to users of the Lynx text-only browser (used by less than 1 percent of all Web visitors), Yahoo! moved quickly and erased the electronic graffiti within minutes of detecting it. Yahoo! was also forthright about the event and took pains to ensure that customers and journalists understood that there was no way that Yahoo! had been distributing viruses.

The company has had similar challenges in managing abuse of Yahoo! Mail, its free email system, which some unsavory types have used to attempt credit card scams and even to deliver death threats. In these situations as well, Yahoo! has addressed the problems promptly and has been open about what the issues were and how the company dealt with them. Approaching these issues with this direct, honest style has further reinforced the regard in which customers, industry influencers, and others hold the Yahoo! brand.

Yahoo!'s reputation has also been influenced by the company's choice of partners. Yahoo! has historically made good choices when it comes to such partnerships; as its influence has grown over time, it has been even easier to attract name-brand allies. Visa, for example, sponsors the Yahoo! Shopping Guide. ZDNet provides the latest high-tech news for Yahoo! Computers. National Geographic Traveler offers travel articles and photographs for Yahoo! Travel. As described earlier in the "Strong Content and Distribution Alliances" section, Yahoo!

has lined up some attractive deals, associating itself with known brands from companies that provide valuable information and services. By aligning itself with leaders, Yahoo! has enhanced the perceived quality of its own offerings, building on the positive brand associations of these companies.

Yahoo! has further reinforced its reputation for quality by providing good customer support. Wendy Yanowitch, Yahoo!'s former vice president of member services, has characterized customer support as "an important extension of our product and brand."[46] Yahoo! responds to customer inquiries via email, fax, telephone, and even snail mail. In the future, it is likely that Yahoo! will drive to develop still more ways of staying in touch with its users, turning to technologies such as chat and the Yahoo! Messenger to facilitate communications. The company's goal has been not just to provide answers for problems, but to strengthen the ties that customers have to the company. As Yanowitch noted, "We see this emergence of customer care being more than just guys who say, 'Thank you for your note, sir. Here's your answer. Bye-bye.' We are looking for engagement over time, and we see our 'customer care' folks as making an important contribution to our relationship with our users."[47]

Building a competency in customer support now is an investment in the future.

Yahoo! spends more on customer support than do many Internet companies. Yahoo! views this expenditure as an investment. As described earlier, good customer care reinforces customer/company relationships and thus the company's reputation as a quality service provider. It also serves as a way to reassert the brand personality. As Yanowitch explains, "In responding to our customers, we try to instill in those responses the fun, casualness, simplicity and honesty that we think is demonstrative of the Yahoo! brand."[48] Finally, building a competency in customer support now is an investment in the future. For as the demographics of the Internet change and the masses begin to move online, providing good customer service will only increase in importance. "The mainstream consumer has 'on land' expectations," said Yanowitch, "and he brings those expectations with him when he comes online."[49]

Value ▼

Yahoo! presents a strong value proposition. At the core of Yahoo!'s value lies the directory, a hand-tailored guide to the Internet that has become more useful each day as the Internet has scaled. The more sites that have come online, the more difficult it has become for people to use a traditional search engine to find what they're looking for. Consider the following example. My wife's grandfather has diabetes. We were recently invited to a family dinner to which we were supposed to bring dessert—a problem given her grandfather's dietary restrictions. We decided to check the Web to see if we could track down a sugar-free dessert recipe online. Our first stop was AltaVista, but when searching on "diabetes" yielded 677,040 entries, we were overwhelmed and decided to check Yahoo! instead. Searching on "diabetes" brought up a listing of seventeen main areas of the directory related to diabetes. We picked the first one listed, "Health: Diseases and Conditions: Diabetes." Clicking on this link took us to a list of ten subcategories, including "sugar free recipes." From there, it was a short hop to Jeanine's Sugar Free Recipes, a site that features a mean recipe for a sugarless carrot cake. If we had had to sort through more than 600,000 entries in order to find a recipe, the Internet would have been worthless to us. With Yahoo!, however, our search took five minutes. In the spirit of Linnaeus, the eighteenth-century botanist whose classification system helped organize the natural world, Yahoo! has made sense of the complex world of information that is the Web. The value that such a guide offers is substantial.

The incremental services that Yahoo! offers are layers of value that supplement the core directory. By turning to Yahoo!, customers can find maps, email, message boards, yellow pages, stock quotes, and other information in a single location. The one-stop shop has appeal, as evidenced by Yahoo!'s high traffic and repeat usage levels. And by offering its customers a useful combination of information and services, Yahoo! in turn has the chance to extract greater value from them. For the more frequently that its customers visit Yahoo!, the larger the number of page views they generate for sale as advertising inventory and the greater the opportunity Yahoo! has to engage these customers in ecommerce.

Chinks in the Armor ▼

Yahoo! faces the ongoing challenge of how to differentiate its service from those of competitive portals. As Patrick Keane of Jupiter Communications puts it, "Considering the fact that you have a number of players doing the same thing, differentiation is very difficult. At one time, differentiation was adding features. Now, the [portals] all provide the same thing."[50] The portal firms study their foes' sites carefully and are quick to imitate one another in the introduction of new features. "Everyone has all their competitors' pages on the wall," says Halsey Minor, CEO of CNET. "There are no secrets. There isn't much you can't copy."[51] The race to add new features is ongoing, but it is a brutal contest and provides temporary advantage at best.

How should Yahoo! respond? The company must continue to compete in the mad dash to add new functionality—this is simply the way the portal space works. But to maximize its gains from adding new features, Yahoo! should turn to other companies for such tools or content whenever possible, either striking strategic partnerships or simply buying the firms outright. Yahoo! has already seen that partnerships and purchases can often enable it to move much faster than developing new functionality itself. And the company is well positioned to pursue either approach. Other firms are eager to partner with Yahoo!, and if a buyout makes more sense, Yahoo! is armed with a valuable currency—company stock—that it can use for acquisitions. By pressing to avoid the "not invented here" syndrome, Yahoo! can roll out new functionality fast, eking the greatest gains from the period in which Yahoo! is the sole portal to offer a particular new service.

Close integration of the features it does offer provides Yahoo! with a further opportunity for differentiation. Although its competitors have also looked to intertwine various elements of their portal services, Yahoo! has done the best job of the lot in creating a network of linked features and information. Consider, for example, Yahoo! Messenger, a Web application originally designed to let Yahoo! users send instant messages to one another—a form of online communication that serves as an alternative to email or chat. Yahoo! has made its Messenger application even more powerful by linking it to other Yahoo! services. Yahoo! Messenger can notify a user when new mail appears in his Yahoo! Mail account, for example. It can also broadcast stock quotes, sports scores, and other information to him that he is tracking via My Yahoo!, his personalized view of the Yahoo! service.

Integration of services offers an opportunity to shine.

Although Yahoo! has done a good job of such integration to date, there is plenty more to be done. For example, Yahoo! Messenger could also be configured to send users the local traffic alerts available through Yahoo! Traffic. Yahoo! Calendar, the portal's Web-based calendar, could be linked to Yahoo! Chat, enabling music fans to automatically populate their calendar with scheduled chat sessions with top bands. The more tightly Yahoo! can interweave those features it offers its customers, the more it will stand out. AltaVista supplements Web searching with a variety of standard portal features—news, yellow pages, stock quotes, and so forth— but the links between these features are loose at best. Disney's Go Network, a network of sites including GO.Com, Disney.com, Wall of Sound, Family.com, Mr. Showbiz, and ESPN.com, feels more like a confederation than a union. For Yahoo!, integration offers an opportunity to shine.

While smart product development can help to set Yahoo! apart, the company's positioning and marketing programs are equally important for differentiation. Yahoo! has already done a good job of defining and articulating a distinctive brand personality. To end users, Yahoo! has positioned itself as quirky yet complete, a slightly zany place to find information on everything from aardvarks to Zoroastrianism. And the company has expressed this brand personality effectively in myriad different marketing programs, as discussed previously. The portal war has not yet descended to the level of "cola combat," where marketing is virtually all that distinguishes different varieties of colored sugar water. But consumer marketing has already had a significant impact on peoples' perceptions of what Yahoo! is and why it is unique. If the company is going to maintain its distinct position in the eyes of both current and prospective customers, Yahoo! will need to invest heavily in marketing programs in the years to come. Just as Coke and Pepsi don't squabble over which company's soft drink contains the higher-quality sweetener, so must Yahoo! avoid feature comparisons with Excite@Home, Lycos, and the rest of the bunch. It is the further development of its spirited, off-kilter brand personality that will separate Yahoo! from its portal peers.

A more granular question for Yahoo! is how the company should make better use of online marketing to grow its business. Unlike many of the other companies reviewed in this book, Yahoo! has never invested a substantial amount in online marketing. The firm has done a small amount of barter advertising, that is, swapping banner ad impressions on Yahoo! for inventory on other popular sites. But the dollar value of these barter deals has been modest.

Why has Yahoo!—a company that makes a good part of its living through the sale of online advertising—limited its own efforts in this area? Karen Edwards just hasn't seen the need. She explains, "I've been questioned by a lot of people in new media. 'Why are you such a big proponent of TV and radio when you sell online advertising?' When 72% of the people on the Internet are already using you, it's really hard for us to get any incremental reach through new media."[52]

While I agree that it does not make sense for Yahoo! to be spending large sums online to build awareness for its core directory service, I believe that Yahoo! has missed an opportunity to make good use of online marketing at low cost. Yahoo! should turn to online marketing to build both traffic and awareness for some of the services that supplement the directory, such as Yahoo! Finance, the company's popular personal finance site, or Yahoo! Mail, its free email system. Yahoo! has supported some of these individual Web properties through print ads. It should also do so through Web advertising. By running such ads through a barter program, it could avoid spending cash on its online advertising. Each month, Yahoo! generates millions of page views' worth of unsold advertising, the equivalent of empty seats on an airline flight. The company has often used this inventory to promote its own Web properties, from Yahoo! Calendar to Yahoo! Messenger. But in doing so, the firm is frequently preaching to the choir, because many of the users of the Yahoo! directory have also dabbled with some of the company's other services. By trading much of this unsold advertising inventory for space on other popular sites, Yahoo! will be reaching out beyond its own customer base, extending its reach to prospective users without spending cash to do so.

Yahoo! is also grappling with the fact that among advertisers, the portal love-fest that began in the mid-1990s is waning. Forrester Research predicts that although the portals' share of total Web traffic will grow from 15 percent in 1998 to 20 percent by 2002, the percentage of online advertising dollars they command will drop from 59 percent in 1998 to 30 percent by 2002.[53] Several issues are behind the predicted drop. One is the simple fact that as the medium matures, advertisers are getting more comfortable buying ad space on a wider range of sites. "No media planner ever got fired for advertising on Yahoo!," notes Forrester Research. "But as marketers get beyond the experimental stage and commit more dollars, they will venture beyond the big name portals."[54] The other problem is that advertisers are beginning to question the value of their investment. Some of these firms are paying princely sums for exposure on portal sites. For example, drkoop.com, a healthcare information site, agreed to pay AOL $89 million over four years for exposure across five AOL brands, including AOL, Compuserve, AOL.com, Netscape Netcenter, and Digital City. As the novelty wears off and their true customer acquisition costs become apparent, companies are beginning to balk. In a recent study of ecommerce merchants—many of whom have paid dearly for portal placement—Jupiter Communications found that more than two-thirds of these merchants failed to generate greater than 30 percent of their sales from these portal deals. Fewer than 5 percent of the executives polled were "highly likely to renew" their portal agreements.[55] As James Vogtle of the Boston Consulting Group notes, "It's still very much an open question whether [these advertisers] are getting a return on their investment."[56]

How should Yahoo! respond to such pressures? For one thing, it must ramp up its end-user research to provide advertisers with even more detail on the kinds of customers they are attracting via Yahoo!. Advertisers are interested in quality leads, and if Yahoo! can offer them more thorough information on the allure of its customer demographics, the propensity of its customers to shop for specific items online, and the like, it will help to reassure its partners that Yahoo! is the right choice. The company should also invest in research that further qualifies and quantifies its customers' feelings about the Yahoo! brand. If Yahoo! can show more information on the affinity that its customers have for the brand—and the halo effect this provides for advertisers associated with Yahoo!—it will be able to further quantify for advertisers the value of a relationship with the company and decrease the likelihood of their abandoning Yahoo! for other advertising venues.

Yahoo! could also solidify its position among advertisers by pushing to offer more unique advertising options. The company sells banners, buttons, and text links by the ton—not highly differentiated ad units. Although it has dabbled with direct marketing, Yahoo! has been conservative in developing this advertising opportunity. In April 1999, the company introduced Yahoo! Birthday Club, a program that offered marketers the opportunity to woo prospects with discounts and special offers included in a birthday email greeting mailed to particular registered users. It could do more to expand this side of the business, however, developing an opt-in "hot deals" newsletter, for example, that featured weekly deals from ecommerce partners.

Although Yahoo! has also shied away from sponsorships in an effort to maintain a feeling of objectivity, I think that the firm has an opportunity to pursue such advertising deals in a tasteful way, one that pairs well-respected brand names with specific Yahoo! categories. American Express, for example, would be an excellent match for the travel category. Pampers would be a great sponsor for the parenting area of the site. These are brand names that consumers trust, and I believe that by pursuing sponsorships with such top-tier advertisers, Yahoo! could open up new revenue opportunities and reinforce its own credibility in particular categories.

The advent of broadband communications offers even more intriguing advertising opportunities for Yahoo!. As high-speed Internet access becomes more common, Yahoo! can develop advertising options that feature sound, video, and graphical images; such rich-media advertising will undoubtedly be attractive to many companies and their ad agencies that are frustrated by Internet bandwidth constraints. The more Yahoo! can do to devise such online marketing opportunities for its advertisers, the greater chance it will have to hold on to the advertising dollars that the portals are predicted to lose in the next several years.

Yahoo! also needs to rethink Yahoo! Shopping, an amalgamation of hundreds of online stores thrown together like a virtual bazaar. Online commerce has the opportunity to become a significant part of Yahoo!'s revenue base in the future. But the way Yahoo! has developed its shopping section does not meet the same quality standards as many of Yahoo!'s other Web properties. Yahoo! has created a series of tools that make it easy for companies to open an online store, which is then included within Yahoo! Shopping. The cost to run such a store is as low as $100 per month, which means virtually any company can secure a spot within Yahoo!'s shopping channel. Many have; search for sports equipment, for example, and you'll find 140 different vendors offering ice hockey products, and more than a thousand with baseball and softball gear for sale. This vast array of vendors is likely overwhelming for customers. And as Keith Benjamin of BancBoston Robertson Stephens has noted, Yahoo!'s "plethora of options" approach signals merely quantity, not quality. "The Yahoo Shopping Brand does not seem to have the aura of quality that AOL has achieved by using high rents to screen out weaker tenants," according to Benjamin. "The functional focus seems to remain price, providing a listing of product availability, highlighting stores paying rent. The issue with this model is that it does not differentiate enough by quality of service."[57]

Yahoo! does provide some online stores with greater visibility than others (it calls them "featured stores") within Yahoo! Shopping. I believe that the company should take this one step further and provide prominent exposure to name-brand vendors. Some, such as Sharper Image and Smith & Hawken, already maintain stores within Yahoo! Shopping. Other big names would likely join the fold as well were they to get preferential treatment—and they'd pay for the privilege. By creating this clear two-tiered vendor structure within Yahoo! Shopping, Yahoo! would both increase the perceived quality of its shopping area and generate incremental revenues from companies paying for spots as anchor tenants.

The Competitive Threat   ▼

Yahoo! faces competition from a diverse cast of characters. Large players such as AOL, Excite, and Microsoft have good product offerings themselves, along with the marketing knowledge and resources required to cause great trouble for Yahoo!. Vertical portals such as CNET are zeroing in on specific subject areas, developing content depth that Yahoo! cannot match. Traditional media companies have also entered the fray, and as shown by NBC's investment in Snap, the offline advertising these firms can devote to supporting their Web ventures can have a substantial impact on traffic and brand awareness. LookSmart has developed a strong "ingredient brand," a Web directory that it is in turn licensing to hundreds of partners, all of which threaten Yahoo!. Overseas, from Brazil to China, home-grown competitors are sparring with Yahoo! in international markets. Back in the United States, Yahoo! is facing a challenge from a whole new generation of search sites, from Google to GoTo.com. Although Yahoo! is well positioned to defend itself against these rivals, the range of foes looking to unseat the company from its leadership position is daunting.

AOL represents Yahoo!'s single biggest worry. The company is a behemoth. With over 18 million members, AOL accounts for 40 percent of all traffic from the home to the Web. AOL customers send over a billion email messages each month and generate more than 1.3 billion Web hits *each day.*[58] AOL has reached these stratospheric levels of activity by building a brand designed for the very user of greatest interest to Yahoo!: the online newbie.

AOL has chased these prospective customers with a vengeance, doing all it could to expose them to the AOL brand and get them to try the service. To gain visibility, AOL has done everything from arranging for product placement on *Baywatch* to developing a seven-story-tall hot air balloon embossed with the AOL logo (now on a three-year, 100-city tour). To generate trial of the service, AOL has been equally creative. The company is most famous for carpet bombing the country with disks and CDs offering potential users a one-month free trial. You've probably received one of these trial packages in your mailbox at some point. You may also have found the ubiquitous AOL disks in a box of Rice Chex Cereal, in a package of Omaha Steaks, even in a United Airlines in-flight meal—just a few of the unique distribution channels with which AOL has experimented. ("We want to get the disks wherever people are, whenever they might be going online," said AOL spokeswoman Ann Brackbill.[59]) The company has also developed OEM (original equipment manufacturer) deals with some of the biggest computer manufacturers around—Compaq, Packard Bell, and IBM—in which the AOL software is bundled on their consumer PC models. This way, prospects don't even have to install the software—it's ready to go from the moment they turn on their computers.

When customers try the service, they're generally pleased with what they find. With its simple interface and solid, AOL-specific content, AOL represents the shallow end of the great online/Internet pool. Many people feel most comfortable entering here and splashing around in an environment in which their feet still touch the bottom. If they care to venture into the deep end, they can do so as well—AOL makes Internet access easy. But even if they spend most of their time within the world of AOL's proprietary content and services, there is plenty to explore right there. ("The secret sauce is convenience," explains Bob Pittman, AOL's president and COO.[60]) While AOL has created some of this content itself, it has also teamed up with other trusted brands to offer information and services ranging from personal finance help (Intuit) to real estate information (Century 21) to online stock trading (E-TRADE).

Although the company had customer service issues for a while (a $146.8 million marketing blitz drove demand to the point at which AOL's 200,000 phone lines were swamped, making it impossible for some members to access their accounts), AOL fixed this problem by investing more than $350 million to upgrade its system. To avoid repeating the mistakes of the past, the company continues to add 25,000 new modems each month to keep the system accessible. And it is now beginning to form partnerships with companies such as Bell Atlantic to offer customers even better access through high-speed technologies such as DSL (digital subscriber line, a fast Internet access solution that uses existing phone lines rather than cable). By fixing the service issues, delivering a strong product, and driving awareness, AOL has developed an extraordinarily powerful brand over the last several years. In my opinion, the company represents the most significant threat to Yahoo! in the market today.

Yahoo! faces another potent challenger in Excite@Home. Excite has long played Avis to Yahoo!'s Hertz. But this "we try harder" portal player has invested substantially in building its own brand and has emerged as a feisty, successful contender. To raise awareness, Excite has devoted substantial dollars to advertising and promotion. For example, the company kicked off its nationwide marketing efforts with an integrated TV, radio, outdoor, and print campaign asking prospects, "Are You Experienced?" This large-scale program was designed to inspire potential Excite users to explore the Web, with Excite as home base. More recently, the company introduced a print and outdoor campaign that used signatures of well-known personalities as a tool to convey the degree of personalization possible through a customized MyExcite page. To supplement these substantial offline media buys, Excite has invested in online advertising as well under the guidance of Modem Media/Poppe Tyson, one of the smarter interactive agencies around.

The company has also run numerous promotions. With its "Who Excites You?" push, for example, Excite prompted users to submit stories of people from their past who excited or inspired them, but with whom they had lost touch. The company then made hay out of attempting to reunite the people mentioned in some of the most intriguing entries. To increase awareness of the service among college students, Excite even drove a large Winnebago plastered with the Excite logo to college campuses throughout California and gave the students a chance to win a week on the road in the Winnebago with their buddies. Excite poured more than $65 million into such marketing efforts between 1995 and 1998. Although this figure may seem modest to marketers of offline products such as cars or financial services, in the nascent Internet space this is a large investment and shows Excite's commitment to emerging from the ongoing portal melee as one of the market's top players.

In addition to driving awareness, Excite has also nailed many of the other factors that we have seen contribute to the strength of a major Internet brand. For example, it has focused on delivering a high-quality service. The company has been a champion of the Web personalization movement and was the first portal site to convert its front page (www.excite.com) to a Web start page that customers can tailor to their unique interests. The firm has also worked hard on improving usability, adding, for example, the ability to point and click on options that will help customers narrow their searches, rather than requiring them to enter complex, structured Boolean searches (e.g.,

Shakespeare AND Romeo NOT Macbeth). Like Yahoo! and AOL, Excite has also done a great job recruiting top-notch information and commerce partners. Onsale serves as the company's principal online auction house, for example, and Auto-By-Tel provides Excite's customers with the ability to research and buy a car online. In addition, through its recent merger with @ Home, a high-speed Internet access and service provider, Excite has secured the chance to get a jump start on the industry shift toward broadband communications. Excite is doing just what it needs to do to forge a leading Internet brand. If the company continues to execute well, I believe it is headed for long-term success.

Although the Microsoft Network (MSN) has been only moderately successful to date, you just can't write off Microsoft. The company is well known for introducing mediocre products or services (Windows, Money, and Encarta, just to name a few) on the first go and then dutifully refining them over time. Several of the underlying properties available through the Microsoft Network, such as MSNBC (news), HotMail (free email), Expedia (travel services), and CarPoint (ecommerce), are high-quality services that draw plenty of traffic. In addition, Microsoft has announced that it will be spending buckets of money on MSN marketing. Microsoft also controls the Internet Explorer Web browser; as a result, it can determine the default start page for the millions of people who access the Internet using this tool. As Chris Charron of Forrester puts it, "They are winning the browser battle and that's huge. [Browser share] is one of the reasons Netscape has become the third most trafficked site on the Net."[61] (Microsoft now has majority market share in the Web browser category.) Thus far, Microsoft has proved to be more successful as a technology company than as a media player. But for Yahoo! to underestimate Microsoft would be dangerous. It has a powerful corporate brand, deep pockets, and the patience to do things right the third or fourth time around.

Yahoo! will also face a challenge from vertical portals—sites that provide rich content and functionality related to specific subject areas or interest groups. As Patrick Keane of Jupiter Communications has put it, "As users become more savvy, they ultimately have less need of a meta-aggregator of content and may choose a really specific niche along their own demographic or content preference."[62] iVillage, which we've examined in detail, is an excellent example of a vertical portal designed for a particular constituency: women. CNET, the technology news and information company, is another example of this type of competitor. With its "all technology, all the time" focus, CNET offers a depth and breadth of technology content that Yahoo! cannot match. CNET's network of sites offer extensive high-tech news and analysis, downloads of the latest shareware (free software designed for public distribution), and auctions of goods that range from modems to monitors. In addition to providing extensive information and services for propeller-head types, CNET has also marketed its network of sites aggressively. In 1999, the company left profitability behind in a drive to build both awareness and usage. Since then, the company has invested substantial funds in a full range of marketing programs, from television commercials to outdoor advertising, from banners to print. Halsey Minor, CNET's CEO, is committed to making CNET known nationally as *the* place to turn for those interested in technology. This is an audience that is clearly important to Yahoo!, and CNET is pushing hard to siphon these users away.

Traditional media companies also pose problems for Yahoo!. Yahoo! has established a larger monthly audience than many large offline media properties (CNBC, ESPN2, and Showtime, to name a few), and the old-world players have taken notice. Initial forays into the online world by some of the offline media companies were only moderately successful despite the strength of their real-world brands and the money at their disposal. In developing Pathfinder, for example, Time Warner failed to create a strong Internet brand and lost a ton of money in the process. (Time Inc. Chairman Don Logan once said that Pathfinder gave new meaning to the term "black hole.") But a number of these firms went on to partner with Internet players. NBC, for example, bought a minority share of CNET's Snap, and Disney nabbed a large chunk of Infoseek. Such relationships ideally combine the financial resources, content, and brand names of these offline media players with the technology, market savvy, and Internet brands of the online partners. How well these assets mix remains to be seen; at this point, the devil is in the details. But Disney plans to use everything from theme parks to cruise ships to build awareness for GO.com, the portal site it has developed with Infoseek. And NBC is running television ads that have exposed hundreds of millions of people to Snap. Yahoo! should fear such competitors. For while these media traditionalists are only beginning to prove their mettle on the Internet, the Internet itself is evolving into much more of a mass medium, which is territory they understand well.

Another Yahoo! adversary, LookSmart, not only runs a portal site of its own but also syndicates content to other companies interested in enhancing their sites with portal-style tools and information. Looksmart.com, the company's destination site, is one of the top twenty most heavily trafficked sites on the Web and offers much of the same content available on Yahoo!: a hand-crafted directory of the best sites on the Web (the company employs a team of 200 people to develop and maintain the directory), news, maps and directions, stock information, weather, and the like. In addition, however, LookSmart licenses this content to Excite@Home, Cox Interactive Media, IBM.net, AltaVista, and a network of more than 220 Internet service providers. LookSmart's partners can select the information they want from a cornucopia of content options and integrate this content into their sites. The information appears on co-branded Web pages, preserving the look and feel of partners' sites while featuring LookSmart as an ingredient brand. This approach has proved to be popular with partners and has magnified the danger that LookSmart poses to Yahoo!. Not only has LookSmart mimicked much of the information and functionality available on Yahoo!, it has also made this same content available to hundreds of its partners, weakening Yahoo!'s ability to differentiate itself from competitors.

Yahoo! is one of the few Internet companies that has expanded aggressively overseas. The firm has created localized versions of its popular portal for eighteen different countries. Pursuing this international growth strategy has widened Yahoo!'s competitive scope even further, bringing the company into conflict with a variety of local rivals. In China, for example, Yahoo! has sparred with China.com, a public company that is partially owned by AOL and has strong ties to Xinhua, China's government news service. In Latin America, Yahoo! has clashed with Telmex, the Mexican telephone giant, and with Starmedia, a portal player that has tailored its service for Web users in each of nine Latin American countries. In the United Kingdom, Yahoo! has tangled with U.K. Plus, whose parent company, Daily Mail & General Trust, owns newspapers such as the *Daily Mail* and the *London Evening Standard.* These companies all have alliances, content, and local knowledge that will help them to defend against Yahoo! as the Silicon Valley native looks to grow its business internationally.

Finally, Yahoo! is also seeing competition from a new generation of companies focused on the core service that made it famous: search. As the volume of information available online has multiplied, the challenge of finding what you're looking for has grown progressively harder. These firms are taking different approaches to making Web searching easier and more accurate, and they've devised some ingenious solutions to the problem. Ask.com, for example, enables visitors to pose simple English-language questions (e.g. ,"Who won the world series in 1985?"), as opposed to using Boolean search logic (e.g., "baseball AND world series NEAR 1985"). This approach, called *natural language searching,* represents a substantial change from the keyword-based searching available on many of the Internet's major portal sites. Direct Hit, another Web search contender, has developed a technology it calls the Popularity Engine, which ranks search results based on the frequency with which users have clicked on particular listings. By analyzing the activity of millions of previous Internet searches, Direct Hit can highlight the Web destinations most likely to be relevant to a customer query. Google, another Web directory started by Stanford Ph.D. candidates, takes a different intriguing approach to improving the quality of search results. Google ranks a site's quality based on the number of other sites to which it is linked, as well the importance of those partner sites ("importance" is again defined the same way—by the number and value of links). Just as a company might value an executive recruiter for the number and quality of his contacts, so does Google evaluate a site based on the strength of its "network." When a user searches with Google, the more "important" a site, the more likely it is to be included in Google's search results. GoTo.com has taken the most blatantly commercial approach of all by turning the standard search results page into an auction. Companies can bid on search terms of interest to them. The higher the bid, the closer to the top of the results page a company's information will appear when a visitor searches on a particular word or phrase.

Yahoo! may eventually decide to buy out one of these firms to build its technology into the Yahoo! directory. Those that don't make the company's shopping list, however, will continue to make trouble for Yahoo!, either as direct competitors or by providing their technology to others that will in turn tussle with Yahoo!. And while there are already plenty of young companies vying for leadership in the "next-generation search" category, Yahoo! will see even more competition in the near future. Timothy Draper, a managing partner with venture capital firm Draper Fisher Jurvetson, reports that his firm invested more than $30 million in search services— and it isn't finished yet. Says Draper, "Search is going to be hot as long as people continue to be frustrated."[63]

"Search is going to be hot as long as people continue to be frustrated."

The proliferation of new search engines raises an important question: What barriers to entry protect Yahoo! from competition? As we've seen with other firms in this book, technology often provides little competitive advantage. An aspiring portal player can license a similar directory structure from LookSmart, as well as additional content and tools. Other tools and information providers can easily fill in the gaps. Yahoo!'s substantial brand awareness, in contrast, serves as a deterrent to companies evaluating an entry into the portal space. To build similar awareness levels for a new service would be hugely expensive now, a fact that should make any firm think twice about challenging Yahoo! directly. Yahoo!'s customer relationships also serve as a competitive roadblock. Millions of people visit Yahoo!

frequently and know how to put the service to good use. Many of them also have entered information about themselves, the stocks they follow, the sports teams they care about, and the weather forecasts they want by registering for MyYahoo!. Large numbers of these customers also depend on Yahoo! Mail as their primary email provider. The switching costs for these entrenched customers are high, and companies attempting to enter the portal arena will have to spend a lot of money to win over these loyal users.

Yahoo! has also locked up many of the more alluring distribution opportunities; newcomers will be left to deal with second-choice partners. Such relationships provide a key advantage for Yahoo!. Jamie Corroon of Hambrecht & Quist has stated that "exclusive distribution deals are perhaps the most significant, and effective, barriers to entry in markets when product differentiation is slight."[64] As the material in this section indicates, there are certainly plenty of companies that are attempting to work one angle or another to snare a piece of the portal business. ("Competitors are nibbling at Yahoo! from every direction," warns venture capitalist Mike Moritz.[65]) On the other hand, Yahoo! has developed some core assets that will hinder many from being successful and that will dissuade others from getting into the business in the first place.

On the Horizon   ▼

As Yahoo! charts its future, one of the most significant decisions the company will have to make is whether it should remain entirely independent. As the Internet matures, the value of offline media as a tool for building awareness among and traffic from the masses is becoming increasingly clear. A number of portal players have opted to ally themselves with traditional media companies to gain the broad exposure these partners can offer through television, film, and other offline properties. Snap, for example, has teamed up with NBC. Infoseek sold out to Disney. And Yahoo! is facing pressure to cut a deal of its own. The comments of Andrea Williams, an analyst with Volpe Brown Whelan & Company, reflect the sentiments of a growing number of Yahoo! watchers: "At some point [soon], I think they'll pursue something deeper, probably a media empire. I think they're going to want ownership of brands other than their own that can drive people to their site. [They] need some offline assets—some real world assets."[66]

Of all of the competitors in the portal space, Yahoo! is the company that has the greatest chance of success if it chooses to go it alone, because its brand awareness is already strong and its traffic levels are high. I do think, however, that Yahoo! could increase its market power even further through an alliance with a major media company. As Jamie Corroon, an analyst with Hambrecht & Quist, has noted, "The company with the largest megaphone will reach the widest audience and attract the most eyeballs. In the same way the broadcast networks like ABC are now being leveraged by entertainment giants like Disney to promote their amusement parks, movies, music events and other businesses, promotion in far-reaching traditional media will be critical for portals going forward."[67] Yahoo! certainly doesn't need to sell the company to an old-school media player. But by taking on a strategic investor from the offline world, Yahoo! could gain access to a level of media exposure that would widen the gap between it and its ever-hungry competitors.

Yahoo! could also sell or ally itself with a high-speed Internet access provider. Ron Rappaport, an analyst with Zona Research, has said, "It's inevitable that audio and video will be the very heart of the Internet experience. The only question is when it will happen."[68] The growth in use of such rich media is tightly linked to the proliferation of high-speed Internet access. Broadband has been slow to spread because of the huge infrastructure investments required in order to make broadband communications a reality. However, many people in the high-tech and communications businesses see high-speed access as "the next big thing"; in the portal space, this belief has translated itself into a flurry of deals. Excite's merger with @Home, the cable-based broadband pioneer, signified Excite's management team's belief that high-speed Internet communications are the future and that if Excite is going to be best positioned to lead the portal sector, it needed to fuse itself with a premier access provider. Although others in the portal arena have not gone so far as to merge with communications companies, they have announced broadband initiatives of their own. Snap, for example, announced that it would create a rich-media version of its site called Cyclone specifically designed for high-speed use, and that high-speed providers GTE, SBC Communications, and Bell Atlantic would carry Cyclone. AOL has said it will offer high-speed connections via Bell Atlantic.

Yahoo! has announced a broadband initiative called Yahoo! Turbo. But it has avoided rushing into the broadband space; instead, it has opted to let the market evolve a bit before taking decisive action. (COO Jeff Mallet has poked fun at competitors that have jumped immediately into broadband, saying that "the companies missing the boat on today's services are trying to cash in on tomorrow's technology."[69]) Yahoo! has also shied away from teaming up with any one access provider. As Mallet has described it, "The way we've approached this is we've built the business and plan on continuing to build this business, access-independent. If we build the largest audience, a broad suite of services, critical demand, and a brand that people will recognize, then we can get access. The great thing about the Web is that it doesn't matter how—you can always get access from any point."[70] I agree with Mallet that this access-independent model is the best way to go . . . at least for a while. As the broadband space begins to mature and as clear leaders emerge, Yahoo! may want to revisit the decision to strike a distribution relationship, pursue a strategic investor, or even discuss a merger. Even at that point, however, I think that Yahoo! may be better served by an alliance with a traditional media company than with an access provider. "It's far from clear that the model of linking access with content is working," notes Barry Parr, an analyst with the research firm IDC. "The only positive example of vertical integration is AOL. Everyone wants to be AOL, but the opportunity to be AOL is gone."[71]

Another issue on which Yahoo! will need to focus is the emerging conflict of interest with some of its ecommerce partners. Although advertising is still its mainstay, Yahoo! is committed to making ecommerce a key component of its revenue mix over time. With Yahoo! Shopping, for example, the company is striving to become a Web destination to which people can come to buy everything from consumer electronics products to music. And in pursuing this vision, Yahoo! is headed for an eventual clash with partners such as Amazon.com, online retailers who are positioning *themselves* as "Web shopping central." These partners are paying big money for the distribution deals they've struck with Yahoo!. They're important customers, and Yahoo! clearly does not want to anger them.

How can the company best manage the problem? For one thing, it should be straight with its partners, acknowledging that there is an overlap in strategic goals rather than attempting to sidestep the issue. Partners will appreciate the candor, and given that "coopetition" (simultaneous cooperation and competition) is common in the Internet space, many companies should be willing to put up with situation—as long as they feel that Yahoo! is delivering the customers and brand awareness they expect from the relationship. However, Yahoo! should show its intent to continue as a committed partner by looking for new ways to highlight its ecommerce tenants. Can it give them premier placement within Yahoo! Shopping, for example? Can it feature these ecommerce allies in direct marketing offers, as mentioned previously? As it rolls out new Yahoo! services, can it develop innovative ways to work exposure for its merchant partners into these new portal pieces? The convergence of Yahoo!'s ecommerce aspirations with those of its partners certainly has the potential to be awkward. But if Yahoo! can manage the expectations of its partners effectively—as well as look for new ways to serve their interests—the company may be able to minimize the conflicts that arise with these important customers.

As Yahoo! matures, it is likely to try its hand at subscription services, a change that will be both promising and tricky. Paul Noglows, an analyst with Hambrecht & Quist, recently wrote, "Yahoo! is cautiously pursuing opportunities for subscription fees and paid premium services. Expect Yahoo! over time to layer on new fees for other premium services, including high-end stock and financial information, auction listings (mirroring eBay's auction charges), and technical services for power computer users."[72] The company's general inclination is to offer free rather than for-pay services. As Jeff Mallet has said, "If we can do a free service, that is our goal. We'll do everything within our powers to create a free service when people come to Yahoo. The good thing is we get this critical mass and it gives us greater leverage. It allows us to carry stuff that may have been paid before and not even available before."[73] Providing its customers with useful information and services for free has long been at the core of Yahoo!'s value proposition; this shouldn't change. I do believe, however, that the company is well positioned to market additional, premium services to its large and loyal installed base.

How should it develop such for-pay offerings? First, Yahoo! must craft services of extremely high quality if they are to be consistent with peoples' expectations of the Yahoo! brand. If Yahoo! were to add a subscription component to Yahoo! Finance, for example, it would need to include elements such as research reports from top-notch financial service firms, news from sources such as the *Wall Street Journal* and Bloomberg, and the ability to make a certain number of stock trades each month (in conjunction with a leading online brokerage such as E-TRADE). It then must price such services aggressively. Some critics will give Yahoo! grief for launching for-pay features, no matter what the cost, because they will see this as a departure from the firm's roots as a pioneer of free Web services. But I believe that this approach—the development of premium services that are high value but low cost—would be a way for the company to add subscription revenues to its bag of tricks in a fashion that is true to the spirit of the Yahoo! brand.

Finally, Yahoo! faces the ongoing struggle to avoid being afflicted with "big company syndrome." Although the firm has grown to employ several hundred people, Yahoo! has long maintained a culture that feels more like that of a start-up than a large corporation. The question, however, is whether Yahoo! can maintain that small-company spark. As it acquires a growing number of companies, it will become harder and harder to keep the original culture intact as acquisitions bring into the fold employees who have not been exposed to the Yahoo! value set. International expansion brings challenges as well, because exporting a culture overseas can be tough, and the relentless pace of life in the Internet space may be a difficult sell in countries with a more sane work ethic than that of the United States. Even basic domestic expansion threatens to dilute Yahoo!'s corporate culture. The larger the firm gets, and the more people are removed from Jerry, David, and the rest of the original Yahoo! crew, the less people will feel the entrepreneurial energy that characterized the company in its early days.

The challenges associated with cultural evolution issues are new for companies in the Internet space because the sector is still young and there simply aren't many Web companies that have grown to Yahoo!'s size. So how can Yahoo! maintain its start-up culture? For one thing, the company should enlist Jerry and David as champions of the Yahoo! ethos. Yahoo!'s founders symbolize the creative, bust-your-tail, do-more-with-less-style culture that was Yahoo! in its early days. To keep this image in the forefront of people's minds, the founders should serve as internal cultural ambassadors. They should talk at new employee orientation sessions. They should visit Yahoo!'s international offices and tell tales of the company's early days. They should invest the time to get to know a broad range of people at the company's Santa Clara headquarters. When Hewlett-Packard was young, Bill Hewlett and David Packard spent significant time and attention on issues of corporate culture. The fact that the company's founders focused so intensely on developing a distinctive culture had a huge impact on HP. Decades later, the company is still known and respected for the culture and associated values that

> **The challenges associated with cultural evolution issues are new for companies in the Internet space.**

Hewlett and Packard helped to build. Jerry and David should take this example to heart as they look to crystallize and communicate the entrepreneurial culture that has made Yahoo! so successful.

Yahoo! can also do a great deal to maintain the start-up feeling through the way it structures the company and runs projects. For one thing, Yahoo! should strive to minimize organizational hierarchy. To win in the Internet space, companies must be able to make and implement decisions quickly. By keeping its organizational structure flat, Yahoo! should be able to keep up a brisk pace. In addition, Yahoo! should take a cue from Microsoft's playbook and push responsibility far down within the organization. Microsoft's product teams run much like independent businesses, yet have the resources and industry clout of the world's leading software manufacturer behind them. This empowerment strategy has enabled Microsoft—a company many times Yahoo!'s size—to continue to move quickly, for the approach yields teams that are impassioned about the businesses they command. Yahoo! should follow suit, vesting the producers of the different Yahoo! services with the authority they need to drive the business forward. Finally, Yahoo! should continue to challenge these teams with sophisticated projects and aggressive goals. Given how fast the Internet landscape is changing, there should be no shortage of meaty projects for the Yahoo! crew to tackle. By allocating difficult business and technical problems to its teams and establishing audacious goals, Yahoo! can maintain the dynamism that characterized the company when it first set out to help people to wend their way through the Web.

www.**Fogdog**.com

In 1993, three Stanford seniors talked seriously about going into business together after graduation. The three had known each other since their first year at Stanford, when they had lived in the same all-freshman dorm. Exactly what they would do was unclear, but Brett Alsop, Rob Chea, and Andy Chen felt strongly that they should pass on the standard corporate jobs that the on-campus recruiting office was dishing out and do something entrepreneurial.

As the spring quarter progressed, however, it began to look like the trio's aspirations to form a new venture would come to naught. Andy, who was midway through a master's degree in electrical engineering, decided he should try to finish it. And Brett and Rob, who had done some interviewing "just in case," were both offered good jobs. They took them. While Rob remained in Silicon Valley in his job as an engineer with Award Software, Brett left for Ohio to join a management training program with West One Bank. As often happens, entrepreneurship had yielded to pragmatism.

After only a year, however, Rob and Brett got restless. Both of them hated their corporate jobs, and talk soon resumed about founding a company. Andy still hadn't finished his master's, but by now he too was interested in picking up the conversation where it had left off the year before. The group decided to focus on Web site development for the sporting goods industry. Brett's dad had great connections in the field (he owned a bicycle company, SoftRide, and had been on the board of the Skiing Industry Association), and Brett was confident that they could leverage these relationships to provide enough business to get the company started. Brett and Rob quit their jobs, Andy left Stanford, and the Cedro Group—named after their freshman dorm—was born.

Brett's connections served them well. The Cedro Group landed a deal with the Sporting Goods Manufacturers Association to provide its members with Web development services. The team went on to develop more than 110 Web sites for some of the biggest names in the sporting goods industry—Mizuno, Top Flight, Trek, and others. They soon had a "healthy little business," as Alsop described it.

But it wasn't enough. The group wanted a business that could scale rapidly, and a services firm just doesn't work this way. Eventually, the trio began to look at electronic commerce. While companies like Amazon.com and CDNOW were changing the retailing landscape in categories such as books and music, the sporting goods industry— a fragmented, regional, old-school business—was functioning just as it always had. It was a segment worth attention; in 1996, worldwide sporting goods retailing was a $150 billion market.[1] By now, the Cedro Group had a rich network of relationships within the industry—the kind of connections they'd need to build a successful Web-based sporting goods store.

The company's management team made the decision to make the move to ecommerce in 1998. Since then, the firm now known as Fogdog Sports has developed quickly. (The company was originally known as Sportsite.com, but changed its name to Fogdog Sports in October 1998.) It has recruited managers with experience at companies like GolfWeb, Mizuno Sports, and General Mills. It has lined up $25 million in venture capital. It has sold off its Web site development business. And it has built a first-rate online sporting goods store, a destination site designed for athletes (as opposed to couch-bound sports fans) that offers products from more than five hundred different manufacturers.

"We want to be the biggest name in sporting goods retailing," says Fogdog vice president of marketing Tom Romary. "It's a very

Fogdog Sports Snapshot (1999)

URL: www.fogdog.com
Ticker symbol/Exchange: N/A **Headquarters:** San Jose, CA
Year founded: 1998 **CEO:** Tim Harrington

Business concept:	Online sporting goods retailer.
Brand assets:	Strong supplier and distribution alliances; early mover advantage; customer and market intimacy; reputation for excellence
Initial investors:	Draper Fisher Jurvetson, Intel, J.H. Whitney & Co., Marquette Partners, Novus Venture Partners, Sprout Group, Venrock Associates, Vertex Management
Primary competitors:	Online: REI, Gear.com, CBS SportsLine, ESPN Sports-Zone, Global Sports Offline: Sports Authority, The Athlete's Foot, Sport Chalet, MC Sports, Sports & Recreation
Major strategic partners:	AOL, Women.com, Key suppliers and manufacturers (e.g. Baseball Express, Reebok)

Major milestones:

May 1998	Company launches as Sportsite.com
June 1998	Raises $5 million in venture capital round
September 1998	Passes one million shopper mark
October 1998	Launches affiliate network
November 1998	Renames company Fogdog Sports
February 1999	Strikes distribution agreement with Women.com
April 1999	Raises $20 million in venture capital round
June 1999	Launches national television advertising campaign
July 1999	Affiliate network reaches 50,000-member mark
August 1999	Strikes distribution agreement with AOL
August 1999	Acquires Sports Universe

Financial summary (CY 1998):	**Revenue: Not available** **Net income (loss): Not available**
Shares outstanding:	Not available
Number of employees:	90

aggressive vision, but I think that it is achievable."[2] Fogdog has made good progress, but it has much yet to do before achieving this vision. Fogdog Sports is far from a household name; one of the firm's biggest challenges is to build awareness in a market characterized by increasing media costs and a growing number of "dot coms" clamoring for attention. As a company that works with a variety of different suppliers to fulfill its orders, Fogdog must also overcome numerous logistics and customer service difficulties as it strives to present a single face to its customers. And although Fogdog has avoided price-based competition so far, the company will surely face greater pricing pressure in the future, both from traditional retailers making their way online and from a growing number of Internet ventures that have made discounting a core element of their value propositions.

Fogdog Sports represents a classic Internet start-up. Given that the majority of the firms covered in this book are relatively well established, I thought it was important to include a young company in the mix. For readers interested in smaller companies, the Fogdog story presents a good look at the myriad challenges a start-up faces in its attempt to build a brand from the bottom up.

Best of Brand   ▼

Fogdog has developed a surprisingly solid set of brand assets during its short operating history. It has built a network of relationships with suppliers in multiple sporting goods categories and has lined up distribution through partners big and small. Fogdog has moved both early and fast and has benefited from the attention paid to a company that pioneers the development of a market category. The firm has done its homework; the customer and market knowledge that have come from its research have helped Fogdog to make more informed product and marketing decisions. Finally, it has developed a good reputation among its customers by providing a broad range of products, quality customer service, and insights from experts to help people make their purchasing decisions.

Strong Supplier and Distribution Alliances ▼

Fogdog has forged tight relationships with both suppliers and distribution partners. These alliances have emerged as some of the company's most important assets, providing Fogdog with a rich mix of products to sell and helping it to reach large numbers of prospective customers in a cost-effective manner.

Supplier Deals   Through its early work developing Web sites for the sporting goods industry, Fogdog came to know a wide range of companies at different levels in the industry's value chain. The company capitalized on these relationships to pull together the network of suppliers it needed to offer a broad range of sporting goods products. Fogdog implemented this patchwork supplier strategy out of necessity. The sporting goods industry is a fragmented business with no major distributors. Tim Harrington, Fogdog's president and COO, notes that "For Amazon to be up and running, it could go sign Ingram [Books] and Baker Taylor and have access to millions of books by signing two contracts. But in the sporting goods industry, there really aren't any distributors. There are about 4,500 manufacturers, and each of the retailers has to deal with all of those manufacturers, so it is a logistics nightmare."[3]

To overcome this lack of a major, one-stop-shop type of distribution partner, Fogdog partnered with a variety of vertically focused catalog companies such as TSI Soccer, Baseball Express, and Mountain Gear. These are small companies with modest Web sites (at best) that simply don't have the capital to launch major Internet-based promotional efforts. Fogdog has been transforming these catalog companies into distributors. "We're turning them into mini Ingrams," says Brett Alsop.[4] For Fogdog, these relationships have provided the company with the scope of products it has needed to position itself as an online superstore. For the catalog companies, partnering with Fogdog have produced valuable incremental business. In this arrangement, all parties win.

Distribution Deals   Fogdog has not pursued the quantity of large-scale distribution alliances that companies such as CDNOW and Barnesandnoble.com have struck, because such mega-deals are simply too pricey for a firm its size to do en masse. As Tom Romary explains, "We will do portal deals selectively—we can't afford to do them everywhere. But in those portals that put an emphasis on sports and have a strong base of people who shop—specifically for sporting goods—we want to be there."[5] One of the company's more significant distribution agreements is with AOL. In 1999, Fogdog struck a two-year, multimillion dollar agreement with AOL to sell sporting goods in Shop@AOL, the shopping section of AOL and AOL.com. With this agreement, Fogdog secured placement in four departments within Shop@AOL, including the Sports & Fitness, Camping & Outdoors, Golf & Recreation, and Footwear & Apparel areas. This partnership has exposed Fogdog to millions of mainstream prospects with an interest in specific sporting goods categories—a combination of volume and focus that has made good sense for the company.

Fogdog has also struck an alliance with Women.com Networks, the iVillage competitor we saw earlier in the book. This vertical portal aggregates large numbers of active, female cybershoppers, and Fogdog has worked with the company to secure real estate within Women.com's gift and health/weight loss centers to pitch fitness apparel, logo merchandise, and sports equipment for moms. Women represent the fastest-growing segment of the online population. By aligning itself with Women.com, Fogdog has secured a distribution partner that has helped it to zero in on this attractive audience.

Fogdog's most important distribution effort, however, has been the development of an affiliate network similar to those crafted by other companies we've seen in this book. A recent study by Forrester Research found affiliate networks to be the most cost-effective type of marketing program available, beating out public relations, television, and even email campaigns to existing customers as a mechanism for driving site traffic.[6] With more than fifty thousand sites already signed onto the program, Fogdog has built one of the ten largest affiliate networks on the Web. Partner sites generally have a strong thematic focus. Take the Running Network, for example. The organization is a network of local running publications such as *Michigan Runner* and the *Washington Running Report*. The Running Network site provides information on how to subscribe to the various print publications, as well as pointers to their Web sites. The Running Network also offers an online running shoe store, courtesy of Fogdog. Such relationships are symbiotic; they provide partners with the opportunity to generate incremental revenues with little effort, while Fogdog gets exposure to the athletes it is hoping to reach.

> **"If you're second, you're lost."**

The Early Mover Advantage ▼

Fogdog is one of the first horizontally focused sporting goods retailers to have carved a place for itself on the Web. As we've seen with other players in this book, the early mover advantage has significant value in the brand-building process. According to Warren Packard of Draper Fisher Jurvetson, one of the venture capital firms that funded Fogdog, "If you are out there first, people will spread the brand by word of mouth. It's incredibly efficient and incredibly cheap."[7] Keith Benjamin of BancBoston Robertson Stephens escalates the value of timing even further: "If you're second, you're lost."[8] Although this comment may be overly dramatic, it certainly is true that it becomes more expensive for companies to establish a market position for themselves if they enter a market late. For example, Barnesandnoble.com has built a solid brand in the online book retailing category, but it has been an expensive exercise. Start-ups like Fogdog simply don't have the financial resources to enter markets fashionably late. They need to *define* their chosen categories, and then race to scale before imitators catch wind of the opportunity and sashay into the market to set up shop. Although being early provides no guarantees, it does offer small companies the greatest probability of success.

Customer and Market Intimacy ▼

For a company its size, Fogdog has devoted a good deal of time and energy to gathering market knowledge and researching customer needs. For example, the firm regularly surveys site visitors about the sports in which they participate to be sure that the store best reflects the interests of its customer base. In addition, Fogdog contrasts this data with information from the Sporting Goods Manufacturers Association (SGMA) to see how its own research compares with general industry numbers. If the SGMA shows more people interested in hockey than are showing up at the Fogdog site, perhaps this is because Fogdog is not offering a rich enough selection of hockey products. The company can then tune its product offerings to increase the probability of capturing the sporting goods purchases of hockey enthusiasts.

Fogdog has also done a fair amount of qualitative research, primarily one-on-one interviews. Like other companies in the book, Fogdog has used such interviews to ferret out usability issues and modify the site accordingly. The firm has also used this research technique to probe broader marketing issues, such as positioning and naming. It was this work, in fact, that convinced the company that it had to change its original name, Sportsite.com, to something more memorable. As Tom Romary remarked, "The research showed that the recall on the brand name 'Sportsite' was poor, and that's where we really decided to kill the name. There's SportsZone, SportsLine, Sportscape and more. People couldn't remember what our site was called, which really hampers word of mouth."[9] Based on this study, the company retained a naming firm to help it dream up new options, ultimately settling on Fogdog Sports. (For the curious, "fogdog" is a real word that means "a bright or clear spot that appears in breaking fog."[10])

A Reputation for Excellence ▼

Fogdog has understood early in its evolution that one of the best things it could do to develop its brand was to forge a reputation for excellence. The management team knew that by doing so, those people who tried Fogdog would not only come back to purchase again, but would also tell their friends about the site. And as we've seen throughout the book, word of mouth is crucial to the success of any Web-based company. To build buzz about its service, Fogdog has cultivated quality in numerous ways. First of all, as mentioned earlier, the company offers a wide selection products. Telemark skis, soccer uniforms, hunting boots, jogging bras, golf umbrellas—all are available on Fogdog.

Not only does Fogdog offer breadth and depth, it also aims to provide high quality merchandise. As Tom Romary remarked, "We offer the best there is. You build trust with a customer when you have the best ski jacket available—that Marmot jacket that costs $400. That doesn't mean that's the only thing you carry. You may also carry some middle-end products, as they may offer a better solution for some customers. But if you don't carry the high-end stuff, you are never going to win the trust of the serious athlete."[11] By wooing these serious athletes, Fogdog is leveraging the classic "pyramid of influence" model used by sporting goods manufacturers. The model works like this: The manufacturer cuts a deal with a respected athlete, whose support for a product influences the opinions—and purchasing decisions—of more casual athletes. For example, by signing baseball star Ken Griffey Jr. as a spokesperson, Nike has leveraged the appeal of the accomplished center fielder to sell millions of pairs of cross-training shoes. If Fogdog can get hardcore sports enthusiasts to shop at its online store, they will spread the word, and the weekend warriors will follow. They, too, will appreciate both the quality and the range of products available, and may tell others.

Fogdog has also bolstered its brand by providing Web shoppers with the kind of information they need to make smart buying decisions. Product photos and descriptions are a help (imagine buying a tent online if you couldn't see what it looked like). But Fogdog has gone beyond the basics to provide supplementary content. For example, for shoppers looking to interpret terminology that they might find in a product description, Fogdog offers a glossary of sports terms that ranges from "activent" to "yoga." In select areas of the site, Fogdog provides advice from category experts. In the outdoor products section, for example, customers can get counsel from outdoorsman Michael Hodgson on what to look for in products such as sleeping bags and water filters. (In case you're ever in the market for a water filter, note that a filter with a pore size efficiency of less than 0.4 microns will remove bacteria and protozoa such as *Giardia* and cryptosporidium, as well as parasitic eggs and larva.) Fogdog also enables customers to add reviews of their own to any product listing, thus providing customers with additional guidance. If you're shopping for a baseball glove, for example, a comment from a customer in Albuquerque, New Mexico, about Easton's Redline Infielder's glove may give you that additional bit of information you need to make your choice. (He rates it a four out of five and notes, "This glove's leather is extremely hard when you first get it. It does take a long time to break it in, but once you do it sucks the grounders right up.")

Fogdog is leveraging the classic "pyramid of influence" used by sporting goods manufacturers.

Fogdog supports its online store with excellent customer service. The company refers to its customer service representatives as "sports consultants" and works to imbue the service staff with company, product, and customer knowledge. Customers can pose their questions by email as well as by phone; the latter is uncommon among Internet companies. If a prospect cannot find what he is looking for, the Fogdog search squad—a special customer service unit—will track it down for him from alternative sources. For example, when an ice climbing enthusiast recently contacted Fogdog in his quest to find a particular kind of crampon, the search squad stepped in. A squad member consulted with an expert in the field, called the manufacturer that the expert had recommended, and tracked down the elusive gear. The customer was pleased with the company's effort to find the product he needed. Not only will he be likely to shop at Fogdog again, he has probably told this tale to others. Such Nordstrom-style customer service has been foreign to traditional sporting goods retailing. And the search squad concept is unique to the Web: I haven't seen a single other Web retailer go this far to make customers happy. By providing quality customer service, Fogdog is differentiating itself from the competitive set and is building brand awareness through word of mouth.

Finally, Fogdog has also built an image of quality by offering a generous returns policy. As Tom Romary notes, a liberal approach to returns is a must if Fogdog is going to beat out traditional sports retailers. "When someone buys a tennis racquet from us, if it's not the right grip size or the right racquet, we take it back, no questions asked. If we don't do that, we are not going to be able to overcome what the local specialty store can do for you."[12] On the Web, customers don't have the opportunity to physically inspect a product before buying. By making it easy to return a product purchased in the Fogdog store, the company has eliminated an element of perceived risk that could preclude some shoppers from buying online. Such a policy can be costly, because processing returns is expensive. But if Fogdog does a good job of providing product information, reviews, and advice, it will limit the number of returns it must handle. Being open to returns will then enable Fogdog to build customer loyalty among that small subset of buyers who do need a refund or exchange.

Chinks in the Armor ▼

As a start-up, Fogdog's single greatest challenge has been to build brand awareness. The online sporting goods retailer with the funky name simply has not been top of mind for most athletes, and Fogdog has much work to do to change this. The good news is that the company's marketing fundamentals are solid; it has been running the kind of marketing programs that will help it cultivate the awareness it seeks. For example, Fogdog has worked hard on public relations and has received coverage in consumer publications such as *Cosmopolitan,* business journals such as *Sporting Goods Intelligence,* and technology publications such as *PC Week.* It has invested in online advertising, buying ad space on specific, sports-oriented sites, such as runnersworld.com, as well as buying sports keywords such as "running," "baseball," and "soccer" on portal sites such as Yahoo!, Lycos, and Excite. It has dabbled with radio, running sixty-second spots in five major U.S. cities over the course of a week during the 1998 holiday season. And in the summer of 1999, the company launched its first national television campaign, pitching Fogdog as "your anywhere, anytime sports store" on ESPN, Golf Channel, Outdoor Life Network, and other sports-oriented venues.

A start-up's greatest challenge is to build brand awareness.

How can Fogdog take its brand awareness to the next level? There is no easy fix; the company has already engaged in the kind of marketing programs that will take it where it wants to go. With those programs that Fogdog has found to be effective, the key is to keep them going and to expand their scope. For example, the company should certainly increase the intensity of its radio campaign, as studies have shown radio to be an offline medium that is particularly effective in increasing both site traffic and brand awareness. Fogdog has made good use of PR, but there is much more the company could do with this marketing vehicle. As a case in point, the proliferation of magazines covering individual sports (e.g., *Bowling Digest, Horse & Rider,* and *Snowboarder*) presents the company with the ideal opportunity to influence athletes with particular interests. An ongoing PR push focused on key vertical markets could help Fogdog to establish itself as *the* online sporting goods store for runners or golf enthusiasts.

To increase its influence without breaking the bank, Fogdog should also add a guerrilla marketing effort to its marketing mix. Companies such as Powerfoods (makers of PowerBars) and Rollerblade have received substantial exposure for their brands by sponsoring marathons, in-line skating races, and other athletic events. Given the range of sports represented on the Fogdog site, the company could sponsor a plethora of different events, such as beach volleyball tournaments, triathlons, and cross-country ski races. Fogdog could also sponsor local community or corporate sports leagues. By focusing on geographic areas with significant Internet penetration, the company could maximize the overlap between the wired and the wiry. Getting involved at the grass roots level would both show Fogdog's commitment to the athletic community and boost site traffic as word-of-mouth support for the company spread.

Fogdog must also look at ways in which it can increase its customer loyalty. In contrast to companies such as CDNOW and Onsale that have repeat purchase rates of 50 to 75 percent, only 20 to 30 percent of those customers who bought from Fogdog in 1999 were repeat customers. How can Fogdog improve these figures? One change that would help would be to build a greater sense of community on the site. REI (which I will profile later in the chapter) has done an excellent job of cultivating community by building virtual spaces in which sports enthusiasts can trade information with others who share their athletic passion. Fogdog should take a page from the REI playbook, developing sport-specific message boards, for example, in which runners can swap training tips, skiers can exchange views on Utah resorts, and tennis players can talk about the latest advance in carbon fiber rackets. By adding such community features, Fogdog would increase the frequency with which its customers visit the site. With each visit, the company would have another opportunity to pitch those who stop by on products that might intrigue them.

Fogdog could also increase customer loyalty by personalizing its communications with its customers. Today, if you sign up for the company's email newsletter, you receive the same message regardless of the particular sport that interests you. But Fogdog knows the kinds of merchandise you like based on what you've bought before. Just as CDNOW customizes its *CDNOW Update* based on past purchases, so should Fogdog tune its email communications to proffer specific offers to customers who have shown a prior interest in certain categories. If you bought a basketball and a game jersey on your last visit to Fogdog, your customized newsletter should let you know when Reebok introduces a hot new basketball sneaker. If you picked up a pair of Fischer Voodoo skis through Fogdog, your newsletter should tell you when the North Face Mountain Patrol parka goes on sale. By personalizing its communications in this way, Fogdog would make customers feel like it shares their passion and is anticipating their needs. Adopting this role of trusted advisor through mass-customized email communications would be an effective way for Fogdog to both sell more product and to further strengthen customers' ties with the brand.

Another problem for Fogdog is the fact that a number of sports and brands are either underrepresented or are missing altogether. For example, although Fogdog does offer some products for athletes interested in fishing, sailing, and rugby, its selection of goods is limited. Sports enthusiasts interested in kayaking, ice skating, and canoeing are simply out of luck. Fogdog offers a variety of shoes in multiple categories available from Reebok and New Balance. Its Nike selection, however, is weak. And Fogdog does not carry any products at all from Shimano, Giro, or Bell, three of the premier manufacturers of cycling accessories. By failing to cover a particular sport or carry an important brand, Fogdog is missing the opportunity to sell to athletes with an interest in that specific sport or manufacturer. Offering limited gear for a certain activity or a weak range of products from a particular vendor may be an even worse offense, because this may lead a shopper to infer that the full range of products available on Fogdog is narrow. Fogdog must continue to add new sports and brands to its roster to fill in existing gaps. Before it does so, however, the company should ensure that those sports it does feature and the brands it currently represents are well covered. (When I visited the site in the fall of 1999, the sailing section contained only three products, and outdoor expert North Face offered only two types of gloves through Fogdog—sure signs of room for improvement for the aspiring online merchant.)

Fogdog also needs to enhance the supplemental content it provides for customers to help them with their buying decisions. Its commerce content is spotty: Fogdog offers the "how to buy a water filter" style advice mentioned earlier in only a few categories within the store. The company should expand this supplemental content to cover all of the store's primary sections. In addition, it should broaden the scope of its editorial content beyond "how to buy" into "how to use"—at least for some of the more exotic equipment it offers. Some shoppers may be reluctant to buy certain gear because they are unsure of exactly how to use it. For example, the novice fisherman might be interested in that $49 fishing knife that Fogdog offers, but since he has never cleaned a fish, he is unsure whether to buy the knife. A page of information on how to clean a fish (along with a diagram) that was available as a link off of the product description could be exactly what Fogdog needs to close the sale.

Finally, Fogdog faces coordination challenges that stem from working with so many different suppliers in a fragmented industry. Some of the companies with which Fogdog has partnered were not ready to leap into ecommerce; Fogdog has had to supply them with the hardware and software required to work with its virtual store. And because customer orders often include multiple items sourced from different vendors, Fogdog is faced with fulfilling the order in several separate packages and absorbing the added shipping costs. What should Fogdog do to improve the situation? Although providing suppliers with technology and educating them on how to use it may be a burden, it also helps Fogdog to strengthen a unique competitive advantage: a network of vendors across a range of sport types, vendors that have distinct relationships with and loyalty to Fogdog. The company should continue to invest in the equipment and training required to bring these suppliers online and into Fogdog's sphere of influence.

The fact that the customer may receive multiple packages is

unfortunate, because it can be confusing (the purchaser may open a partial shipment and think that Fogdog has forgotten to send products he has ordered). But it's something that Fogdog will have to live with, because the company doesn't want to warehouse and ship more products itself (an approach contrary to its current model) or consolidate shipments from multiple vendors and reship to the customer in a single package. Both would be expensive alternatives. Instead, to make the best of the situation, Fogdog should work with its suppliers to ensure that all of them fulfill its orders within a certain time period. This way, the outdoor enthusiast who ordered gear from Fogdog doesn't receive his ski poles one week and his compass two weeks later. And if Fogdog can commit to using a primary shipping company, it should be able to negotiate rates that take some of the sting out of sending multiple packages to fulfill a single order.

The Competitive Threat   ▼

Fogdog faces competition from multiple directions. Among the stronger contenders are the larger, well-capitalized vertical players. Many of the smaller, sport-specific companies are catalog-only operations that don't have the financial resources or Web knowledge to develop a robust Internet presence. Indeed, Fogdog has already partnered with a number of these firms, which are happy to get the incremental business that comes their way by fulfilling orders for Fogdog. A handful of these niche players, however, pose a challenge to Fogdog in specific markets. Take REI, the well-known outdoor sports store. REI has both a powerful brand in the traditional sports retailing world and a well-developed Web site. The selection is excellent: Whether you're looking for an ice ax or a paddling jacket, a compass or a weather radio, you can find it at REI. The site offers online primers on cross-country skiing, kayaking, and other outdoor sports. It also hosts online communities focused on subjects such as hiking and climbing, giving outdoor enthusiasts a home on the Web to which they keep returning to meet and exchange information with other athletes. Of all of the vertically focused sports retailers I've encountered, REI is the one that has made the most of the Web. Fogdog should expect stiff competition in outdoor sports categories from this well-known crossover marketer.

Most of the horizontally focused, traditional retailers pose less of a threat, for several reasons. First of all, there are no national "big box" stores. While a retailer such as Copeland's may be relatively well known on the West Coast, it has no presence in other parts of the country and thus does not benefit from the strength of a powerful offline brand in its efforts to establish a presence online. Second, many traditional sporting goods retailers have been slow to make much use of the Internet. Typical is Big Five Sporting Goods, a large retailer with 210 stores in nine western states. Its Web site is anemic. Visit and you'll find background information on the company, the addresses of its stores, and "Big Five Web Site Special Coupons" that you can print out and use for discounts on the purchase of products such as daypacks and parkas at its retail stores.

> **Traditional sporting goods retailers have been slow to make use of the Internet.**

"The leading sporting goods retailer in the western United States" has no online store at all. Slightly better is the Web site of Herman's World of Sports, another regional player. At the Herman's online store, visitors can shop for products in categories such as baseball, volleyball, basketball, and soccer. But the selection is marginal. At the Herman's virtual store, I visited the football section and found eight footballs. When I checked Fogdog, however, I found 27 footballs . . . as well as cleats, kicking tees, helmets, and elbow pads. The Herman's site also lacked any of the supporting content that Fogdog has, the kind of information that helps customers to make informed purchasing decisions.

A handful of these traditional retailers, however, may cause trouble for Fogdog through their alliance with Global Sports, Inc. Global Sports has cut exclusive agreements to run the Web sites of a number of old-school merchants, including the Sports Authority, the Athlete's Foot, Sport Chalet, MC Sports, and Sports & Recreation. While the merchants must still handle the marketing of the sites, Global Sports takes care of site development and maintenance, product distribution, and customer fulfillment. In return, Global takes 90 to 95 percent of the revenues and passes on the remaining 5 to 10 percent to its partners (an arrangement the retailers consider to be good, because they generally see margins of only 3 to 5 percent on the merchandise they sell in their stores). Although some of these companies did run basic Web sites of their own prior to developing relationships with Global, they were modest efforts with little corporate support. (An article in the April 1998 issue of *Forbes ASAP* revealed just how clueless one such company was about the Web. "Sports Authority CEO Jack Smith admits he doesn't know what to do with his company's site," wrote the author. "'We've gotten a few hits,' Smith said. 'Isn't that what you call them?'"[13]) Partnering with Global, however, has helped these retailers to develop a credible Internet presence quickly. If they invest in adequate marketing support, the members of the Global Sports cabal may prove to be more capable online competitors than Big Five and others who have tackled the Web on their own.

What about Fogdog clones? Are there other horizontally focused online purists that are poised to challenge the company? The short answer is: not many. The good news for Fogdog is that the competition from fellow Web-based retailers is weak. Browse the sporting goods retailers section of Yahoo!'s directory and you'll see that there are a decent number of companies attempting to build something similar to what Fogdog has created. But when you visit the sites of companies such as Sports N' More, Overdrive Sports, and Sports Superstore Online, prepare to be underwhelmed. Many of these sites are slow to load and appear to have been designed by amateurs. Product selection is modest. And it's doubtful they have much capital to spend on building awareness. To date, Fogdog appears to have a substantial lead over most similar Web-based sporting goods retailers.

The only other pure online player of note in the sporting goods category is Gear.com. Like Fogdog, Gear.com offers brand-name products in a broad range of sports categories, from badminton to wakeboarding. In contrast to Fogdog, however, Gear.com sells only closeout goods. Closeouts may come from overproduction; changes of style, color, or function; or the cancellation of preseason orders placed by retailers. Gear.com has partnered with 150 different manufacturers looking for distribution for their closeout goods. With prices that range from 20 to 90 percent off retail, reasonable selection, good customer service, and a thirty-day, 100 percent satisfaction guarantee, Gear.com would make for a worrisome challenger to Fogdog on its own. But Gear.com is not operating alone. In July 1999, Amazon.com purchased a 49 percent stake in Gear.com. As part of its efforts to expand into new categories, Amazon has made similar investments in start-ups in other markets, such as Drugstore.com (an online health-care products retailer) and Pets.com (a Web-based pet store). It has given these companies exposure on the Amazon.com home page, provided them with strategic counsel, and given them access to the software code for valuable site functionality, such as one-click ordering. Gear.com will likely get similar treatment, and if the online sporting goods category proves hot, Amazon may just buy the company altogether. Given its close ties to Amazon, Gear.com could prove to be the wild card of the sports sector. To help decrease the threat posed by Gear.com, Fogdog could certainly steal from the company's business model, selling closeout goods in a special "hot deals" section of its site. But the greatest danger posed by Gear.com comes from the potential impact of Amazon's marketing support. Unfortunately for Fogdog, there is nothing much the company can do to limit this threat.

Fogdog also faces competition from sites such as CBS SportsLine and ESPN SportsZone. These highly trafficked Web properties represent Mecca for sports fans, providing detailed coverage of everything from NFL football to college basketball, from professional golf to NHL hockey. Both are backed by deep-pocketed parent companies with powerful offline brands. And both happen to have online stores of their own. For Fogdog—a company that is tiny in comparison—the good news is that CBS SportsLine and ESPN SportsZone focus on the fan, not the athlete. As a result, their stores tend to focus more on "logo wear" than on serious sports equipment. Is there some overlap between the products these two sports monoliths offer and the selection available at Fogdog? Absolutely. But the true danger to Fogdog lurks in the possibility that either of these two firms could decide to expand beyond NHL jerseys and autographed boxing gloves into a broader range of sporting goods. Were one of these companies to make such a strategic shift, it could cause trouble for Fogdog. Given, however, that the target customer for SportsLine and SportsZone is the sports fan, not the sports participant, I don't think that Fogdog is likely to end up competing head to head with these firms. As an insurance policy, however, I'd recommend that Fogdog pursue discussions with one or both of these companies about developing a co-branded sporting goods store that could be built into the SportsLine or SportsZone store. If these companies want to expand their ecommerce efforts, Fogdog would thus benefit as a strategic partner rather than getting outgunned as a competitor. And if the firms show a lack of interest in such a partnership, Fogdog will know that the probability of competing directly against SportsLine and SportsZone is low and can focus its attentions instead on other adversaries.

A final source of competition for Fogdog will come from some of the sporting goods manufacturers themselves. Most of them have been too worried about angering their distributors to sell online. Visit the sites of manufacturers such as Fila or Reebok and you'll see fancy graphics of shoes and clothing, but if you want to buy their products on the Internet, you'll have to go to a Web-based retailer such as Fogdog to do it. Some manufacturers, such as Healthrider, the creator of the well-known Healthrider exercise machine, do sell their wares on the Web, but for the most part these are companies that have made direct sales a core element of their business model and thus are not worried about disrupting relationships with channel partners. These smaller companies will steal little business from Fogdog through their

Web stores. The bigger threat comes from megabrands such as Nike, a company with significant market share and market power based on consumer demand for its products. Like the Fila and Reebok sites mentioned above, Nike's Web site is currently not much more than a big online brochure, although it does sell a limited set of its high-end products online. But Nike has a strong enough presence in the sporting goods market that when (not if) it ultimately decides to expand its online store, its distribution partners will simply have to grin and bear it. When Nike does ramp up its online efforts, it will certainly pull sales away from Fogdog, for some shoppers will want to go right to the source. But the company has been late to the Web, and for every day that Nike and its big brand brethren lack robust online stores of their own, Fogdog benefits.

Although Fogdog has not yet established the extensive barriers to entry erected by other companies profiled in this book, it has forged two that will help it to protect its position. The first is its affiliate network, the largest of any player in the category. While Amazon could eventually make sporting goods available to its affiliate network members through its relationship with Gear.com, it is the only company that could come close to matching the size of Fogdog's affiliate program in the next several years. An even more valuable defensive asset, however, is Fogdog's supplier network. In CD retailing, if a company wants to open a new online music store, it can line up a solid supply source by partnering with a single company: Valley Records. But for an aspiring online sporting goods retailer to be able to offer the same breadth and depth of products that Fogdog does, it will need to develop the equivalent of the Fogdog supplier network . . . one partner at a time. Therefore, not only does Fogdog's supplier network enable the company to offer its customers a wide range of products under one roof, which feeds their excitement about and loyalty to the Fogdog brand, it also enables the firm to hold competitors at bay. Once potential adversaries realize the complexity of establishing such a rich collection of suppliers, some may reconsider whether to even enter the category.

On the Horizon   ▼

As its market matures, Fogdog will be faced with increasing price competition. The company has initially taken the high road. Tom Romary explains:

> We are not positioning on price, as a lot of online retailers have done. That doesn't mean that we won't offer deals on occasion. But we are not going to position ourselves as a discounter. With sporting goods, I think we can take this angle. People have a unique passion for sports and are willing to spend top dollar on gear that will help them tweak out that extra 30 seconds on their 10K time or work in those last couple of ski runs that they may have been too tired to take before.[14]

I think that Fogdog is correct in assuming that there will always be a set of customers for whom price is less relevant, namely, athletes who are committed to finding the gear that will help them to perform at their peak. However, this market segment is modest in size compared with the "weekend athlete" segment, the kids market, and other more mainstream customer groups. The majority of customers don't need to spend the extra $250 for the expedition-grade tent that has been weather tested in Everest-like climes; they're happy with the $179 special meant for summer camping at the lake. They don't want to shell out $249 for a tennis racket suitable for pros; instead, they're more comfortable paying $119 for a basic model that they will use for an occasional weekend doubles game.

If Fogdog is going to appeal to such mainstream shoppers, it will need to pay more attention to price in the future. If it doesn't, it may well get aced by the growing number of competitors in this market who are catering to the value conscious. Gear.com, as we saw earlier, serves the needs of price-sensitive customers well through the sale of closeout goods. Onsale, the online auctioneer that we will investigate later in chapter 6, has considered adding sporting goods to the roster of products it sells at auction, offering customers both great deals and an entertaining new way to shop. Accompany, a start-up with funding from Netscape co-founder Marc Andreessen, enables shoppers to get products they want for less by banding together to make group purchases (for example, a group of eight people might team up through Accompany to buy North Face down sleeping bags at a discount). And as traditional retailers such as Sports Authority gain greater headway on the Web, they may use price as a tool to gain market share on the Web in their effort to make up for lost time.

How should Fogdog respond? At a basic level, the company will need to be sure that it offers value-priced selections in all categories and that it merchandises these deals effectively. As suggested earlier, Fogdog could also add a Gear.com-like closeout section to the site, enabling it to serve effectively both serious athletes (for whom quality matters more than price) and more mainstream consumers. **More intense price competition is inevitable among online sporting goods retailers in the future.** Along similar lines, Fogdog could also add a sporting goods auction section to its store. There are a growing number of vendors who sell the technology required for a Web site to implement online auctions. Fogdog could turn to such a company to help it implement auctions of either closeout goods or seconds (products with slight defects that manufacturers would wholesale to Fogdog at substantial discounts). All three approaches—or some combination of them—could work if implemented correctly. What is important is that Fogdog take action. More intense price competition is inevitable among online sporting goods retailers, and if Fogdog wants to be a market share leader, it needs to evolve in synch with the market.

Another challenge that Fogdog will face is growing competition for affiliate partners. As mentioned earlier, Fogdog's sizable affiliate network is one of its greatest corporate assets. Fogdog will want to maintain its existing advantage by continuing to add members to its growing group of partners. But as the effectiveness of affiliate networks becomes common knowledge and as the competition in the online sporting goods retailing market intensifies, Fogdog will have to work harder to fend off other companies from snaring the affiliates it wants to recruit. Some firms may provide co-marketing funds for their affiliate partners. Others may offer better sales commissions or attractive bonuses for partners that achieve certain sales goals. For Fogdog to keep its lead, it is going to have to ante up. If it doesn't, potentially valuable distribution partners will gravitate toward Fogdog's opponents.

Fogdog will also grapple with numerous tricky issues as it attempts to build its business overseas. The company has established a small office in Europe and is trying to determine the best way to attack the European market. Should it build the business itself, or should it team up with local partners in the countries it targets? And which countries should it target first? The United Kingdom and Germany are obvious choices: They have large populations, fair Internet penetration rates, and robust markets for sporting goods. But what comes next? Should Fogdog try to tackle France, a large country with sizable sporting goods sales but low Internet usage? Or should it take the other extreme and pursue some of the Scandinavian countries, much smaller markets, but ones in which a much greater percentage of the population is online. Then there is the challenge of staffing these businesses. What sort of mixture of local talent and U.S. managers makes sense? And how can Fogdog attract the people it needs, convincing U.S. managers to take a European career detour and selling Europeans on a start-up they've never heard of? (Fogdog? Qu'est-ce que c'est?)

Developing the right product mix will be tough as well, because the interest in specific sports varies significantly from country to country (e.g., the Brits love cricket, whereas the Germans could not care less about it). So just what products should each country's site carry? Crafting supplier relationships will also be hard. Many of the biggest sporting goods brands have exclusive relationships with European distributors, which means Fogdog won't be able to sell products from these prominent vendors in Europe. The alternative is for Fogdog to work with smaller companies that have not yet struck such agreements, or with European manufacturers. Which suppliers should Fogdog Europe pursue for which sports? How open will the Europeans be to brands they don't know? Does it make more sense to source product primarily from local manufacturers? These are some of the myriad questions that Fogdog will have to resolve as it expands into Europe. The opportunity for Fogdog is substantial, because the markets are good sized and the competition nascent. But for Brett Alsop, who heads the European operation, bringing Fogdog to Europe will undoubtedly feel like doing a start-up all over again.

CHAPTER 6

www.**Onsale**.com

In the fall of 1993, Jerry Kaplan was making the rounds up on Sand Hill Road the nexus of Silicon Valley's venture capital community—to raise money for his latest high-tech venture: Onsale. Kaplan's goal was to use the Web as a venue for an online auction house. The problem, however, was that at this point, the Web had yet to take off. And Kaplan's last start-up, GO, which had attempted to develop a new pen-based computer, had failed, burning through more than $75 million in venture capital before its remnants were finally sold off . . . at auction. Financiers weren't exactly rushing to invest in Onsale.

Although the financing picture looked grim, Kaplan decided to launch the company, leveraging a charity auction planned by the Boston Computer Museum to gain publicity. The auction would be conducted entirely online, with Onsale wielding the virtual gavel. It was a risky move, because both the concept and the supporting software were unproven. On May 29, 1995, Kaplan recalls, "The clock ticks 8:00 A.M., and all these items open, and bids start flying in. By 8:15, Alan [Onsale's co-founder] and I looked at each other and knew we were looking at the future of retailing."[1]

Onsale began with a focus on auctioning excess merchandise, such as closeout and refurbished products, to small businesses. (Although it sold to consumers as well, 80 percent of its revenues came from businesses with under 100 employees.) In three years, Onsale itself went from nothing to a company with $208 million in annual revenues and almost a million registered bidders. What's more, during that time online auctioneering grew from a concept to an established way to purchase goods on the Internet. According to Jupiter Communications, online shoppers bought more than $461 million in merchandise from auction sites in 1998, with PC hardware and software together accounting for 12.9 percent of that total.[2] As the market took hold, however, the competition intensified quickly. Auction Universe, uBid, DealDeal, WebAuction, Cyber Swap, and countless other auction sites sprang up that were interested in selling computer gear at auction to Onsale's target market. And when Onsale moved to expand its focus by selling goods at fixed prices as well (the auction business became known as Onsale @ Auction, the retail business as Onsale @ Cost), it found itself in one of the most competitive segments in ecommerce. As margins narrowed to almost nothing, companies looked for ways to shore up the strength of their businesses. For Onsale, reinforcement came through a merger. The firm recently decided to join with Egghead.com, the Web-based reincarnation of the former brick-and-mortar software vendor, to form a single entity named Egghead.com.

Egghead.com is the product of a radical transformation. A symbol of the early days of the software business, the Egghead retail chain thrived during the 1980s and at one point included 250 stores. In the 1990s, however, competition from numerous sources forced the company to take drastic action to survive. In 1998, Egghead closed *all* of its remaining stores and became a pure Web-based retailer—the only major brick-and-mortar company ever to make such a shift. Time has proven Egghead's choice to be the right one. Egghead.com has built a base of 1.8 million customers (there is little overlap with Onsale's customer list) and boasts a 65 percent repeat purchase rate. Its brand recognition and merchandising skills are assets that, when joined with Onsale's direct marketing and cross-selling skills, operational talents, and distribution and supplier alliances, could make for a strong combination. Jerry Kaplan expects combined monthly traffic of 3.1 million visitors per month to the Egghead.com site once the Egghead

Onsale Snapshot (1999)

URL: www.Onsale.com
Ticker symbol/Exchange: ONSL/Nasdaq   **Headquarters:** Menlo Park, CA
Year founded: 1994   **CEO:** Jerry Kaplan

Business concept:	Sells computer products to small business customers via both auction and fixed-price formats.
Brand assets:	Customer commitment; distribution and content alliances; early mover advantage; customer and market intimacy; reputation for excellence; value
Initial investors:	Founders provided seed funding
Primary competitors:	Online: Buy.com, Beyond.com, Outpost.com, Amazon.com, eBay, Dell Offline: CompUSA, Wal-Mart, PC Connection
Major strategic partners:	AOL, CBS Sportsline, Excite, ZDNet, Intuit, Yahoo!

Major milestones:

November 1996	Exceeds $4 million per month in sales
April 1997	$15 million IPO
September 1997	Forges distribution agreement with AOL
September 1997	Strikes distribution deal with CBS Sportsline
September 1997	Announces distribution agreement with Excite
October 1997	$48 million secondary stock offering
October 1997	Announces Onsale Exchange
January 1998	Strikes distribution agreement with ZDNet
February 1998	Announces first $1 million customer
April 1998	Announces distribution agreement with Yahoo! Computers
May 1998	Logs five-millionth bid
September 1998	Begins to offer vacations at auction
September 1998	Teams with Yahoo! to offer person-to-person auctions
December 1998	Forges distribution agreement with Yahoo! Small Business
January 1999	Announces one-millionth registered customer
March 1999	Logs ten-millionth bid
April 1999	Offers free shipping
May 1999	Ranked as one of the fastest-growing companies in Silicon Valley
June 1999	Strikes distribution agreement with Intuit
July 1999	Signs merger agreement with Egghead

Financial summary (CY 1998):	**Revenue: $207.8 million** **Net income (loss): ($14.7 million)**
Shares outstanding:	19.5 million
Number of employees:	200

and Onsale Web properties have been joined. Combined revenue in 1999 could be as high as $500 million, he said, "which would make us the second-largest publicly traded online retailer, after Amazon.com."[3]

The future looks intriguing for the new Egghead.com. But Onsale has had more ups and downs than any other company featured in this book, and the evolution of Onsale and its fusion with Egghead.com is a story worth a closer look. How has Onsale leveraged online marketing effectively to build its business? How have its supplier relationships served to bolster the Onsale brand? In a market characterized by fierce price competition, how can the company afford to provide the level of customer service it aims to offer? With the merger, how will the firm expand the definition of the Egghead brand to mean more than software? And what will happen to the Onsale brand itself? These are several of the issues we'll explore as we examine both the history and the future challenges of the company that first brought auctions to the Web.

Best of Brand   ▼

Onsale has performed well on multiple fronts in its drive to build its business. It has developed a focused, effective Web advertising campaign. It has built an extremely loyal customer base. Onsale has struck critical deals both with suppliers and with distribution partners. It identified a market opportunity and moved quickly to exploit it. It has invested in understanding the preferences and specific needs of its customers. The company has crafted a well-designed service and supported effectively those customers who have required help. And it has offered Web shoppers first-rate deals. Onsale has had problems that have served to counterbalance these successes, but we'll start with an analysis of those things the company has done best.

Online Marketing ▼

Online marketing has been one of Onsale's principal tools for build-ing awareness and generating sales for both @Auction and @Cost. (Note: Because @Auction generates more than 70 percent of the company's sales, I'll emphasize the auction side of the business in this chapter.) The company has developed and implemented its online marketing strategy in conjunction with Lot21, a San Francisco–based interactive agency. Onsale has concentrated the majority of its advertising dollars on a network of large sites it refers to internally as "The Big Five": AOL, Yahoo!, Excite, HotBot, and CNET. With some of these partners, Onsale has also forged distribution deals (see the section "Strong Supplier and Distribution Alliances" later in this chapter) and has thus been able to obtain attractively priced, well-targeted ad space as part of the arrangement. With others, the relationship has been limited to straight ad buys. Between them, the Big Five have enabled Onsale to reach an esti-mated 70 percent of the online population. Given the reach and efficacy of these sites, the company has concentrated the majority of its online advertising dol-lars on this group. The company has also bought space on a network of niche sites such as fastcompany.com, entrepreneur.com, and smalloffice.com. These sites can't deliver significant volume—their traffic numbers are just too low—but because they present a fo-cused target audience, Onsale has found this group to be worth pur-suing.

First and foremost, Onsale has pitched value.

The messaging of the banners that have run on all of these sites, large or small, has been similar. First and foremost, Onsale has pitched value. "Say Cheese!," read a banner for a digital camera, its strobe flashing. "Digital Cameras—Bids Starting at $99." Onsale has also promoted the fact that it offers good deals on well-known brands. "Get the picture with HP Scanners," read another ad. "Bids as low as $99." And of course, the company has striven to communicate the excitement of participating in an auction. "Get in the Action!" urged a third banner. The letter *u* then slid in between the *a* and *c* of the final word, transforming "action" into "auction." Onsale's banner messages have been simple and clear, communicating the value proposition and driving prospects to experience the brand first-hand at the Onsale site.

Onsale has searched for the most relevant opportunities to present these messages. On the sites described previously, for example, the company has purchased particular keywords whenever possible. Thus, if people were searching on words like "auction," "modem," or "laptop," Onsale has had the opportunity to make its pitch at the moment that a prospect may have been considering a purchase. In addition, Onsale has lobbied to secure the most relevant placement for its ads within the sites on which it has advertised. If partner sites have had particular sections dedicated to auctions or to computer gear, for example, Onsale has opted for this real estate first.

In addition to the online advertising it has run on sites across the Web, Onsale has also done a fair amount of advertising on its own site. The goal has been to educate visitors about the noncomputing products available through Onsale, from Caribbean vacation packages to Callaway golf clubs. These consumer offerings are well beyond the scope of the company's focus on computing equipment—an issue we'll address again later in the chapter. But carrying such products—and plugging them with on-site banners—has generated incremental revenue for the company. "Our customers are omnivores," Jerry Kaplan has said. "They will eat just about anything that can be sold in the on-line auction."[4] By dedicating roughly 20 percent of its advertising inventory to such house ads, Onsale has helped satiate the appetites of hungry customers. The strategy makes sense: Onsale has focused its external advertising resources on bringing in high-value customers. It has then maximized the value of these buyers—as well as generating revenue from visitors who happened upon the site on their own—through cross-selling.

Customer Commitment ▼

Onsale has the highest repeat usage figures of any company featured in this book. Seventy-seven percent of its customers are repeat buyers. When Onsale celebrated its three-millionth bid in January 1998, it revealed that the Wichita, Kansas, customer who placed the bid had made almost 500 bids through the service since first encountering Onsale a year earlier. So what has kept these customers coming back?

For one thing, whereas the process of buying through Onsale @ Cost is pretty straightforward (find it, buy it), purchasing products at auction can turn shopping into entertainment. When an Onsale customer finds a product he wants for sale via @ Auction, he begins the bidding process by checking the current status of the auction (he'll see the number of products available, the current high bid, the number of auction participants and what they have bid, and so forth). If he wants to partici-pate in the auction, he places a bid through the site. If he is outbid, Onsale emails him to tell him so and encourages him to go back to @ Auction and bid again. If he wants to give it another go, the customer will return to the

> **"We've figured out a magical way to sell to men."**

site and place a new bid. When the auction closes and a particular player has won, he'll be notified by email and can then complete his transaction. When the bids are flying in the midst of an online auction, these auctions are dynamic, competitive, and frankly, a lot of fun. Onsale's customer base is almost 90 percent male, and the auction has proved to be particularly successful with this audience. "We're creating a whole new way to sell goods that appeals to male hunting instincts, to male gamesmanship, competition and skill," says Jerry Kaplan.[5] "We've figured out a magical way to sell to men."[6] Kaplan's claims are boastful, but he has bragging rights: Men have shown a particular affinity for the auction format.

Onsale customers are also getting good deals, whether they buy at auction or pay wholesale prices through @ Cost. On a recent visit to Onsale, I saw a 3Com Palm V personal organizer available on @ Cost for $349.95, and an HP ScanJet 5200CXI (a color scanner) selling for $239.94—good deals both. On @ Auction, I found an HP Vectra desktop machine that was originally priced at $1499 going for $529, a Kenwood home theater receiver that listed for $850 selling for $271, and an eleven-day Greek island cruise for two from Renaissance Cruises, which had a list price of $5000, going for $3251. These auctions were still in session, so prices undoubtedly came up somewhat before the auctions closed, but you get the idea. Customers are getting bargains, the kind that both drive repeat usage and compel satisfied customers to tell others about the deals they got through Onsale.

The service is designed in a way that makes shoppers feel smart. For example, Onsale includes original prices in the descriptions of many of the goods it sells via @ Auction. By doing so, the company has taken a page from the playbook of companies such as Staples, the office superstore, which lists the amount saved over retail by shopping at Staples at the bottom of its receipts. And when an Onsale customer places a bid that is accepted, the resulting email note he receives tells him that he has "won," a word that reinforces that he has gotten a good deal by shopping with Onsale. As Martha Greer, Onsale's former vice president of marketing, said, "We are trying to inject signals into this process that communicate not only that the deal is smart, but more importantly that the shopper is smart. We want to say to the customer, 'You are a smart guy—look how much you saved!'"[7] Such positive reinforcement confirms the customer's purchasing decision and strengthens his relationship with the company.

Strong Supplier and Distribution Alliances ▼

Onsale's management team understands well the interdependent nature of the Web. Over the last several years, the company has secured a valuable and diverse set of partnerships.

Merchant Deals   Whereas content-sharing partnerships have been key to many of the other companies we've looked at thus far, for Onsale the critical relationships have been with its suppliers. "Strong relationships with over 275 existing name brand suppliers give the company its edge over the competition," Jerry Kaplan has said.[8] It is this network of suppliers that has provided the company with a decent volume of products to channel through the auction side of its business. In a business that sells excess merchandise, when the supply flow slows, so does growth. Onsale actually has not been able to find the volume of closeout and refurbished goods required to expand the business as fast as it would have liked. (In fact, the company avoided investing heavily in marketing—a problem we'll address later—out of fear that it would not have enough supply to service the demand it would have generated through such programs.) But as an early entrant with a well-established supplier network, Onsale has had better luck securing inventory for auction than have many of the smaller players in the auction market, companies that were late to the scene and could not purchase the same quantities of goods as could Onsale.

In addition to providing Onsale with a fair quantity of merchandise, these suppliers have delivered products with known brand names—Sony, Casio, IBM, Doubletree Hotels, Dunlop, and others. The Onsale brand has gained prestige by keeping good company. And customers have had an easier time buying brands they know and have felt better about the deals they have gotten. For Onsale, therefore, these supplier deals have been essential to building the auction side of its business.

Distribution Deals   Onsale understands that a strong distribution network can do much to boost an Internet brand. As Jerry Kaplan has explained, "The economics of distribution on the Web are changing. We believe sporadic banner advertising is less effective than creating permanent links from high-affinity sites. Market leaders, such as Onsale, are purchasing permanent 'real estate' on related sites to reach key target consumers and are creating extensive cross-links to drive traffic from the sites."[9] One of the company's most important distribution alliances has been with AOL. Onsale has secured prime real estate within the electronics and computer hardware departments of AOL's popular shopping channel. As we've seen in the analysis of other companies featured in this book, such as Barnesandnoble.com, AOL has traffic volumes that can deliver large numbers of new customers to its strategic partners. By allying itself with AOL, Onsale has secured the equivalent of a combination billboard/tollbooth on one of the online world's busiest thoroughfares.

Onsale has also developed a broad strategic partnership with Yahoo!, another crucial pipeline of online traffic. The relationship has multiple dimensions. On the one hand, Onsale serves as the exclusive auction sponsor for Yahoo! Computers, a resource guide for computer enthusiasts that features industry news, product reviews, message boards, and online shopping. Onsale provides Yahoo! Computers with a live data feed of current auctions for products such as desktop computers, printers, and scanners. Yahoo! thus offers its visitors a useful service, while Onsale gets brand visibility and a high-volume source of qualified leads.

In addition to securing a spot on Yahoo! Computers, Onsale has teamed up with Yahoo! to pursue an entirely different segment of the online auction market: person-to-person auctions. In person-to-person online auctions (popularized by the success of eBay), people sell all manner of goods directly to one another—baseball cards, jewelry, Barbie dolls, and more. No third party takes possession of the merchandise; it's a bit like a giant cyber swap-meet. Onsale experimented briefly with person-to-person auctions on its own through a service called Onsale Exchange, but became concerned that Exchange was a distraction from its focus on selling to small business customers. By serving as a back-end technology provider for Yahoo! instead of running a person-to-person site of its own (Onsale retired Exchange upon closing the Yahoo! deal), Onsale has been able to direct its attention toward its business customers while at the same time benefiting from technology licensing fees and shared ad revenues from the Yahoo! Auctions site. Some market analysts have praised the move. "If they were going to be serious about going into the person-to-person market, they had to forge an alliance with a major portal," said Fiona Swerdlow of Jupiter Communications. "Yahoo! is the creme de la creme."[10] But one can't help but wonder: Given how popular person-to-person auctions have become, if Onsale had kept Exchange going rather than providing its technology to Yahoo!, could it have seen the outrageous stock appreciation that has made billionaires of the eBay management team? Onsale made a decision to focus on a specific facet of its business. The Monday morning quarterback, however, would ask: Did it make the right choice?

The Early Mover Advantage ▼

Like other companies we've profiled, Onsale has benefited from being early to market. As the originator of online auctions, the company received good press coverage (although as you'll see later, Onsale has also made some fundamental PR errors). Developing a niche early on has also spurred word-of-mouth recommendations. The company has been around long enough to have built a sizable base of enthusiastic customers, repeat buyers who have told friends and colleagues about their experiences with Onsale. Such third-party recommendations carry influence; given that five of six customers who visit the site today reach it by simply typing in the URL rather than via an online ad or through a distribution partner, such referrals are clearly making a valuable contribution to Onsale's business.

Customer and Market Intimacy ▼

Onsale is a data-driven firm; company managers focus on studying their customers' needs and the dynamics of the service. These managers believe that the information will enable them to add to and refine the service in ways that result in success in the marketplace.

For example, the company recently conducted a series of focus groups to help it understand more about what its customers thought about buying vacation packages on Onsale (such vacation deals are part of the set of products that the company cross-sells to its current customer base). Through conversations with shoppers, Onsale managers found that customers saw these vacations as a risky buy. As one person told them,

> You know, if I buy this week-long stay in New Hampshire's White Mountains, the issue is not the fact that I paid $99 for the vacation. That's really inexpensive. I know that's a really great deal. But what if I don't like the place? The cost isn't $99. It's a week of my vacation time. I've taken my family there. There's the embarrassment of oh, my gosh, this place isn't any good.[11]

Based on comments such as these, the company decided to add content to the site that customers told them would make them more comfortable making purchasing decisions: more photographs of the resorts, images of the cruise ships and ports of call, and detailed itineraries. By carefully probing customer needs, Onsale was able to unearth the information it required to make its Vacations & Travel section more successful.

Onsale has also done quantitative research to help it make pricing decisions. With the activity on the site serving as a living laboratory, the company has varied opening bid pricing on many types of items sold via Onsale @ Auction and analyzed the results. If you decrease the price by a certain amount, how does this affect demand? What if you decrease it further still? You want plenty of "auction action," because this is what leads the winners to feel like they got a good deal. On the other hand, you don't want too many people to walk away empty handed. Such experimentation has helped Onsale to make the kind of informed pricing decisions that keep its auctions dynamic and rewarding for customers.

The company has also invested in product research. In its usability testing, for example, Onsale staffers assign test subjects certain tasks and watch as they work to complete them on the site. How many clicks did it take them to find what they were looking for? Did they move straight through the bidding process, or did they get distracted along the way? Based on such information, Onsale might revise the site's navigational structure, making changes that simplify the purchasing process for its customers. The firm has also used surveys to unearth service issues that could be improved. In a recent survey, for example, the company asked respondents, "What would it take for you to buy more frequently from Onsale?" For many corporate cus tomers, the answer was simple: If they could buy on an approved account rather than via credit card, they would buy more often and in greater quantities. Soon after the results of the study were out, the development team began work on adding open accounts. It is the sum total of many such decisions—decisions guided by a research-driven knowledge of its customers and markets that has made Onsale a useful, usable service.

A Reputation for Excellence ▼

The Onsale staff has a deep-seated belief that offering a quality service is one of the core tenets of brand development. As former Onsale executive Martha Greer told me, "You build a brand from the inside out, not from the outside in, and it's all about the customer experience."[12] To make that experience a good one, Onsale must begin by cultivating the trust of its customers. Although all companies selling online must win trust, Onsale has the additional challenge with its @ Auction business of making buyers comfortable with the idea and process of purchasing at auction. To help customers familiarize themselves with Onsale and the auction format, the company provides ready access to background information. The @ Auction New Visitors information center includes a bidding guide, an online tutorial that coaches people on how to participate in auctions. In addition to getting bidding tips, prospective auction participants can review information about the different auction formats that Onsale uses, such as the Yankee Auction and the Express Auction. The firm has found that candor leads to comfort. To make customers feel good about buying from Onsale, the company has worked to take the mystery out of online auctions.

There have also been shoppers who have questioned just how Onsale @ Cost can offer products at wholesale prices. To temper this skepticism, Onsale provides an overview of exactly how the @ Cost pricing policy works. (Customers pay invoice price plus a 2.6 percent transaction processing fee and a modest shipping charge, and the company offers shoppers the chance to review a detailed pro forma invoice before completing their orders.) The @ Cost New Visitors material also includes in-

Candor leads to comfort. formation on the various ways to locate an item you're looking for and a step-by-step guide to placing an order. Again, Onsale has aimed to resolve any potential customer concerns by making the pricing and purchasing processes clear.

In addition to offering information on how to shop at Onsale, the company provides customers with a buyer's guide to help them make more informed purchasing decisions. To develop this guide, Onsale teamed up with pcOrder.com. With information from pcOrder.com's ContentSource, a content library designed to provide online retailers with point-of-sale information on computer products, Onsale fashioned a resource containing detailed data and advice on desktop computers, graphics cards, printers, and other such devices. Whether a customer is attempting to determine how much hard drive space he needs or whether he needs a full-duplex sound card (if he wants to use the card for recording sounds, the answer is yes), the Onsale buyer's guide can give him the guidance he requires to make an intelligent product choice.

Onsale has also worked to convey quality by paying close attention to operational details. "Brand building is operational excellence," Greer has said.[13] In her opinion, the customer experience is affected significantly by the sum of myriad details, and Onsale has focused on getting the details right. For example, as mentioned earlier, the company lists the original price of almost all of the products it sells at auction. This helps customers to get a feeling for how much they've saved by shopping on the site, reinforcing their purchasing decision. Onsale also communicates actively with its customers during the buying and shipping processes. When a customer places a winning bid through @Auction, for example, the company sends him an email note to confirm that he has won. When it ships the product, it sends another note to alert the buyer that his purchase is on its way. Finally, Onsale sends him a third email to confirm that the product has been delivered successfully (thus, if someone other than the purchaser has signed for the product, the buyer immediately knows and, if necessary, can file a claim). By actively communicating with its customers, Onsale aims to make them feel that they are in control at all points of the purchase and delivery cycle. In a shopping scenario in which buyers don't see the physical products until shipments arrive, such attention is reassuring and makes customers feel confident about their choice of vendors.

Onsale has also enhanced its reputation through its choice of suppliers. The company has focused on forming partnerships with name-brand partners for both @Auction and @Cost. As a result, the laptops sold on Onsale come from companies such as IBM, the golf clubs are supplied by manufacturers such as Mizuno, and the camcorders come from firms such as JVC. The fact that customers are getting good deals on brands they know has a positive impact on their opinion of Onsale.

Finally, Onsale has capitalized on the opportunity that providing prompt, thorough customer service offers to reinforce its good name. The company has built a team of service representatives that regularly fields a broad range of issues—from handling returns to addressing detailed product questions. ("How does the resolution of the Casio digital cameras you offer compare with that of the Vivitar cameras?" "Do your Amptron motherboards come with warranties?") By managing these inquiries quickly and well, Onsale knows that it can win points with its customers at critical moments in their interactions with the service.

Value ▼

Through both @ Cost and @ Auction, Onsale offers its customers a good value. The prices are competitive. The brands are ones that shoppers know and like. The selection is good. The purchasing experience ranges from straightforward (@ Cost) to engaging (@ Auction). And the customer service is both helpful and efficient. The Onsale value proposition, in sum, is simple and strong. It has resonated with Internet shoppers. With more than a million registered customers to its credit, Onsale offers buyers an online shopping experience that works.

Chinks in the Armor   ▼

Some of Onsale's greatest short-term challenges are associated with its merger with Egghead; how to upgrade the meaning of the Egghead brand stands at the top of the problem list. When the two firms decided to join, they ran studies to evaluate the awareness levels of both the Egghead and Onsale brands. They found that among small businesses, Onsale had an aided awareness level of 6 percent. Egghead, on the other hand, had 32 percent aided awareness. The results of the research had a major influence on the decision to name the combined company Egghead.com. As Barry Peters, Onsale's director of customer acquisition, described it, "We thought, 'OK, we can take the Onsale brand and build it up to the awareness levels of our three biggest competitors [Outpost.com, Buy.com, and Beyond.com, all of which had 15 to 16 percent awareness]. Or we can take the Egghead brand and start ahead of those guys and just work on crafting the message and polishing up the Egghead brand."[14]

This process will not be an easy one, however, for there is plenty of polishing to do. Founded in 1984, Egghead had 250 stores at its peak in 1995. But the software retailer came under pressure from all sides. Computer superstores such as CompUSA, mass retailers such as Wal-Mart, and online vendors such as Outpost.com all attacked Egghead's market. Unable to compete based on its traditional business model, Egghead closed its remaining 80 retail outlets in February 1998, laid off 600 of its 800 workers, and bet its future on the Internet with the opening of its virtual store, Egghead.com. So although the Egghead name is well known, people see the brand as dated. As one article put it, "To many on the Street, the name Egghead still conjures up images of a crappy has-been retailer."[15] For most, the Egghead name represents nothing beyond software—a problem given that Egghead and Onsale want to sell a broad range of computing products. And the average small businessman is unlikely to associate Egghead with the Web, much less with online auctions, which will now represent an important facet of the company's business.

So how can the new Egghead.com upgrade the associations linked to its brand? Running a first-rate Web store will be critical, that is, one that offers a broad range of computing products at attractive discounts— whether the user purchases at auction or through the fixed-price format. Securing wide distribution through respected partners will also be important, because it will link the Egghead name with the brands of well-known Web players and will lure potential customers to the Egghead.com site, where they'll get to know the brand firsthand.

How can the new Egghead.com upgrade the associations linked to its brand?

At this point, however, it is offline advertising that will provide the firm with the opportunity to influence the largest number of people quickly. A significant investment in such brand-building advertising will be a major change for both companies. Although Egghead has done some offline advertising since it made the move to the Web (the company has run print ads in *Business Week, Small Office Computing,* and the *Wall Street Journal,* for example), the ads have had a merchandising mentality: "Here is a product at a price." These ads have been meant to stimulate sales, not to communicate the new nature of the Egghead brand. Onsale has done little advertising offline. The reluctance to invest in this type of advertising stems partially from Onsale's direct marketing orientation. Since it has been harder for Onsale to measure the impact of traditional advertising on sales, it has also made the company averse to investing large amounts in offline media. Barry Peters has described the situation this way: "One of the greatest things we've accomplished with our online advertising is being able to track results to the penny. This online tracking makes it challenging to justify ad spending offline as we do not have such perfect tracking for these dollars. While the ROI on online ad dollars can be measured virtually perfectly, results of spending offline are more difficult to quantify."[16]

The limited availability of excess merchandise required to feed its auction business has also led Onsale to temper its offline advertising efforts. As Jerry Kaplan has explained, "a multi-million dollar ad campaign . . . would be unlikely to have an effect on our sales, because our constraint has been getting enough supply to sell, not getting enough customers to buy. At Amazon, by contrast, if you drive more traffic, you sell more stuff. Not the case here. If I double my traffic tomorrow, it would have a negligible effect on the company. So demand is not the constraint to the growth of our business. Supply is the constraint."[17] Kaplan made these comments before the introduction of Onsale @ Cost. Although supply issues have continued to hamper the growth of Onsale @ Auction, the development of @ Cost, which sells first-run goods rather than closeout and refurbished products, has enabled Onsale to open the advertising throttle further without worrying that it would disappoint customers when the products they wanted were sold out. The firm has run a modest print campaign in magazines such as *Homeoffice Computing* and *Small Business Computing*. It has also run radio advertising in ten U.S. cities. In comparison with other Web companies in its market, however, Onsale's commitment to offline marketing has been tepid. As Barry Peters has said, "We have baby-stepped our way into offline media."[18]

Changing public perceptions of the Egghead.com brand will take more than baby steps, however. If the revitalized firm is going to affect the opinions of large numbers of people quickly, it will need to invest a healthy sum in traditional mass media to do so. Radio, print, and television should all be on the docket. The new Egghead.com will need not only to reach small business customers, but also to reach out to industry influencers such as financial analysts, Internet pundits, and journalists. As this book makes clear, a company cannot build a brand through sheer media spending alone. But if Egghead.com is going to jump-start a change in the way its brand is viewed, aggressive offline advertising will be a must.

A renewed focus on public relations will also help. When Onsale first introduced the auction concept, it got plenty of media attention. But when eBay unveiled person-to-person auctions, Onsale let itself get shoved out of the limelight. The concept of consumers purchasing Beanie Babies through a giant online flea market (eBay) resonated with the press more so than the idea of businesses buying closeout computer gear at auction (Onsale). Had Onsale been more aggressive in its PR work, it could have received much more coverage—after all, it was the inventor of the online auction. The company also did little to educate the press about the difference in the two companies' business models (eBay's main focus is on consumers, whereas Onsale targeted small businesses). eBay seized the position of auction innovator in the minds of the press; if journalists wrote about another player in the field, it was Amazon.com, which soon mimicked eBay's auction service. Onsale was an afterthought.

Egghead, too, lost PR momentum. Its transition from brick-and-mortar retailer to a 100 percent Web-based venture captured headlines, but after this initial burst of press attention the company sank into press obscurity. At this point, it's time for the Egghead.com marketing team to revitalize its PR push; as the combined Egghead/Onsale venture comes together, the company will have much to talk about. Although the new Egghead.com will be one of the biggest retailers on the Web, few people know this; it is important to tell that story. The revitalization of the Egghead brand is another tale worthy of attention, one that will generate renewed interest in the company if the firm educates journalists and pundits on how it is approaching the makeover. Egghead can also leverage the intensely competitive nature of its market to gain attention. As Egghead gains ground versus the companies with which it is sparring—potentially absorbing some of them as the computer products market consolidates—the press will want to follow the market's evolution. Both Onsale and Egghead have made poor use of public relations in recent times. The new Egghead.com has an opportunity to turn this around, and should.

In addition to updating the image of the Egghead brand, the new Egghead.com will need to determine a strategy for the Onsale brand and its two sub-brands, Onsale @ Cost and Onsale @ Auction. Although Egghead.com will be the mother brand, Onsale does have brand recognition, primarily as an auction provider. And although Egghead is known as a software retailer, it is not generally associated with auctions—despite the fact that it offered such auctions before it agreed to merge with Onsale. (Egghead purchased a small online auction vendor called Surplus Direct in 1997, leveraging the technology but essentially ignoring the Surplus brand.) How should the company manage its brand portfolio? My suggestion is that the two Onsale sub-brands—@ Auction and @ Cost—be abandoned, because Onsale's brand equity rests in the name of the company and not in the names of the individual Web properties. Egghead's auction site can be branded as "Egghead Auctions, Powered by Onsale." By using the Onsale name in this way, Egghead.com will get the most out of the Onsale brand, because those who know it equate it with auctions. And by positioning Onsale as an ingredient brand, the company can focus its attentions on building a single superbrand—Egghead.com—rather than attempting to build and sustain multiple high-visibility brands.

Another immediate merger-related challenge will be how to fuse the two organizations—companies with markedly different histories and orientations. Egghead is a "click-and-mortar" player, a retailer from the old school that got the Internet religion late in life when its traditional business fell apart. Onsale, on the other hand, has been 100 percent Web based from the start. Egghead has long had what is known as a "box pusher" mentality (the focus is on moving product; building brand is secondary). Onsale, in contrast, is a direct marketer, with a dash of brand thinking thrown in for good measure. Egghead has been sequestered in Issaquah, Washington, a small town about 110 miles southeast of Seattle. Onsale, meanwhile, has grown up in Silicon Valley, the Internet's ground zero (and the headquarters of the new Egghead.com). The contrasts between the two companies are significant, and to make this union work, the company's management will have to be attentive to problems that may emerge and attempt to resolve them quickly. How well will the Washington transplants adapt to the culture of Silicon Valley and to that of Onsale itself? How effectively can the marketing managers from both companies reorient their thinking to focus on brand development, not just sales and customer acquisition, and work together to implement the appropriate marketing programs? Jerry Kaplan is a serial entrepreneur, an independent thinker. How will Kaplan, the new president of Egghead.com, adjust to reporting to George Orban, the head of the original Egghead and the chairman of Egghead.com? These are all issues that may cause friction as Egghead and Onsale attempt to combine their two organizations. Such problems could be distracting for the new Egghead.com, causing people to focus inward rather than on the market as they grope toward solutions. Given the intensity of the competitive situation, distraction is the last thing that Egghead.com can afford.

The new Egghead.com will also need to tune the mix of products it offers for sale if it is going to be consistent with its computer-focused positioning. The pre-merger version of Egghead focused primarily on high-tech products, although it sold products such as jewelry, coffee makers, and bread machines at auction. Like Egghead, Onsale offered plenty of tech gear. But as mentioned earlier, Onsale has also cross-sold a variety of other products to its deal-hungry customers. Shoppers may have come to Onsale hunting for a twenty-one-inch monitor or a color printer. But while they were there, the company tempted them with a broad assortment of other products. A remote control airplane, a South Park alarm clock, an eleven-day cruise of the Greek islands, even tee times at ritzy golf clubs in California and Arizona—all were up for auction at Onsale. If the revitalized Egghead.com is going to forge a brand that stands for computers, those products that are not consistent with the company's new strategy are going to have to go. This may prove a bit painful for the firm's CFO because some of these auxiliary products have offered better margins than those that can be made on modems and mice. So be it, however. Egghead.com won't be taken seriously as a computer products specialist if it's also hawking binoculars and tennis equipment.

The Competitive Threat   ▼

The competition Egghead.com faces is both extensive and brutal. Closest to home are the other online retailers of computing products, of which Cyberian Outpost (Outpost.com) is a good example. Like Egghead.com, Cyberian Outpost is targeting the small business market with a full range of computer hardware, software, and peripherals. The company has built awareness through a series of outrageous television commercials (one featured scenes of wolves attacking a high school marching band, while another showed a cannon shooting gerbils at a brick wall). What did these commercials have to do with laptop computers or accounting software? Absolutely nothing—but they made effective use of edgy humor to cut through the "dot-com" advertising clutter and gain the attention of prospective customers.

Cyberian Outpost has cut marketing and distribution deals with a variety of popular sites, including Lycos, Excite, theglobe.com, and MetaCrawler. It, too, offers computer product auctions (although not as extensive as those hosted by Onsale). And it has gained traction both with customers (the firm has sold to more than 330,000 people in 150 countries) and pundits (in December 1998, Cyberian Outpost was ranked as providing the number one shopping experience on the Web by the online rating services firm BizRate). Granted, the Cyberian Outpost brand is not nearly as well known as Egghead.com. And its customer base is a tenth the size of Egghead.com's (between them, Onsale and Egghead brought together an unduplicated 3.1 million customers through the merger). But Cyberian Outpost is already the one-stop-shop computer products retailer/auctioneer that Egghead.com aspires to become. And as Egghead and Onsale spend time working out the kinks associated with their union, Cyberian Outpost will be solidifying its position as *the* place on the Web for small businesses to do all their shopping for high-tech equipment.

More worrisome than Cyberian Outpost, however, is Buy.com. This retailing rebel is selling hardware, software, videos, books, games, and music with *zero margins* in an attempt to build a well-known brand and a massive customer base. The goal is to eventually make money from this huge audience through a mixture of advertising sales, services (such as equipment leases and warranties), shipping charges, and the like. It's a business model that is extremely controversial. It does have its fans. "Products are content!" exclaims J. Neil Weintraut of 21st Century Internet Venture Partners. "Companies use products to attract a critical mass of customers and make profits through a smorgasbord of collateral revenue streams!"[19] But the zero-margin concept also has plenty of detractors, Jerry Kaplan among them. Buy.com's approach "won't be sustainable," he has said. "No one can stake a business on negative margins."[20] Toby Lenk, CEO of eToys, seconds Kaplan's dim view. "The bottom line is, you end up getting what you pay for—even on the Internet," Lenk has said. "We'll see how long some of these bargain-basement Web sites last."[21] But whether or not Buy.com succeeds is irrelevant. As John Hummer of Hummer Winblad Venture Partners notes, "They don't have to be successful to have a huge impact on all of business."[22] Prices are falling and margins dwindling for all under the impact of this grand experiment. The good news for Egghead.com is that it has $163 million in cash to help it survive the pricing mayhem instigated by Buy.com. The bad news is that it will have to spend plenty of this money to weather the storm.

Another source of competition for Egghead.com will be the auc-

> **The competition Egghead.com faces is extensive and brutal.**

tioneers. Hundreds of online auction sites have sprung up since On-sale first pioneered this category in the mid-1990s. Search under "auction" within Yahoo! and the results are overwhelming. Auction Universe, uBid, DealDeal, WebAuction, Cyber Swap . . . the list continues ad infinitum. Many of these companies are small, business-to-business and business-to-consumer sites that are more a nuisance than a threat. Much more troublesome will be the so-called person-to-person auction giants, eBay and Amazon.com.

Consider eBay. Although Onsale has positioned itself as occupying a different market niche than eBay, the amount of overlap between the two firms is more than Onsale has cared to admit. Whereas Onsale has connected manufacturers and customers by serving as a distribution channel for refurbished or closeout products, eBay, an online trading community, has focused on bringing individual buyers and sellers together through online auctions. Each day, eBay hosts more than 2.5 million auctions, with 250,000 new items joining the "for sale" list every twenty-four hours. Yes, plenty of these auctions involve consumers selling Star Wars trading cards or antique train equipment to one another. But eBay also hosts volumes of auctions every day in which small businesses are purchasing everything from CD-ROM drives to network routers, sometimes from individuals and other times from entrepreneurial companies that have turned to eBay as a new distribution channel. By serving small businesses effectively, eBay has provided competition for Onsale and will continue to prove problematic for the emerging Egghead.com.

How has eBay built such an extraordinarily successful business in so short a period of time? Much of the company's growth happened organically. As sellers discovered eBay as an efficient, effective way to sell their goods, and as buyers began finding bargains on the site, people began to spread the word about this burgeoning online marketplace. The more people that came to eBay to buy and sell, the more useful a resource it became, which in turn spurred its growth further. In Internet industry parlance, this concept is known as the *network effect.* It's a phenomenon that we've seen play out in other sectors as well. The proliferation of the fax machine is a case in point. When the fax machine was first introduced, it was expensive and only moderately useful, because the number of other people or companies to whom one could send faxes was limited. But as the idea caught on, more people purchased the machines. And the larger the installed base of fax machines, the more useful the device became—which accelerated fax adoption even more. Why didn't Onsale see similar growth? With Onsale, the transaction was one way. Buyers purchased a product from Onsale, but couldn't put goods of their own up for sale. It was the development of an open, bidirectional auction environment that led to eBay's stellar growth.

The company has reinforced this natural growth with a variety of marketing and distribution programs. eBay has worked the press hard to feed journalists' excitement about online auctions. The result has been a wave of articles with titles such as "The Auction Economy" in which auctions have been described as revolutionizing the way in which products are bought and sold. "Pandora's E-box is now open,"*Business Week* opined in one column, "and pricing will never be the same."[23] The substantial increase in the company's stock price has also made it easy for eBay to grab journalists' attention, and the company has been featured in scores of magazines and newspapers as a leader of the Internet economy.

To complement its PR efforts, eBay has invested in offline advertising. The company's "What Are You Searching For?" campaign, for example, ran on more than ten thousand radio stations during a five-week blitz, as well as in print publications such as *Parade, People,* and *Newsweek.* The firm has dabbled in guerrilla marketing as well. During the summer of 1999, eBay staffers drove two wildly decorated, "Internet ready" RVs across the country, visiting more than thirty different towns to spread the word about eBay at local community events. The company has also struck a number of large distribution deals. For example, eBay developed a co-branded version of its site in partnership with AOL that will be heavily marketed to AOL's 18 million customers. So while eBay may attribute much of its success to the organic growth described above, the company's marketing team is bringing a rich set of programs to bear to further increase both brand awareness and site traffic.

In growing its auction business, eBay is unlikely to focus aggressively on the business market any time soon; CEO Meg Whitman has called the segment a low priority. But in a move that would cause even greater trouble for Egghead.com than it already has, eBay is looking seriously at supplementing auctions with the sale of goods at fixed prices. The company recently polled its members on whether they'd like to see "fixed price auctions"; many said yes. One way in which eBay might pursue the sale of fixed-price goods would be to enable small businesses to rent virtual storefronts on the eBay site for a fee. Some 20 percent of its sellers account for 80 percent of the transaction volume on eBay; many of these high-volume sellers are probably businesses. By pursuing the virtual storefront model, not only could eBay collect both "rent" and transaction fees from these companies, it could also keep more traffic on its site (these businesses have often steered shoppers to their own retail Web sites from their listings on eBay).[24] Although it's not assured that eBay will pursue fixed-price sales, Egghead.com should not be surprised if it does. When asked if the company would expand in this way, Whitman has said, "There is a better than even chance. The question is, exactly when, and what format we will do it in. It's this notion of choosing what you're going to focus on. And I have this philosophy that you really need to do things 100%. Better to do five things at 100% than 10 things at 80%."[25] Egghead.com may have a reprieve here, but it's probably only temporary.

Amazon.com has already introduced a hybrid retailing/auction model. Through its electronics store, Amazon sells a broad range of computer equipment: PDAs, printers, scanners—virtually everything except computers themselves, which the company decided to avoid given the competitive intensity of the market. However, any gear that is not available through the firm's electronics store is probably up for bid on Amazon Auctions. Experts estimate that Amazon spent up to twelve months and $12 million to develop its extensive auction site, a site that looks very similar to eBay.[26] ("It's kind of frightening—they cloned eBay," said Larry Schwartz, president of Auction Universe.[27]) Shoppers in the market for techno-tools can buy desktop computers, utilities software, laptops, and other such products at extremely low prices. For small businesses, Amazon makes a great place to shop because it offers good selection and value from a brand name they know and trust. (According to a study by the Brand Institute, roughly 101 million U.S. adults recognize the Amazon name —which makes it number one in ecommerce—while some 63 million know the eBay brand, which ranks third.[28])

Amazon launched its auction site in March 1999. The company opened its electronics store only four months later, and some analysts have suggested that it was the threat posed by Amazon's expansion that threw Egghead and Onsale together. "When they heard about Amazon, they probably panicked," said David Cooperstein of Forrester Research. "Smaller companies will try to hold hands as the ship

Consolidation of demand and customer cross-selling offer a critical advantage.

goes down."[29] Although this may be an extreme view, I agree with Cooperstein that like eBay, Amazon represents a significant danger to Egghead.com, and that Amazon's invasion of the electronics market likely accelerated the pace of the Onsale/Egghead merger discussions.

Amazon has had its marketing engine running flat out to build awareness and spark trial of both its electronics store and its auction service. The company has invested in outdoor advertising in major U.S. cities (in the San Francisco Bay area, for example, Amazon supported the launch of its auction service with billboards along Highway 101, Silicon Valley's main thoroughfare, and with bus placards on MUNI, San Francisco's public transit system). It has run extensive radio advertising in these same cities, and has done plenty of online advertising as well.

Perhaps most important, however, is Amazon's push to cross-sell these new services to its current customers. With the launch of both Amazon auctions and the electronics store, the company sent "personalized" email notes from Jeff Bezos to its entire customer base—

millions of online shoppers—to tell people about the latest additions to Amazon.com and urge them to give the new services a try. It has given both auctions and the electronics store significant exposure throughout its Web site (in a recent visit to Amazon.com, for example, I found an offer for a Palm V organizer from the electronics store highlighted on the site's home page). The firm is even adding inserts to the orders it ships to its customers to pitch them on auctions and electronics (case in point: The Amazon box that contained the *Sesame Street 1–2–3* video that I recently ordered for my daughter also included a cardboard mailing piece that looked like a digital camera and urged me to visit the company's electronics store). In short, Amazon is doing all it can to leverage its customer base to jump-start its sales in new categories and to extract the maximum value from these shoppers. According to Erik Byrnjolfsson, a professor at the MIT Sloan School, this sort of consolidation of demand and customer cross-selling offer a critical advantage. "A large aggregator can put a company selling a narrow product line out of business," he says.[30] While I don't think that Amazon will crush Egghead.com, I believe that the competitive friction between the two will be intense in the years to come.

In addition to the threat it faces from pure Web retailers, Egghead.com must also deal with competition from a variety of players with a presence both online and off. Take PC Connection, for example. The company started back in 1982 as a computer products mail-order house. In the years since, PC Connection has built a thriving catalog business (the company sends out millions of its familiar *PC Connection* and *MacConnection* catalogs each month, and since 1995, the firm's compound annual growth rate has averaged more than 42 percent year after year). In 1997, PC Connection also began selling on the Web, and its pcconnection.com and macconnection.com stores have proved to be popular with the small and medium-sized businesses it targets (business customers account for roughly 85 percent of the company's sales).

Why has PC Connection been a success? Its product selection is good. The firm sells both through catalogs and on the Web, enabling it to reach a broader range of customers than just those comfortable buying online. Most distinctive, however, has been PC Connection's focus on customer service. Since the firm began, PC Connection has turned to service as a way to set itself apart from the pack. In fact, the company introduced a number of service innovations that are now standard throughout its industry. In 1982, for example, PC Connection was the first computer products direct marketer to offer toll-free technical support. In 1991, before caller ID had been widely introduced, PC Connection worked with Northern Telecom and IBM to use the emerging technology to develop a service called "One Minute Mail Order." The resulting application enabled customer account information to appear on a customer service representative's computer screen immediately when the call connected. Customer service continues to be a weak point for many Internet retailers. PC Connection, on the other hand, has had a focus on service for almost twenty years. The price competition that has swept through the computer products industry will exert margin pressures that may make it difficult for PC Connection to continue to provide the level of service it is used to offering. On the other hand, if the company can regain margin in other ways (such as selling more of its house brand PCs, machines it assembles from standard parts) and maintain this point of differentiation, PC Connection will continue to be a thorn in the side of Egghead.com.

CompUSA, another Egghead.com competitor, is the largest computer store chain in the United States. With 210 superstores in eighty-two cities across the country, CompUSA has a significant physical presence. The cavernous stores sell a huge collection of computer products, and prices are low—too low to provide the company with decent margins given the cost structure associated with running this brick-and-mortar business. "They are getting the crap beat out of them quarter after quarter financially," according to Roger Kay, an analyst with International Data Corporation. "They have not been able to turn a buck in that business, and they're one of the better-established, higher-volume outlets. That's pretty bad for the others . . . [because] CompUSA is probably the premier outlet in retail."[31] In an effort to stem its losses, CompUSA has shuttered unprofitable stores and laid off thousands of employees. It has also begun to focus more of its efforts on building its online store, CompUSA Net.com. Like Egghead, CompUSA's offline stores have helped the company to build brand awareness that has contributed to the growth of its Web business. But with a moderate selection and an unsophisticated site, CompUSA is a long way behind most online retailers in its drive to sell via the Web. Between its offline woes and its modest online success, CompUSA poses a much lesser threat to Egghead.com than do other firms in this arena.

Although Egghead.com need not fret about CompUSA, it should pay close attention to Wal-Mart. Wal-Mart is monolithic. The company operates 2,300 stores and 440 Sam's Club membership warehouses in the United States and employs more than 600,000 Americans. Roughly 100 million people are estimated to shop at a Wal-Mart store each week—including plenty of small business owners looking to take advantage of the value-priced products Wal-Mart offers its customers. The stores don't carry the breadth and depth of computer products available at a CompUSA or an online retailer. Instead, Wal-Mart pitches a carefully selected set of best-selling high-tech products. This is the same formula that the company used to surpass Toys 'R' Us as the country's leading brick-and-mortar toy retailer, and it's also working well for computers, peripherals, and other high-tech gear.

Fortunately for Egghead.com, Wal-Mart has been slow to exploit the Web. Although the company did begin selling online in July 1996, it initially focused on big-ticket items such as appliances. It took another year for Wal-Mart to begin selling books and CDs via the Web, and computer products came later still. As Wal-Mart ramps up its Web retailing efforts, it is likely that the company will follow a similar strategy online as it has offline when it comes to computer equipment, that is, offering a focused selection of the most popular products. It will also supplement the lower margins from such products with higher margins from the sale of private-label, build-to-order PCs, a business that is already showing promise for Wal-Mart. In addition, the company plans to experiment with the sale of software via digital downloads. As we'll see in greater detail later in this chapter, this is a trade that could be tremendously profitable for Wal-Mart, and one that Egghead.com will undoubtedly pursue as well. So although Wal-Mart is not yet a Web powerhouse, the odds are likely that it will eventually carve out a chunk of the online computer products retailing market for its own. According to Michael Niemira, a retail analyst for Bank of Tokyo-Mitsubishi in New York, "It may not be a story for this year or next, but as time goes on, Wal-Mart will be something to be reckoned with."[32]

Egghead.com will also spar with a number of computer product manufacturers, most notably Dell. Dell has been a direct sales company from the start and took to the Web naturally. By 1999, the company was selling more than $18 million in goods through its online store each day. Building on the success of its PC sales, the company then introduced Gigabuys.com, a shopping site aimed at small and medium-sized businesses that offers a variety of high-tech products from multiple vendors. "We get about 25 million visitors to our Web site a quarter," said CEO Michael Dell at launch. "[The goal is] to be able to sell those customers anything they buy that goes along with their PC—printers, software, modems, networking cards, add-ons—and to have one common shopping cart."[33] By cross-selling add-on products to its customers through Gigabuys.com, Dell has the potential to be not only a major PC vendor, but a sizable retailer of complementary products as well. To make matters worse for Egghead.com, Dell has also entered the auction space with the introduction of dellauction.com. Through its auction site, the company not only enables shoppers to bid on used or refurbished Dell PCs (computers that have been leased from the company and then returned), but also to put their old computer systems up for auction, regardless of brand. As these initiatives show, Dell is driving hard to provide its customers with a full range of products and purchasing options. It is succeeding—which means trouble for Egghead.com.

As this section makes clear, the computer products market is already quite crowded. What barriers to entry will discourage additional competitors from joining the fray and making life even more complicated for Egghead.com? One factor that protects Egghead.com (as well as several others in the space) is brand awareness. As we saw earlier, although Onsale has relatively low levels of brand awareness, the Egghead name is much better known—as are brands such as Amazon, Dell, and Wal-Mart. Any company that enters the computer products sector now is going to go head to head with such players and would need to spend significant sums on marketing to establish the kind of awareness and consumer confidence that market leaders like these already have. Low margins will also help to scare off new entrants. The computer products market is likely to consolidate in the future, and when it does, the financial picture will improve. But in the near term, however, margins will continue to be skinny. Unless a company has plenty of cash on hand to help it through the tough times, it won't survive. It simply can't count on profits from operations to fund its business in the next several years. Egghead.com has $163 million in cash at its disposal—almost triple the cash reserves of Cyberian Outpost. Strong customer relationships (both Egghead and Onsale have their loyalists) will also dissuade firms from entering the space. And on the auction side of the house, as mentioned earlier, Onsale has brought to Egghead.com good relationships with suppliers of excess merchandise, alliances that would be difficult for others to replicate.

On the Horizon   ▼

As we look at what the future will likely bring for Egghead.com, there are a number of pending challenges worth exploring. For example, as auctions increase in popularity as a way to purchase goods online, the Onsale section of Egghead.com will lose its uniqueness. Indeed, many stand-alone auction sites have already taken root since Onsale first introduced the concept. The emergence of auction technology vendors such as FairMarket and OpenSite, however, is making it possible for all manner of sites to host auctions. "People think of auctions as destination sites," says Michael Brader-Araje, OpenSite's founder, "but auctions are going to become a natural component of all e-commerce site initiatives. You will see thousands of manufacturers and retailers start to use auctions as a component of their Internet presence."[34] It's not as if the name-your-price model is going to dominate the economy. Bargaining takes work, which is why fixed prices appeared in the first place. As Amazon's Jeff Bezos puts it, "Would you want to negotiate the price of the *New York Times* every time you bought it?"[35] But online auctions are certainly an idea that has caught on. And the further they spread, the less of a differentiator Onsale's auctions become for Egghead.com.

Another issue with which Egghead.com will wrestle is how to provide quality customer service to support a business with such thin margins. As PC Connection has shown, providing outstanding customer support can differentiate companies competing in a commodity business. Yet offering good service doesn't come cheap. So what is Egghead.com to do? For one thing, it must invest further in site content and features that enable customers to help themselves. Well-indexed, searchable databases of common questions and expanded buyer's guides are good examples of self-help tools that empower customers to be their own first line of support. The company should also look into technologies such as real-time chat that will enable it to provide a high level of service while decreasing support costs. And to offset the expense associated with good customer service, Egghead.com will need to actively explore new revenue sources, such as the sale of service contracts.

Given how competitive computer products retailing has become, it is certain that a number of the current players won't be able to make it on their own. "Every company is vulnerable, every company is under attack," says Buy.com CEO Scott Blum.[36] The market is ripe for consolidation, and based on its relative market strength, Egghead.com is well positioned to roll up smaller Web properties looking for a white knight. The opportunities that come with such acquisitions could be attractive for Egghead.com. By absorbing such smaller players, the company could add large numbers of people to its customer base quickly, boost its revenue figures and market share, and acquire scarce managerial and technical talent. As we've seen, however, the implementation of these mergers can be tricky. Cultural differences can be jarring. The fusion of different technical systems can be complex. And management friction is not uncommon as roles and responsibilities shift when companies join. Egghead.com stands to gain a lot by exercising its market power to digest smaller players. It's important to realize, however, that such mergers come with associated costs as well.

A final opportunity that will be attractive though not trouble free for Egghead.com will be the shifting of its software sales to a digital download model. Most software is still manufactured and sold in a traditional manner. The product is duplicated on CD-ROM or floppy disk, packaged in a box along with documentation, and then shipped to a distributor. The distributor in turn sells the product to the retailer, who then sells it to the customer. Sometimes, the retailer can arrange for the software package to be sent directly from the distributor to the consumer. Other times, however, the retailer takes possession of the software and then either sells it to the customer in a physical store or, in the case of a Web-based merchant, ships the product to the purchaser from a warehouse. The process is an inherently inefficient one, with costs mounting as the software is manufactured and then shipped from here to there. But software is a purely digital product—a long series of zeros and ones. If a retailer can deliver this product directly to the customer via the Internet (and now it can), it can substantially reduce its costs and thus increase its margins.

We've seen this concept before in looking at the book and music markets. The idea is equally compelling in the software world, and if Egghead.com is going to improve its financial picture, moving aggressively into digital downloads is a must for the company. Numerous challenges stand between Egghead.com and success with this effort. Although network bandwidth is constantly increasing, slow Internet access speeds can still make downloading software a long, painful process. The number of titles that software manufacturers have made available for download is modest. And there are psychological barriers to overcome as well, because some shoppers may feel that there is something less valuable about an application that is just downloaded to the hard drive, as opposed to software that comes in a box, on a tangible storage medium, along with a manual. Other companies in this space, however, have already made good progress in selling digital downloads despite such problems. By the summer of 1999, for example, Beyond.com, an online software retailer, had already completed more than one million digital downloads for its customers, a sales volume equivalent to 1.6 million pounds of cardboard boxes, or a software stack twenty-nine times the height of Mount Everest. Egghead.com has dabbled tentatively in the digital download space. But it will take a more concerted effort if the company is going to take a leadership role in the development of this new software distribution channel.

Conclusion

As we've seen in the preceding chapters, the development of an Internet brand is a holistic process. Building awareness—the activity that many equate with "branding"—is just one aspect of brand development. Crafting a powerful online brand requires paying just as much attention to developing other facets of the brand as well, such as customer loyalty and influential distribution partnerships. There is no silver-bullet solution for the development of a substantial Internet brand. Instead, dominant ebrands emerge when companies invest in a rich mixture of marketing and business practices.

The companies we've analyzed in this book understand this. Although the Web will continue to change and expand with phenomenal speed, I think you'll find the best practices they share will remain fairly constant. So whether you're attempting to develop your own Internet brand, looking to invest in a Web-based business, studying the Internet business landscape, or evaluating competitors, the knowledge you've gained from this set of case studies should hold you in good stead.

To keep you abreast of the latest developments in Internet marketing, I've created a companion Web site for this book, which you'll find at http://www.ebrands.homestead.com. Here, you'll find additional writings on the topic of building Internet brands, the latest news on our case study companies, a virtual bookstore featuring other marketing books I recommend, and a detailed directory of other Web-based marketing resources that I've found useful.

Best of luck in all your ebranding efforts!

Coordinates

Company or Site	URL
AltaVista	www.altavista.com
Amazon.com	www.amazon.com
AOL.com	www.aol.com
Armchair Millionaire	www.armchairmillionaire.com
Ask.com	www.ask.com
@ Home	www.athome.com
@ Plan	www.Webplan.net
BabyCenter	www.babycenter.com
Barnesandnoble.com	www.barnesandnoble.com
Barnes & Noble, Inc.	www.shareholder.com/bks
Bertelsmann	www. bertelsmann.com/index.cfm
Beyond.com	www.beyond.com
Big Five Sporting Goods	www.bigfivesportinggoods.com
Blockbuster	www.blockbuster.com
Book Stacks Unlimited	www.books.com
Borders	www.borders.com
Burson-Marsteller	www.bm.com
Buy.com	www.buy.com
CBS Sportsline: The Sports Store	www.thesportsstore.com
CDNOW	www.cdnow.com
CNET	www.cnet.com
Columbia House	www.columbiahouse.com
CompUSA	www.compusa.com
Cone Communications	www.conenet.com
Cunningham Communications	www.ccipr.com

Cyberian Outpost	www.outpost.com
DDB Needham	www.ddbn.com
Dell	www.dell.com
Direct Hit	www.directhit.com
Disney	www.disney.com
eBay	www.ebay.com
Egghead.com	www.egghead.com
Electra	www.electra.com
ESPN: The Store	http://store.espn.go.com
E-TRADE	www.etrade.com
Excite	www.excite.com
FairMarket	www.fairmarket.com
Fatbrain.com	www.fatbrain.com
Firefly	www.firefly.com
flamenco-world.com	www.flamenco-world.com
Fogdog Sports	www.fogdog.com
gap.com	www.gap.com
Gear.com	www.gear.com
GeoCities	http://geocities.yahoo.com
Global Sports Interactive	www.gs-interactive.com
GoTo.com	www.goto.com
Google	www.google.com
Hearst Home Arts	www.homearts.com
Herman's World of Sports	www.hermansports.com
HotBot	www.hotbot.com
IN2	www.in2.com
InsWeb	www.insWeb.com
i-traffic	www.i-traffic.com
iVillage	www.ivillage.com
LookSmart	www.looksmart.com
Lot21	www.lot21.com
Manning Selvage & Lee	www.mslpr.com
Martha Stewart Living Omnimedia	www.marthastewart.com
Media Metrix	www.mediametrix.com
Microsoft Network	www.msn.com
Middleberg Associates	www.middleberg.com
Modem Media	www.modemmedia.com
MySimon	www.mysimon.com
NBC	www.nbc.com
Netcentives	www.netcentives.com

Net Perceptions	www.netperceptions.com
Netscape	www.netscape.com
New York Times on the Web	www.nytimes.com
Niehaus Ryan Wong	www.nrwpr.com
Nielsen/NetRatings	www.nielsen-netratings.com
Nike	www.nike.com
The Onion	www.theonion.com
Onsale	www.onsale.com
OpenSite	www.opensite.com
Oprah's Book Club	www.oprah.com/bookclub/book-club.html
Organic Online	www.organic.com
Oxygen Media	www.oxygen.com
Parent Soup	www.parentsoup.com
PC Connection	www.pcconnection.com
Planet Out	www.planetout.com
Playboy Enterprises	www.playboy.com
REI	www.rei.com
RocketCash	www.rocketcash.com
Roger Black's Interactive Bureau	www.iab.com
SonicNet	www.sonicnet.com
Spumco	www.spumco.com
TBWA/Chiat/Day	www.tbwachiat.com
Tower Records	www.towerrecords.com
Tripod	www.tripod.com
Virgin Megastores	www.virginmega.com
Virgin Records	www.virginrecords.com
Waggener Edstrom	www.wagged.com
Wal-Mart Online	www.wal-mart.com
Weiss, Stagliano and Partners	www.wspworld.com
Women.com	www.women.com
Yahoo!	www.yahoo.com
Yahoo! Calendar	http://calendar.yahoo.com
Yahoo! Clubs	http://clubs.yahoo.com
Yahoo! College Search	http://features.yahoo.com/college/search.html
Yahoo! Finance	http://quote.yahoo.com
Yahoo! Insurance Center	http://insurance.yahoo.com
Yahoo! Messenger	http://messenger.yahoo.com
Yahoo! Shopping	http://shopping.yahoo.com

Notes

INTRODUCTION

1. Robert D. Hof, Seanna Browder, and Peter Elstrom, "Internet Communities—Forget Surfers. A New Class of Netizen Is Settling Right In," *Business Week,* 5 May 1997, 66.
2. Maryann Jones Thompson, "Tracking the Internet Economy: 100 Numbers You Need to Know," *The Industry Standard,* 13 September 1999, <http://www.thestandard.net>.
3. Ibid.
4. Ibid.
5. Heather Green and Linda Hamelstein, "To the Victors Belong the Ads," *Business Week Online,* 4 October 1999, <http://www.businessweek.com>.
6. David Aaker, *Managing Brand Equity* (New York: Free Press, 1991), 7.

CHAPTER 1: iVillage

1. Robert D. Hof, Seanna Browder, and Peter Elstrom, "Internet Communities—Forget Surfers. A New Class of Netizen Is Settling Right In," *Business Week,* 5 May 1997, 64.
2. Candice Carpenter, interview by author, tape recording, Redwood City, CA, May 1998.
3. Media Metrix, World Wide Audience Ratings, March 1999.
4. Ibid.
5. Regina Joseph, "Will It Take More Than iVillage?" *Forbes.com,* 16 December 1998, <http://www.forbes.com>.

6. MacDara MacColl, interview by author, tape recording, Redwood City, CA, May 1998.

7. Ibid.

8. Carpenter, interview.

9. Louis Trager, "Women Even Score on Net Use," *Inter@ctive Investor,* 29 March 1999, <http://www.zdii.com/fp.asp>.

10. Jason Stell, interview by author, tape recording, Redwood City, CA, May 1998.

11. Hof, Browder, and Elstrom, "Internet Communities," 64.

12. Joe Berwanger, interview by author, tape recording, Redwood City, CA, May 1998.

13. Stell, interview.

14. Carpenter, interview.

15. Hillary Graves, interview by author, tape recording, Redwood City, CA, May 1998.

16. Danny Sullivan, email exchange with author, 1 June 1999.

17. Graves, interview.

18. Ibid.

19. Ibid.

20. Heather Campbell, interview by author, tape recording, Redwood City, CA, May 1998.

21. Paul Ahern, interview by author, tape recording, Redwood City, CA, May 1998.

22. Campbell, interview.

23. Ahern, interview.

24. Gregg Greenberg, interview by author, tape recording, Redwood City, CA, May 1998.

25. Sandeep Junnarkar, "NBC to Invest in iVillage," *CNET News.com,* 30 November 1998, <http://www.news.com/>.

26. Greta Mittner, "NBC Swaps Promos for iVillage Equity," *Redherring.com,* 30 November 1998, <http://www.redherring.com>.

27. iVillage, "iVillage Survey: What Turns Women On-Line" (press release, New York, 5 February 1998).

28. Paul Eng, "A Coffee Klatch for Moms and Dads," *Business Week,* 5 May 1997, 76.

29. iVillage, "iVillage Survey."

30. MacColl, interview.

31. "The IQ Q&A: Nancy Evans & Candice Carpenter," *Advertising Week,* 23 September 1996, 25.

32. Hof, Browder, and Elstrom, "Internet Communities," 64.

33. Ibid, 64

34. Carpenter, interview.

35. Ibid.

36. Glen Gamboa, "Special Sites for Her Eyes Only," *Buffalo News*, 21 April 1998, E8.

37. Jupiter Communications, "Jupiter Communications Sprint 1997 Projections."

38. Netsmart Research, "What Makes Women Click?," (Fall 1997).

39. Jonathan Gaw, "Programmer Gives Birth to Internet Success Story," *Minneapolis Star-Tribune*, 27 November 1997, B5.

40. iVillage, "iVillage and Simon & Schuster's Red Rocket Announce Broad-Based Sponsorship Agreement" (press release, New York, 2 December 1997).

41. John Hagel III and Arthur G. Armstrong, *Net Gain: Expanding Markets Through Virtual Communities* (Boston: Harvard Business School Press, 1997).

42. Carpenter, interview.

43. Joshua Levine, "A Place to Chat," *Forbes*, 9 September 1996, 167.

44. MacColl, interview.

45. Chuck Schilling, interview by author, June 1998.

46. Email note from NestMom to iVillage, <http://www.ivillage.com>.

47. MacColl, interview.

48. Craig Bicknell, "A Profile in Ferocity," *Wired News*, 8 February 1999, <http://www.wired.com/news/>.

49. Ibid.

50. Craig Bicknell, "Exec Questions iVillage Books," *Wired News*, 27 May 1999, <http://www.wired.com/news/>.

51. Ibid.

52. Greta Mittner, "iVillage Is Expecting," *Redherring.com*, 14 December 1998, <http://www.redherring.com>.

53. Christopher Byron, "It Takes an iVillage to Raise Millions," *MSNBC*, 24 March 1999, <http://www.msnbc.com/news/>.

54. Eric Fleming, "iVillage: Singing an E-commerce Tune," *Inter@ctive Investor*, 19 February 1999, <http://www.zdii.com/fp.asp>.

55. Darren Chervitz, "Not Alone in This iVillage," *CBS MarketWatch*, 19 March 1999, <http://cbs.marketwatch.com/news/newsroom.htx>.

56. Carpenter, interview.

57. Chip Bayers, "Push Comes to Shove," *Wired*, February 1999, <http://www.wired.com>.

58. Bicknell, "Profile in Ferocity."

59. Ibid.
60. Molly O'Neill, "But What Would Martha Say?" *The New York Times Magazine,* 16 May 1999, <http://www.nytimes.com/library/magazine/millennium/m2>.
61. Lori Waffenschmidt, "Martha Stewart Puts Her Taste Online," *CNN Interactive,* 16 September 1997, <http://www.cnn.com>.
62. Carpenter, interview.
63. Gary Stern, "It Takes iVillage," *Link-Up,* September/October 1996, 7.
64. Lisa Napoli, "Despite a Passion for the Net, Many Online Volunteers Want Pay," *The New York Times on the Web,* 19 April 1999, <http://www.nytimes.com>.

CHAPTER **2: CDNOW**

1. John Grossman, "Nowhere Men," *Inc.,* June 1996, 63.
2. Troy Wolverton, "CDNOW, N2K Strike First Note After Merger," *CNET News.com,* May 18, 1999, <http://www.news.com>.
3. Jupiter Communications, "Music Industry and the Internet," (report, New York, 1997).
4. Ibid.
5. Anonymous CDNOW manager, interview by author, tape recording, Redwood City, CA, May 1998.
6. Rod Parker, interview by author, tape recording, Redwood City, CA, May 1998.
7. Arielle Dorros, interview by author, tape recording, Redwood City, CA, May 1998.
8. Parker, interview.
9. Dorros, interview.
10. *Select,* April 1998, 97.
11. Parker, interview.
12. Deborah Kania, "Branding.com," *ClickZ,* 6 July 1999, <http://www.clickz.com>.
13. Kevin Perlmutter, interview by author, tape recording, Redwood City, CA, May 1998.
14. Ibid.
15. "CDNOW and MTV Networks Announce Premier Integrated Marketing Alliance," *PR Newswire,* 19 May 1998.
16. Michael Tchong, *ICONOCAST,* 1 July 1998, <http://www.iconocast.com>.

17. Frederick F. Reichheld, *The Loyalty Effect: The Hidden Force Behind Growth, Profits, and Lasting Value* (Boston: Harvard Business School Press, 1996).

18. Jason Olim, interview by author, tape recording, Redwood City, CA, May 1998.

19. Don Peppers and Martha Rogers, *The One to One Future: Building Relationships One Customer at a Time* (New York: Currency Doubleday, 1993).

20. Parker, interview.

21. Ibid.

22. Patrick Keane, interview by author, tape recording, Redwood City, CA, May 1998.

23. Matt Broersma, "Strike Up the Band—This Music Man Means Business," *ZDNet News Channel,* 25 August 1997, <http://www.zdnet.com/zdn>.

24. Ibid.

25. CDNOW, "CDNOW Launches Next Generation of Highly Successful Cosmic Credit Program" (press release, Fort Washington, PA, 28 April 1998).

26. Neil Weintraut, "Building the Bulletproof Net Start-up: The Five Critical Ingredients of Online Success," *Business 2.0,* July 1999, <http://www.business2.com>.

27. Mark Hardie, interview by author, tape recording, Redwood City, CA, May 1998.

28. Olim, interview.

29. Bob Trevor, interview by author, tape recording, Redwood City, CA, May 1998.

30. Parker, interview.

31. Michael Tchong, "Branding Redux," ICONOCAST, 16 December 1998, <http://www.inconocast.com>.

32. CDNOW prospectus, <http://www.sec.gov/Archives/edgar/data/1050372/0001036050-97-001094.txt>.

33. Olim, interview.

34. Trevor, interview.

35. Bob Tedeschi, "CDNOW Struggles to Be Heard," *The New York Times on the Web,* 24 May 1999, <http://www.nytimes.com>.

36. Jane Weaver, "More Costly TV Ads Spell Trouble for Internet Companies," *MSNBC,* 10 June 1999, <http://www.msnbc.com/news/>.

37. Janet Stites, "For an Acquisition to Work, Two Cultures Must Merge,"

The New York Times on the Web, 7 December 1998, <http://www.nytimes.com>.

38. Ibid.
39. Reuters, "CDNOW Opens Enlarged Music Site, Set to Go Digital," 18 May 1999.
40. Gabrielle Jonas, "CDNOW's Jason Olim Challenges Amazon," *CMPnet*, 23 September 1998, <http://www.cmpnet.com>.
41. Robert Hof, "Amazon.com: The Wild World of E-commerce," *Business Week*, 14 December 1998, 106.
42. Suzanne Galante, "Bulked-up CDNOW Takes on Mighty Amazon," The Street.com, 30 March 1999, <http://www.thestreet.com>.
43. CDNOW, "CDNOW to Merge with Sony's and Time Warner's Columbia House to Create World's Leading Music and Video E-Commerce Company" (press release, Fort Washington, PA and New York, 13 July 1999).
44. Ken Cassar, "The Online Music Market: Niche Players Will Proliferate Despite Continued Dominance by the Big Guys," Jupiter Communications Analyst Note, 27 April 1998.
45. Hardie, interview.
46. Jupiter Communications, "Music Industry and the Internet."
47. Ibid.
48. Bob Tedeschi, "Online Merchants Grow Uneasy as Web Portals Sell More Goods Themselves," *The New York Times on the Web*, 12 April 1999, <http://www.nytimes.com>.
49. Grossman, "Nowhere Men," 63.
50. Jon Pareles, "With a Click, a New Era of Music Dawns," *The New York Times on the Web*, 15 November 1998, <http://www.nytimes.com>.
51. Neil Strauss and Matt Richtel, "Coalition Sets Plan to Block Internet Music Piracy," *The New York Times on the Web*, 29 June 1999, <http://www.nytimes.com>.
52. Mark Mooradian, "Music: Record Labels and the Imperative for Digital Distribution," Jupiter Communications Analyst Report, July 1998.
53. Bob Tedeschi, "E-Commerce Sites Target Next Generation of Buyers," *The New York Times on the Web*, 29 March 1999, <http://www.nytimes.com>.
54. Ibid.

CHAPTER **3: Barnesandnoble.com**

1. Ben Boyd, interview by author, tape recording, Redwood City, CA, August 1998.

2. Tony Orelli, interview by author, tape recording, Redwood City, CA, September 1998.

3. Ibid.

4. Nicole Vanderbilt, interview by author, tape recording, Redwood City, CA, August 1998.

5. "Barnes and Noble to pay AOL \$40 Million to Be Exclusive Book Supplier," *Dow Jones Online News,* 16 December 1997, <http://www.dowjones.com>.

6. Chris Charron, interview by author, tape recording, Redwood City, CA, July 1998.

7. Barnesandnoble.com, "Barnesandnoble.com Launches Affiliate Network" (press release, New York, 9 September 1997).

8. Fred Rubin, interview by author, tape recording, Redwood City, CA, September 1998.

9. Digitrends, *Digitrends Daily,* 1998, <http://www.digitrends.net>.

10. Boyd, interview.

11. Doreen Carvajal, "In an Age of On-Line Booksellers, Distribution Is the Key," *The New York Times on the Web,* 18 November 1998, <http://www.nytimes.com>.

12. Michael McCadden, interview by author, tape recording, Redwood City, CA, September 1998.

13. Buford Smith, interview by author, tape recording, Redwood City, CA, September 1998.

14. Matt Kelleher, interview by author, tape recording, Redwood City, CA, August 1998.

15. "Booking the Net," *CNNfn,* 27 October 1998, <http://www.cnnfn.com>.

16. Jeanne Dugan, "The Baron of Books," *Business Week,* 29 June 1998, 109.

17. Mary Huhn, "Buy-the-Book Battle," NYPOST.COM 18 May 1999, <http://www.nypost.com>.

18. Ibid.

19. Ibid.

20. Boyd, interview.

21. Rubin, interview.

22. Boyd, interview.

23. James Ledbetter, "Jonathan Bulkeley's Book Values," *The Industry Standard,* 5 March 1999, <http://www.thestandard.net>.

24. David Simons, "Barnesandnoble.com's Golden Gaffe," *The Industry Standard,* June 1999, <http://www.thestandard.net>.

25. Vanderbilt, interview.

26. Advertisement for *The Wall Street Journal* in *Marketing Computers* magazine.

27. *"Even Before Books,"* editorial, *The Washington Post,* 4 August 1997, A18.

28. Clint Willis, "Does Amazon.com Really Matter?" *Forbes ASAP,* 6 April 1998, 55.

29. Gabrielle Jonas, "Amazon.com Beats Wall Street by 7 Cents," *CMPNet,* 27 April 1998, <http://www.cmpnet.com>.

30. "Hot Strategy: 'Be Unprofitable for a Long Time'," *Inc.,* September 1997, 32.

31. "Borders Will Rely on Retail Stores," *CNET News.com,* 12 April 1999, <http://www.news.com>.

32. Paula L. Stepankowsky, "Powell's Books Plans to Thrive Both in Stores and on the Web," *The Wall Street Journal,* 21 September 1998.

33. Michelle Rafter, "The Online Bookstore That Makes Money," *The Industry Standard,* 8 March 1999, <http://www.thestandard.net>.

34. Troy Wolverton, "Amazon Still a Shelf Above the Competition," *CNET News.com,* 2 June 1999, <http://www.news.com>.

35. Barnesandnoble.com prospectus, <http://www.sec.gov/Archives/edgar/data/1069665/0000889812-98-002327.txt>.

36. Ibid.

37. Charles Piller, "Most Net Retailers All Sale, No Service," *latimes.com,* 28 June 1999, <http://www.latimes.com>.

38. Ibid.

39. Ibid.

40. Ibid.

41. "Barnesandnoble.com Cuts Electronic Book Device Price," *CNNfn,* 9 June 1999, <http://www.cnnfn.com>.

42. Jimmy Guterman, "Book Burnout," *The Industry Standard,* 21 June 1999, <http://www.thestandard.net>.

43. "The Deadest Aim in the Branding Shootout," *Business Week Online,* 7 September 1998, <http://www.businessweek.com>.

44. Ledbetter, "Bulkeley's Book Values."

Chapter 4: Yahoo!

1. Robert H. Reid, *Architects of the Web: 1,000 Days That Built the Future of Business* (New York: John Wiley and Sons, 1997).

2. Blaise Simpson, interview by author, tape recording, Redwood City, CA, July 1998.

3. Ibid.

4. Ibid.

5. Ibid.

6. Jon Goldstein and Jerry Yang, "Yahoo Is Worth $1.5 Billion. Insane? Jerrry Yang Thinks Not," *Time,* 1 November 1997, 30.

7. Simpson, interview.

8. "Case Study: Yahoo," *Redherring.com,* January 1998, <http://www.redherring.com>.

9. Simpson, interview.

10. Ibid.

11. Ibid.

12. Karen Edwards, interview by author, tape recording, Redwood City, CA, August 1998.

13. Ibid.

14. Ibid.

15. Simpson, interview.

16. Reid, *Architects of the Web.*

17. Ibid.

18. Patricia Nakache, "Secrets of the New Brand Builders," *Fortune,* 22 June 1998, 167.

19. Randall E. Stross, "How Yahoo! Won the Search Wars," *Fortune,* 2 March 1998, 148.

20. John Yost, interview by author, tape recording, Redwood City, CA, August 1998.

21. Reid, *Architects of the Web.*

22. Edwards, interview.

23. Yost, interview.

24. Ibid.

25. Edwards, interview.

26. Ibid.

27. Lucas Graves, "Marketers of the Year: Karen Edwards, VP, Brand Management, Yahoo!" *Marketing Computers,* February 1998, 28.

28. Edwards, interview.

29. Yahoo!, "NPD Findings Show Yahoo! Ranked Highest in User Opinion" (press release, Santa Clara, CA, 26 August 1997).

30. Michael Krantz, "Start Your Engines," *Time,* 20 April 1998, 50.

31. Bob Tedeschi, "Caught in a Web of 'Sticky' Services," *The New York Times on the Web,* 20 October 1998, <http://www.nytimes.com>.

32. Edwards, interview.

33. Ibid.

34. Yost, interview.

35. Mark Mooradian, interview by author, tape recording, Redwood City, CA, August 1998.

36. Stross, "How Yahoo! Won," 148.

37. Chris Charron, interview by author, tape recording, Redwood City, CA, August 1998.

38. George Anders, "Comparison Shopping Is the Web's Virtue—Unless You're a Seller," *Wall Street Journal*, 23 July 1998, A1.

39. Reid, *Architects of the Web.*

40. Kim Cleland, "Yahoo!," *Advertising Age*, S1.

41. Edwards, interview.

42. Ibid.

43. Stross, "How Yahoo! Won," 148.

44. Jonathan Littman, "Yahoo's Brand of Cool," *Upside Today*, 19 July 1998, <http://www.upside.com>.

45. Don Crabb, "Yahoo! Virus Scare Is Nothing to Fear," *Chicago Sun-Times*, 21 December 1997, 62.

46. Wendy Yanowitch, interview by author, tape recording, Redwood City, CA, August 1998.

47. Ibid.

48. Ibid.

49. Ibid.

50. Jim Hu, "Racing to the Start Line," *CNET News.com*, 14 May 1998, <http://www.news.com>.

51. Amey Stone, Patrick Lambert, and Linda Hamelstein, "The Battle of the Portals: Who Will Be Left Standing in the Fiercest Contest in Cyberspace?" *Business Week Online*, 7 September 1998, <http://www.businessweek.com>.

52. Bernhard Warner, "Brandweek's Marketers of the Year," *Brandweek*, 20 October 1997, 70.

53. Chris Charron, Bill Bass, Cameron O'Connor, Mamie Chen, and Jill Aldort, *The Great Portal Shakeout, Media & Technology Strategies*, Forrester Report, Vol. 2, Number 7, March 1998.

54. Charron et al., *Great Portal Shakeout.*

55. Sandeep Junnarkar and Jim Ju, "How Prime Is Portal Real Estate?" *CNET News.com*, 20 May 1999, <http://www.news.com>.

56. Ibid.

57. Beth Lipton, "Report Details Yahoo Strategies," *CNET News.com*, 5 March 1999, <http://www.news.com>.

58. AOL, "AOL Surpasses 14 Million Member Mark" (press release, Dulles, VA, 12 November 1998).

59. "You've Got More Mail," *Wired News*, 28 September 1998, <http://www.wired.com/news/>.
60. Catherine Yang, "AOL: The Right Kind of Busy Signals," *Business Week*, 23 February 1998, 34.
61. Chris Charron, interview by author, July 1998.
62. Hu, "Racing to the Start Line."
63. Julia Pitta, "!&#$%.com," *Forbes*, 16 August 1999.
64. Jamie Corroon, "H&Q Net Perspectives: Portals Quickly Becoming a Commodity," *Inter@ctive Investor*, 30 June 1998, <http://www.zdii.com/fp.asp>.
65. "Old Souls," *Forbes.com*, 2 October 1998, <http://www.forbes.com>.
66. "Yahoo! Now Goes it Alone," *CNNfn*, 9 February 1999, <http://www.cnnfn.com>.
67. Corroon, "H&Q Net Perspectives."
68. Alan Goldstein, "Yahoo Aims to Transform Itself into Major Media Company," *Knight-Ridder Tribune Business News*, 20 May 1999.
69. Jim Evans and Jason Krause, "Excite Sale Marks New Weapon in Portal Wars: Speed," *The Industry Standard*, 19 January 1999, <http://www.thestandard.net>.
70. Jeff Mallet, "Eyes on the Prize," *CNET News.com*, 11 March 1999, <http://www.news.com>.
71. Jim Hu, "Will Broadband Determine Yahoo's Future?," *CNET News.com*, 21 January 1999, <http://www.news.com>.
72. Lipton, "Yahoo Strategies."
73. Ibid.

Chapter 5: Fogdog Sports

1. John Horan, analyst, Sporting Goods Intelligence, email to author, 10 November 1998.
2. Tom Romary, interview by author, tape recording, Redwood City, CA, October 1998.
3. Tim Harrington, interview by author, tape recording, Redwood City, CA, October 1998.
4. Brett Alsop, interview by author, tape recording, Redwood City, CA, October 1998.
5. Romary, interview.
6. Michael Tchong, ICONOCAST, 1 July 1999, <http://www.iconocast.com>.
7. Warren Packard, interview by author, tape recording, Redwood City, CA, October 1998.

8. Keith Benjamin, interview by author, tape recording, Redwood City, CA, October 1998.
9. Romary, interview.
10. *The American Heritage Dictionary of the English Language* (Boston: Houghton Mifflin, 1992).
11. Romary, interview.
12. Ibid.
13. Review, Sporting Goods & Equipment, *Forbes ASAP,* 6 April 1998, <http://www.forbes.com>.
14. Romary, interview by author.

CHAPTER **6: Onsale**

1. Jonathan Littman, "Gentlemen, Place Your Bids," *Upside,* June 1998, 64.
2. Sandeep Junnarkar, "Cyberian Outpost Bids on Net Auction Trend," *CNET News.com,* 16 March 1999, <http://www.news.com>.
3. George Anders, "Egghead.com and Onsale Inc. Unveil Merger," *The Wall Street Journal,* 15 July 1999, B6.
4. Joelle Tessler, "On-Line Auction House Onsale, Inc. Expanding Beyond Computer Sales," *Dow Jones Online News,* 27 March 1998, <http://www.dowjones.com>.
5. Susan Moran, "Going . . . Going . . . Downloaded. How Onsale, the Leading Web Auctioneer, Outsmarts Rivals," *Business Week,* 29 September 1997, 96.
6. Littman, "Gentlemen."
7. Martha Greer, interview by author, tape recording, Redwood City, CA, November 1998.
8. "Onsale CEO Reports High Growth in Sales and Customer Registrations," *PR Newswire,* 27 April 1998.
9. Onsale, "Onsale Announces Strategic Alliances; Netscape, BetBuyer, CBS SportsLine and Excite Agreements Signed" (press release, Mountain View, CA, 25 September 1997).
10. Fiona Swerdlow, interview by author, tape recording, Redwood City, CA, November 1998.
11. Greer, interview.
12. Ibid.
13. Ibid.
14. Barry Peters, interview by author, tape recording, Redwood City, CA, September 1999.
15. Suzanne Galante and Cory Johnson, "Egghead.com Thinks Up a Plan," *The Industry Standard,* 22 March 1999, <http://www.thestandard.net>.

16. Peters, interview.
17. Jerry Kaplan, interview by author, tape recording, Redwood City, CA, November 1998.
18. Peters, interview.
19. Brian Taptich, "Less Than Zero Margins," *Redherring.com*, March 1999, <http://www.redherring.com>.
20. George Anders, "Online—Web Seller Asks: How Low Can PC Prices Go?" *The Wall Street Journal*, 19 January 1999, B1.
21. Taptich, "Less Than Zero Margins."
22. Linda Hamelstein, "Throw Out Your Old Business Model," *Business Week Online*, 22 March 1999, <http://www.businessweek.com>.
23. Robert Hof, Heather Green, and Paul Judge, "Going, Going, Gone," *Business Week Online*, 12 April 1999, <http://www.businessweek.com>.
24. Robert Hof and Linda Hamelstein, "eBay vs. Amazon.com," *Business Week Online*, 31 May 1999, <http://www.businessweek.com>.
25. Ibid.
26. Troy Wolverton, "Amazon's Auction Options Were Limited," *CNET News.com*, 6 April 1999, <http://www.news.com>.
27. Daniel Eisenberg, "Now It's One Big Market," *Time*, 12 April 1999, <http://www.time.com>.
28. Hof and Hamelstein, "eBay vs. Amazon.com."
29. Tom Davey, "What Were These Eggheads Thinking?" *Redherring.com*, 15 July 1999, <http://www.redherring.com>.
30. David Bank, "A New Model—A Site-Eat-Site World," *The Wall Street Journal*, 12 July 1999, R12.
31. Brooke Crothers and Joe Wilcox, "Will 'Computer Store' Become an Oxymoron?" *CNET News.com*, 13 August 1999, <http://www.news.com>.
32. Abigail Goldman, "Wal-Mart, Fingerhut Alliance Shakes Up Internet Retailers E-commerce," *Los Angeles Times*, 22 June 1999, C1.
33. Michael Kanellos, "Dell to Open Gigabuys.com," *CNET News.com*, 2 March 1999, <http://www.news.com>.
34. Leslie Walker, "Bidding for a Slice of Web Trade," *The Washington Post*, 15 April 1999, E1.
35. Hof, Green, and Judge, "Going, Going, Gone."
36. Bank, "A New Model."

Index

Aaker, David, 7, 152
Advanced Book Exchange, 145
advertising. *See also entries for advertising by media*
  offline
    by eBay, 255–256
    by Fogdog Sports, 216
    by iVillage, 27–30
    by Onsale, 247–249
    purpose of, 8
  online
    by Amazon.com, 257
    amount of, 2
    by Barnesandnoble.com, 114
    by Fogdog Sports, 216
    by iVillage, 25–27, 41
    by Onsale, 235–236
    purpose of, 67
    on Yahoo!, 185
  return on investment (ROI) for, 186–187, 247
Advertising Age, 29, 36, 162
advertising community, advertising to, 29
Advertising Week, 22, 82, 162
Affiliate Network program (Barnesand-noble.com), 124–125, 147
affiliate networks
  of Barnesandnoble.com, 124–125, 147
  of CDNOW, 64, 82–83, 97, 108

of Fogdog Sports, 210–211, 225, 227–228
Ahern, Paul, 28, 29
Album Advisor (CDNOW tool), 65, 76
alliances. *See* strategic partnerships (alliances)
Alsop, Brett, 205–206, 209
AltaVista, 143, 179, 182, 184
Amazon Associates program (Amazon.com), 125
Amazon.com
  brand awareness of, 142–143, 257
  cross-selling on, 55, 93, 98, 125, 201, 223, 225, 249, 256–258
  development of, 4, 110, 142–144
  email marketing by, 127
  executive compensation of, 141
  international sales on, 149
  music sales on, 62, 85, 95–96, 98–99, 108
  pricing on, 134
  product diversity on, 152
  profitability of, 47
  size of customer base of, 98, 144
  strategic partners of, 36, 178
American Baby, 10, 34, 52
America Online (AOL)
  advertising on, 235
  brand awareness of, 189, 190

America Online (AOL) (*continued*)
  cost of advertising on, 186
  customer loyalty to, 191
  customer service on, 191
  marketing by, 167, 190
  music broadcasting on, 103
  size of customer base of, 178, 190
  strategic partners of, 10, 16, 51–52,
      122–123, 143, 147, 210, 240, 255
  use of volunteers on, 33, 57
  vertical integration on, 200
AOL.com. *See* America Online (AOL)
AOL Europe (AOL), 140
Arbitron, 86
Armchair Millionaire (iVillage site), 16,
    22, 38
Armchair Millionaire Action Planner
    (iVillage tool), 32
Armstrong, Arthur G., 38
Arthur Andersen, corporate intranet of,
    125
Ask.com, 16, 196
Athlete's Foot, 222
@ Home, 193, 199–200
Atlantic Monthly, 118
@ Plan, 177
AT&T Internet service, 115
auction sites. *See* eBay; Onsale
Auction Universe, 232, 254
author chats, on Barnesandnoble.com,
    120–121, 130
Auto-By-Tel, 193
Auto Coverage Analyzer (Yahoo! tool),
    171

BabyCenter, 54, 55
Baby Name Finder (iVillage tool), 35–36
Backstreet Boys, sponsorship of, 166
Bane, Melissa, 134
banner advertising
  by Amazon.com, 143
  by Barnesandnoble.com, 115
  by CDNOW, 67–68
  by iVillage, 25–27, 41
  limitations of, 69
  by Onsale, 235–236
Barnes & Noble, Inc. (booksellers)
  brand awareness of, 113, 128

  as crossover marketer, 12, 110
  history of, 4, 109
  music sales by, 99
  sales volume at, 109
  size of customer base at, 110
Barnesandnoble.com
  best practices in developing, 8,
      12–13
  brand assets of, 111, 112–134
  brand awareness of, 113–119
  community on, 120–121
  competition of, 110, 111, 112,
      142–147, 148–149
  cross-selling on, 135
  cultivating reputation of, 128–133
  customer loyalty to, 119–121
  customer service on, 112, 149–151
  description of, 4–5, 111
  development of, 109–112, 211
  email marketing by, 127, 132, 135
  executive compensation of,
      141–142
  fulfillment of, 130, 147
  future of, 148–152
  goals (business concept, mission,
      theme) of, 111, 116, 128, 146,
      152
  international sales on, 148–149
  investors of, 111
  IPO of, 110–112, 134
  leveraging offline assets of, 132,
      136–138
  major milestones of, 111
  market research by, 11, 126–128
  music sales on, 99–100
  pricing issues on, 134–136
  problems of, 128–129, 134–142
  product diversity on, 152
  profitability of, 111, 138, 146
  relaunch of, 116, 137
  repeat purchase rates on, 135
  size of customer base on, 148
  strategic partners of, 110, 111, 112,
      121–126, 139–141, 14
  target market of, 114–115
  value of, 11, 114, 133–134
Baseball Express, 209
B. Dalton (booksellers), 4, 109

Beatrice's Web Guide, 48
Bell Atlantic, 200
Benjamin, Keith, 188–189, 211
Bertelsmann AG, 110, 112, 138–141,
     148–149
Berwanger, Joe, 22
Better Health (iVillage site), 4, 16, 22,
     26, 31, 41
Beyond.com, 146, 246, 265
Bezos, Jeff, 142, 144, 257, 263
Bicknell, Craig, 45
Big Five Sporting Goods, 221
BizRate, 252
Black, Roger, 126
Black Rocket (ad agency), 163–164
Blum, Scott, 263
BMG, 101–102
Boldget, Henry, 143
Bonds, Barry, 71–72
book sales. *See* Amazon.com; Barnes-
     andnoble.com
BooksOnline (BOL, Bertelsmann AG),
     112, 148–149
Borders (booksellers), 134, 144
Borders.com (Borders), 144
bots, defined, 104. *See also* HotBot
Boyd, Ben, 113, 128, 137, 138, 146, 152
Brackbill, Ann, 190
Brader-Araje, Michael, 263
Brady, Tim, 102
brand awareness
   of Amazon.com, 142–143, 257
   of AOL, 189, 190
   of Barnesandnoble.com, 113–119
   of CDNOW, 64–75, 87
   of Excite, 189
   of Excite@Home, 191–192
   of Fogdog Sports, 208, 215–217
   of iVillage, 19–30
   of Microsoft, 189
   of Onsale (Egghead.com), 235–236
   strategies for building, 7, 8
   of Yahoo!, 157–167, 197–198
brand equity, defined, 7
branding, defined, 6–7
Brand Institute, 257
brand loyalty. *See* customers, commit-
     ment of

brand names (brands)
   benefits of, 2
   best practices in developing, 7–13
   cultivating reputation of, 11
   defined, 6–7
   focus on building awareness of, 8
   leveraging key offline assets of, 13,
        132, 136–138, 139
   loyalty to, 1–2, 8–10
   one-upping offline brands, 12–13
   reasons for developing, 2
   respecting core elements of, 12
   and value, 11
Brentanos (booksellers), 144
broadband, development of, 199, 200
browsers. *See names of specific browsers*
Bulkeley, Jonathan, 140, 141, 152
Business Solutions program (Barnes-
     andnoble.com), 125–126
Business Week, 21, 96, 162, 255
Buy.com, 146, 246, 253
Byrnjolfsson, Erik, 258
Byron, Christopher, 46

Campbell, Heather, 28, 29
Capitol Records, 101
Carpenter, Candice, 15, 16, 19, 20, 23,
        31, 32–33, 34, 37, 38, 39, 45, 49,
        56, 58
Carsey-Werner-Mandabach, 51
Carter, Steven, 45–46
Cassar, Ken, 99, 150
"category killers," defined, 145–146
CBS SportsLine, 212, 223–224
CDNOW
   affiliate network of, 64, 82–83, 97,
        108
   brand assets of, 63, 64–91
   brand awareness of, 64–75, 87
   competition of, 62, 63, 95–96,
        97–104, 146
   cross-selling on, 93
   cultivating reputation of, 87–91
   customer acquisition costs of, 81,
        92–93
   customer loyalty to, 75–79
   customer service on, 64, 66, 75–78,
        85, 89–91

CDNOW (*continued*)
  description of, 4, 63
  development of, 61–62, 65–66
  development pace of, 83–84
  feedback teams of, 90–91
  flexibility of, 73
  fulfillment of, 91, 102
  future of, 104–108
  goals (business concept, mission, theme) of, 63, 65–66
  investors in, 63
  major milestones of, 63
  market research by, 84–87
  mergers of, 62, 93, 94–95, 96, 105
  problems of, 92–97
  profitability of, 63, 75
  repeat purchase rate on, 217
  returns policy on, 91
  rewards program on, 78–79, 95
  sales volume on, 61–62
  size of customer base of, 62, 101
  strategic partners of, 63, 73–74, 79–83, 100–101
  target market of, 68, 71, 106–107
CDNOW Update, 76–77, 218
CD Universe, 108
CDworld, 108
Cedro Group, 206
celebrity endorsements, 71–72, 213
Championship Auto Racing, sponsorship of, 175
Charles Schwab, 22, 178
Charron, Chris, 125, 193
Chea, Rob, 205–206
Chen, Andy, 205–206
China.com, 196
CMJ New Music Monthly, 80
CMJ New Music Report, 80
CMPnet, 95
CNET, 154, 189, 194, 235
College Media, 79–80
Columbia House (Sony and Time Warner), 62, 93, 94–95, 105
community, sense of. *See* GeoCities; iVillage; PlanetOut; Tripod; Usenet newsgroups
Compaq Computers, 172–173, 190

competition
  of Barnesandnoble.com, 110, 111, 112, 142–147, 148–149
  of CDNOW, 62, 63, 95–96, 97–104, 146
  of Fogdog Sports, 207, 220–225, 227–228
  of iVillage, 17, 32, 47–56
  of Onsale (Egghead.com), 232, 233, 252–262
  of Yahoo!, 155, 189–198
CompUSA, 259–260
CompUSA Net.com, 260
Computer Science Corporation, Seventh Annual Retail survey, 144–145
CondéNet (Condé Nast), 26, 47, 50
Cone Communications (PR), 20
content, alliances for. *See* strategic partnerships
Cooperstein, David, 257
corporate intranets, strategic partnerships with, 125–126
Corroon, Jamie, 198, 199
Cosmic Credit program (CDNOW), 82–83, 97, 108
Cosmopolitan, 22, 216
crossover marketers
  best practices in developing, 12–13
  defined, 3, 12, 112
  success of, 131
cross-selling
  on Amazon.com, 55, 93, 98, 125, 201, 223, 225, 249, 256–258
  on Barnesandnoble.com, 135
  on CDNOW, 93
  on Onsale, 236
  on Yahoo!, 170
Crotty, Michael, 107
customers
  commitment of (brand loyalty), 1–2, 8–10, 169
  offline advertising to, 29–30
  profile of. *See* market research
customer service
  on AOL, 191
  on Barnesandnoble.com, 112, 149–151

on CDNOW, 64, 66, 75–78, 85, 89–91
on Fogdog Sports, 214–215
on iVillage, 42–43
on Onsale, 245, 263
on Yahoo!, 176, 181–182
Cutie-Patootie Parenting Tips (Rosie
O'Donnell site), 27
Cyberian Outpost (Outpost.com), 246,
247, 252–253
Cybernautics, 24–25
Cyber Swap, 232, 254
Cyclone (Snap), 200

Datek, 92
DDB Needham (ad agency), 28, 29–30
DealDeal, 232, 254
Delhagen, Kate, 48, 62
Dell, 261
development, pace of, 10, 38–39, 83–84,
153, 174–175, 211–212
Digital City (AOL), 123
digital distribution
of books, 151–152
of music, 105–106
of software, 264–265
Direct Hit, 196
direct mail marketing, 67
direct response advertising, 67
Disney, 43, 51. *See also* Go Network
Disney.com (Go Network), 184
distribution, alliances for. *See* strategic
partnerships
Dorros, Arielle, 67, 68
Draper, Timothy, 197
drkoop.com, 186
Drugstore.com, 223
DSL (digital subscriber line), 191

early mover advantage. *See* development, pace of; innovation
eBay, 54, 240, 249, 254–256
ecommerce, global projections for, 2
Edwards, Karen, 157, 159, 162–167, 169,
170, 175, 176, 177, 185
Egghead.com, 6, 146, 232–234,
246–247. *See also* Onsale
Electra (Oxygen Online site), 51
Electric Minds, 32

electronic books, 151–152
Elliot Bay Book Company (Seattle,
WA), 145
email marketing
by Amazon.com, 127
by Barnesandnoble.com, 127, 132,
135
by CDNOW, 76–77
email newsletters, 76–77
Enliven (Excite@Home), 115
Entertainment Asylum (AOL), 123
Entertainment channel (Tripod), 96
Entertainment Connection, 101, 108
entrepreneur.com, 235
Epicurious Food (CondéNet site), 50
Epicurious Travel (CondéNet site),
50
ESPN.com (Go Network), 184
ESPN SportsZone, 212, 223–224
eToys, 145–146
E-TRADE, 92, 191, 202
Euromonitor, 148
Evans, Nancy, 15, 19, 31
Excite
advertising by, 191–192
advertising on, 235
brand awareness of, 189
celebrity endorsement of, 71–72
"mo factor" on, 9
searching on, 24, 178, 192–193
strategic partners of, 38, 193
Excite@Home
Amazon.com's alliance with, 143
brand awareness of, 191–192
development of, 199–200
Enliven technology, 115
Expedia (MSN), 193
Express Lane (Barnesandnoble.com),
129, 132
Eyes (Barnesandnoble.com), 127

Fahle, Rich, 135
FairMarket, 263
Family.com (Go Network), 184
Farrace, Mike, 100
fastcompany.com, 235
Fast Forward Rewards program
(CDNOW), 78–79, 95

Fatbrain.com, 145
Filo, David, 153, 158–159, 161, 178, 203
Financial Times, 66
Fitness and Beauty (iVillage site), 37
Fitness Online, 27
flamenco-world.com, 99
focus groups, 177, 241–242
Fogdog Sports
    affiliate network of, 210–211, 225, 227–228
    brand assets of, 207, 208–215
    brand awareness of, 208, 215–217
    competition of, 207, 220–225, 227–228
    cultivating reputation of, 208–209, 213–215
    customer loyalty to, 217–218
    customer service on, 214–215
    description of, 5–6, 207
    development of, 205–208
    development pace of, 10, 211–212
    fulfillment on, 208, 219–220
    future of, 226–229
    goals (business concept, mission, theme) of, 206–208
    international sales on, 228
    investors of, 206, 207
    major milestones of, 207
    market research by, 212–213
    problems of, 215–220
    product selection on, 218–219, 228–229
    profitability of, 207
    repeat purchase rate on, 217
    returns policy on, 215
    strategic partners of, 207, 209–211
    supplemental content of, 219
    target market of, 226–227
Forrester Research, 39, 75, 150, 175, 186, 210
Frequently Asked Questions (FAQs), 42
Friedensohn, David, 82

Gap, 5, 13, 131, 133, 139
gap.com (Gap), 13, 131, 133, 137, 139
Gartner Group, 151

Gear.com, 223, 225, 226
GeoCities
    development of, 21
    strategic partners of, 81–82, 143
    use of volunteers on, 58
getmusic.com (BMG and Universal Music), 101–102
Gigabuys.com (Dell), 261
Glaxo Wellcome, 41
Global Sports, Inc., 221–222
GO, 231
GO.com (Disney), 44, 184, 195
Go Network (Disney), 44, 174, 184
Google, 190, 196–197
GoTo.com, 179, 190, 197
Graves, Hillary, 24, 25, 26, 27
Greenberg, Gregg, 30
Greer, Martha, 238, 243, 244
GTE, 200
guerrilla marketing
    by AOL, 167
    by eBay, 255
    by Fogdog Sports, 217
    by iVillage, 25, 33
    strategies for, 8
    by Yahoo!, 166–167
Guterman, Jimmy, 151

Hagel, John, III, 38
Hampel/Stefanides (ad agency), 70, 72
Hardie, Mark, 84, 99
Harmon, Steve, 178–179
HARPO Entertainment Group, 51, 122
Harrington, Tim, 209
Healthrider, 224
Herman's World of Sports, 221
Hewlett, Bill, 203
Hewlett-Packard, 203
high-speed Internet access, 199–200
Hindman, Joanne, 45
Hodgson, Michael, 214
HomeArts Network (Hearst Corporation), 47–49
HotBot (search engine), 124, 174, 179, 235
HotMail (MSN), 42, 193
Hummer, John, 253

iBaby (iVillage), 54, 55
IBM, 190
Imagine Radio (Viacom), 103
iMaternity.com (iVillage), 59
Infoseek (Disney), 44, 178, 194, 195,
   198–199
InfoSpace, 26
Ingram Book Group (distributors), 130,
   147
initial public offering (IPO)
   of Barnesandnoble.com, 110–112,
     134
   of iVillage, 46, 47
innovation
   on CDNOW, 83–84
   on Fogdog Sports, 10, 211–212
   on iVillage, 38–39
   on Onsale, 241
   on Yahoo!, 10, 153, 174–175
instant messaging, 184. *See also* Yahoo!
   Messenger
InsWeb, 171
Intel, 164
Interactive Bureau (Web designers), 126
Interactive Pregnancy Calendar (iVillage tool), 35
Intermarket Group, 70
international sales
   on Amazon.com, 149
   on Barnesandnoble.com, 148–149
   on Fogdog Sports, 228
   on Yahoo!, 190, 195–196
Internet. *See* World Wide Web
Internet broadcasting, 103
Internet Explorer (Microsoft), 193
Intuit, 22, 37–38, 191
IN2 (ad agency), 26
i-traffic (ad agency), 67–68, 69
IUMA (Internet Underground Music
   Archive), 67
iVillage (The Women's Network)
   advertisers on, 56–57
   brand assets of, 17, 18–43
   brand awareness of, 19–30
   community on, 16, 17, 19–20, 26,
     30–33
   competition of, 17, 32, 47–56

cultivating reputation of, 42–43
customer loyalty to, 4, 9, 15, 18,
   34
customer service on, 42–43
description of, 3–4, 17, 194
development of, 16–18
development pace of, 38–39
founding of, 15–16
future of, 56–59
goals (business concept, mission,
   theme) of, 16, 17, 19–20, 26
investors in, 17, 23
IPO of, 46, 47
major milestones on, 17
market research by, 11, 39–41
personnel turnover of, 18, 45–46
problems of, 16–18, 43–47
profitability of, 17, 18, 46–47
strategic partners of, 10, 17, 18–19,
   22, 27, 30, 34–38, 51–52
use of volunteers on, 33, 57–58
volume of traffic and membership
   on, 16, 23, 32, 34

Jazz Central Station (N2K), 74
Jupiter Communications, 36, 39, 100,
   106, 187, 232

Kaplan, Jerry, 231, 232–234, 236, 237,
   239, 247, 251, 253
Kay, Roger, 259
Keane, Patrick, 30, 81, 183, 193–194
Kelleher, Matt, 130
Kenner, Todd, 45
Koogle, Tim, 141, 161
Kraus, Joe, 168
Kricfalusi, John, 68

latimes.com (*Los Angeles Times*), 114
Laybourne, Geraldine, 50–51
Lenk, Toby, 253
Levitan, Robert, 36, 45
Levy, Jeff, 168
Logan, Don, 194
LookSmart (Looksmart.com), 189,
   195
Lot21 (ad agency), 235

Lucent Technologies, corporate intranet of, 125

Lycos
  banner advertising on, 27
  development of, 174
  music broadcasting on, 103
  searching on, 24
  strategic partnerships with, 37, 52
Lycos Radio Network (Lycos), 103
Lyons, Jed, 130

MacColl, MacDara, 19, 32, 39, 43
Mallet, Jeff, 161, 175, 200, 202
Marino, Craig, 94
marketing. *See also* advertising; public relations
  offline
    by Barnesandnoble.com, 116–119
    by CDNOW, 70–75
    by iVillage, 27–30
    by Yahoo!, 163–167
  online
    by Barnesandnoble.com, 114–116
    by CDNOW, 66–69
    by iVillage, 24–27
    by Onsale, 235–236
    by Yahoo!, 185–186
  return on investment (ROI) of, 25
Marketplace (NPR), 167
market research
  by Barnesandnoble.com, 11, 126–128
  by CDNOW, 84–87
  focus on, 10–11
  by Fogdog Sports, 212–213
  by iVillage, 11, 39–41
  by Onsale, 241–243
  by Yahoo!, 175–178, 187
Martha Stewart Living Omnimedia, 47, 52–54
mass market. *See* customers
McCadden, Michael, 131
McCain, Ken, 96
MC Sports, 222
Media Metrix, 86, 177
Media Week, 29
microsegmentation, of markets, 82

Microsoft
  brand awareness of, 189
  corporate intranet of, 125
  organization structure of, 204
  strategic partners of, 147
Microsoft Network (MSN), 193
Middleberg Associates (PR agency), 25–26, 65
Miller, Matthew, 145
Minor, Halsey, 183, 194
Mittner, Greta, 46
Modem Media/Poppe Tyson (ad agency), 25–26, 192
"mo (momentum) factor"
  on CDNOW, 66
  defined, 9
  on iVillage, 23
  on Yahoo!, 162
Moms Online (Oxygen Online site), 51
Mooradian, Mark, 174
Moritz, Michael, 154, 157, 198
Mosaic (Web browser), 153
Mountain Gear, 209
MP3 music compression, 105–106
Mrkonic, George, 144
Mr. Showbiz (Go Network), 184
MSN. *See* Microsoft Network (MSN)
MSNBC.com, 114, 193
MTV Networks, 73–74, 80, 101, 107
multicultural issues, in Barnesand-noble.com/Bertlesmann alliance, 140–141
multilingual issues, on CDNOW, 90
Music Boulevard (N2K), 74
music (record) clubs, 93, 94–95
music sales. *See* Amazon.com; Barnes-andnoble.com; CDNOW
MXGonline.com, 107
My CDNOW (CDNOW tool), 78
MyExcite (Excite), 192
MySimon, 104
MyYahoo! (Yahoo!), 168, 172–173, 198

National Geographic Traveler, 180
natural language searching, defined, 196
Netcentives, 79

NetFind (AOL search engine), 143
Net Perceptions, 77
Netscape
strategic partners of, 48, 143, 174
volume of traffic on, 193
Netscape Navigator (Web browser), 174
Netscape Netcenter, 174
network effect, defined, 254–255
newsgroups. *See* Usenet newsgroups
newsletters. *See* email newsletters
Newsweek magazine, 22, 128, 255
New York Times Book Review, 118, 119, 134
New York Times on the Web, 114, 121, 123–124
nexus laws, 136
NFO Research, 163
Niehaus Ryan Wong (NRW, PR firm), 157–159, 161
Nielsen/NetRatings, 86
Nicmira, Michael, 261
Nike, 213, 225
Noglows, Paul, 201–202
NPD group, study by, 167
N2K, 62, 74, 94, 95, 96

O'Donnell, Rosie, 27
OEM (original equipment manufacturer) deals, 190
offline advertising. *See* advertising, offline
offline marketing. *See* marketing, offline
Olenick, Michael, 35
Olim, Jason, 61, 65, 74, 75, 76, 83, 84, 89, 95, 96, 104
Olim, Matthew, 61
O'Neill, Molly, 53
one-to-one marketing, 77
online advertising. *See* advertising, online
Online Anywhere, 173–174
online marketing. *See* marketing, online
Onsale (Egghead.com)
brand assets of, 233, 234–246
brand awareness of, 235–236
competition of, 232, 233, 252–262
cross-selling on, 236

cultivating reputation of, 11, 243–245
customer loyalty to, 237–238
customer service on, 245, 263
description of, 6, 233
development of, 231–234
development pace of, 241
future of, 262–265
goals (business concept, mission, theme) of, 233
investors of, 233
major milestones of, 233
market research by, 241–243
organizational structure of, 250–251
problems of, 234, 246–252
product diversity on, 226–227, 239, 251–252
profitability of, 232–234, 262
public relations on, 9
repeat purchase rate on, 217, 237
strategic partners of, 193, 233, 235, 238–241
target market of, 236
value of, 246
Onsale @ Auction, 232, 235, 237, 250
Onsale @ Cost, 232, 235, 237, 244, 247, 250
Onsale Exchange (Onsale), 240
Oprah's Book Club, 122, 129, 134
Orban, George, 251
Orelli, Tony, 115
Organic Online (ad agency), 114–115, 126–127
outdoor advertising
by Amazon.com, 257
by Barnesandnoble.com, 119
Outpost.com (Cyberian Outpost), 246, 247, 252–253
Overdrive Sports, 222
Oxygen Media (Oxygen Online), 38, 47, 50–52

Packard, David, 203
Packard, Warren, 211
Packard Bell, 190

PageNet, 173
Pareles, Jon, 106
Parent Soup (iVillage site), 4, 15, 16, 26, 31, 34, 43
Parker, Rod, 66, 67, 69, 77, 80, 87
Parr, Barry, 168–169, 200
Pathfinder (Time Warner), 4, 194
PC Connection, 258–259, 263
pcOrder.com, 244
People magazine, 118, 119, 159, 255
Peppers, Don, 77
Perlmutter, Kevin, 71
personalization
    on Barnesandnoble.com, 120
    on CDNOW, 78
    on Excite, 192
    on Fogdog Sports, 217–218
    purpose of, 78
    on Yahoo!, 168, 172–173, 198
Peters, Barry, 246, 247
Peterson's Education Center, 172
Pets.com, 223
Phoenix Technologies, 173
Phys (CondéNet site), 50
Piller, Charles, 149, 151
Pittman, Bob, 191
PlanetOut, 21, 32
Playboy.com (Playboy Enterprises), 131, 133, 139
Playboy Enterprises, 5, 131, 133, 139
PointCast, 115
Polaroid, 29
Polygram Records, 101
Popularity Engine (Direct Hit tool), 196
portal sites. *See also* vertical portals; *names of specific portals*
    customer retention on, 168–169
    development of, 68
    differentiation of, 183–185
    strategic partnerships with, 37, 80–81, 143
    volume of traffic on, 186
Powell's Books (Portland, OR), 145
print advertising
    by Barnesandnoble.com, 118–119
    by CDNOW, 70
    by iVillage, 28–29

by Onsale, 247
by Yahoo!, 166
profitability
    of Amazon.com, 47
    of Barnesandnoble.com, 111, 138, 146
    of CDNOW, 63, 75
    of Fogdog Sports, 207
    of iVillage, 17, 18, 46–47
    of Onsale, 232–234, 262
    of Web brands, 3
    of Yahoo!, 3, 5, 155, 161
Pruett, Scott, 175
psychographic profiles, defined, 114–115
public relations
    by Amazon.com, 142
    by Barnesandnoble.com, 138–141
    by CDNOW, 65–66
    by Fogdog Sports, 216
    by iVillage, 20–24
    by Lycos, 162
    by Onsale, 241, 249–250
    purpose of, 8, 9, 65
    by Yahoo!, 142, 157–163
Publisher's Weekly, 122

Quicken.com, 38

radio advertising
    by Amazon.com, 257
    by Barnesandnoble.com, 117–118
    by CDNOW, 66, 70–72
    by eBay, 255
    by Fogdog Sports, 216
    by iVillage, 29
    by Onsale, 247
    by Yahoo!, 165
Rappaport, Ron, 199
RedRocket (Simon & Schuster), 36
REI (sporting goods retailer), 217, 220–221
Reicheld, Frederick, 75
Reid, Robert, 176
relationship marketing. *See* one-to-one marketing
Relationships channel (iVillage site), 16
reputation
    of Barnesandnoble.com, 128–133

of CDNOW, 87–91
of Fogdog Sports, 208–209,
    213–215
of iVillage, 42–43
of Onsale, 11, 243–245
strategies for cultivating, 11
of Yahoo!, 11, 178–182
return on investment (ROI)
    of advertising efforts, 186–187, 247
    of marketing efforts, 25
reward programs, on CDNOW, 78–79
Rheingold, Howard, 32
Rielly, Tom, 32
Riggio, Leonard, 109, 135, 140
Riggio, Stephen (Steve), 123, 132
RocketCash, 107
Rocket eBook, 151
Rocktropolis (N2K), 74
Rogers, Martha, 77
Rogers, Tom, 30
Rolling Stone, 65, 70, 79, 159
RollingStone.com, 101
Romary, Tom, 206, 210, 212, 213, 215,
    226
Rubin, Fred, 127, 137
runnersworld.com, 216
Running Network, 211
Rushkoff, Douglas, 22

sales tax issues, 136–138, 139
Schilling, Chuck, 40
Schwartz, Larry, 257
search engines. See also bots; names of
    specific search engines
    coverage of, 1
    development of, 129, 196–197
    keyword buys on, 67–68
    seeding of, 24
Secure Digital Music Initiative (SDMI),
    106
Sequoia Capital, 154
Sharper Image, 189
Sherman, Cary, 106
Simons, David, 141
Simpson, Blaise, 157, 159, 160
Smith, Buford, 131, 139
Smith, Jack, 222
Smith & Hawken, 189

Snap (NBC), 154, 189, 194, 195, 198
software bundling, 190
SonicNet, 82
Sony, 178
spiders, defined, 178
Spin, 70, 101
Spinner.com (AOL), 103
sponsorships
    by CDNOW, 69, 70
    by Fogdog Sports, 217
    by Yahoo!, 166–167, 175, 188
Sport Chalet, 222
sporting goods industry. See Fogdog
    Sports
Sporting Goods Intelligence, 216
Sporting Goods Manufacturers Associa-
    tion (SGMA), 206, 212
Sports & Recreation (sporting goods re-
    tailer), 222
Sports Authority, 222, 227
Sportscape, 212
Sports Illustrated, 166
Sportsite.com, 206, 212
Sports N' More, 222
Sports Superstore Online, 222
Spumco.com, 68–69
Starbucks, 29
Starmedia, 196
Stell, Jason, 20, 23
Stern, Howard, 70–72
stickiness, defined, 169
Stites, Janet, 94
StorkSite (Women.com), 48
strategic partnerships (alliances)
    of Amazon.com, 36, 178
    of AOL, 10, 16, 51–52, 122–123, 143,
        147, 210, 240, 255
    of Barnesandnoble.com, 110, 111,
        112, 121–126, 138–141, 147
    of CDNOW, 63, 73–74, 79–83,
        100–101
    of Excite, 38, 193
    of Fogdog Sports, 207, 209–211
    of GeoCities, 81–82, 143
    of iVillage, 10, 17, 18–19, 22, 27, 30,
        34–38, 51–52
    of Lycos, 37, 52
    of Microsoft, 147

strategic partnerships (alliances)
    (*continued*)
  of Netscape, 48, 143, 174
  of Onsale (Egghead.com), 193, 233,
    235, 238–241
  purpose of, 10
  of Yahoo!, 155, 171–174, 180–181,
    201, 240
Sullivan, Danny, 24
Surplus Direct, 250
Swerdlow, Fiona, 241
Swoon (CondéNet site), 50

Tattered Cover (Denver, CO), 145
Taulli, Tom, 47
TBWA/Chiat/Day (ad agency), 116, 117,
    118, 119, 127
TCI, 51
Tedeschi, Bob, 92
television advertising
  by Barnesandnoble.com, 116–117
  by CDNOW, 66, 70, 73–74
  cost of, 92, 175
  by Fogdog Sports, 216
  by iVillage, 29, 30
  by Yahoo!, 163–165, 175
Telmex, 196
Thrive (Oxygen Online site),
    51
Time magazine, 119, 158
Tower Records, 99, 146
Trevor, Bob, 85, 89
Tripod, 21, 96–97
TSI Soccer, 209
TV advertising. *See* television advertis-
    ing
Tylenol scare, 179–180

uBid, 232, 254
U.K. Plus (Daily Mail & General Trust),
    196
Universal Music, 101–102
usability testing, 39, 86, 242–243
Usenet newsgroups, 24–25

Valley Records (distributors), 91, 102,
    147, 225

value equation
  and Barnesandnoble.com, 11, 114,
    133–134
  defined, 11, 133
  and Onsale, 246
  and Yahoo!, 11, 182–183
Vanderbilt, Nicole, 123, 125, 142
Veronis Suhler (investment bankers),
    148
vertical portals, 154, 189, 193–194
Virgin Megastores, 99–100, 146
viruses, 180
Visa, 178, 180
Vogtle, James, 187
volunteers
  on AOL, 33, 57
  on GeoCities, 58
  on iVillage, 33, 57–58

Waggener Edstrom (PR firm), 142
Waldenbooks, 144
Wall of Sound (Go Network), 184
Wall Street Journal, 28, 145, 162
Wal-Mart, 260–261
Warner Brothers, 27
Web. *See* World Wide Web
WebAuction, 232, 254
WebTV, 108
Weintraut, J. Neil, 83, 253
Weiss, Stagliano and Partners (ad
    agency), 116, 117, 118
Whitman, Meg, 256
Williams, Andrea, 199
Winfrey, Oprah, 51, 122, 129, 134
Wired Digital, 124
Wired magazine, 124
Women.com Networks, 47–50, 210
Women's Channel (Lycos), 37
Women's Wire (Women.com), 28, 47,
    48, 49
World Wide Web (WWW)
  advertising on, 2
  branding on, 2
  commercial debut of, 1
  confusion for users of, 1
  customer loyalty on, 1–2, 8–10
  demographics of, 20, 28, 36

entry to, 1
flexibility of, 73
key metrics about, 86, 177
origins of, 1
pace of change on, 1, 23–24, 40, 73, 154
personalization of, 78
size of, 1
URLs of major companies, 269–271

Xoom.com, 46

Yahoo!
    advertising on, 187, 188, 235
    Amazon.com's alliance with, 143
    brand assets of, 155, 156–183
    brand awareness of, 157–167, 197–198
    CDNOW's alliance with, 80–81
    competition of, 155, 189–190
    cross-selling on, 170
    cultivating reputation of, 11, 178–182
    customer loyalty to, 167–170, 197–198
    customer service on, 176, 181–182
    description of, 5, 155
    development of, 153–154, 158
    development pace on, 10, 153, 174–175
    executive compensation of, 141
    expansion of, 202–204
    future of, 198–204
    goals (business concept, mission, theme) of, 155
    international sales on, 190, 195–196
    investors of, 154, 155
    major milestones of, 155
    market research by, 175–178, 187
    problems of, 154–156, 183–189

    profitability of, 3, 5, 155, 161
    size of customer base of, 154, 178
    strategic partners of, 155, 171–174, 180–181, 201, 240
    strength of, 3, 5, 44
    subscription services on, 201–202
    supplemental services of, 168, 169
    value of, 11, 182–183
Yahoo! Auctions (Yahoo!), 240
Yahoo! Birthday Club (Yahoo!), 187
Yahoo! Calendar (Yahoo!), 184, 186
Yahoo! Chat (Yahoo!), 80, 165, 169, 184
Yahoo! Clubs (Yahoo!), 168, 169–170
Yahoo! College Search (Yahoo!), 172
Yahoo! Computers (Yahoo!), 180, 240
"Yahoo! Everywhere" campaign, 173–174
Yahoo! Finance (Yahoo!), 165–166, 170, 186, 202
Yahoo! Insurance Center (Yahoo!), 171
Yahooligans! (Yahoo!), 74, 159
Yahoo! Mail (Yahoo!), 80, 170, 180, 186, 198
Yahoo! Messenger (Yahoo!), 170, 181, 184, 186
Yahoomobile, 167
Yahoo! Shopping (Yahoo!), 102, 146, 175, 188–189, 201
Yahoo! Shopping Guide (Yahoo!), 180
Yahoo! Sports (Yahoo!), 175
Yahoo! Traffic (Yahoo!), 184
Yahoo! Travel (Yahoo!), 159, 165, 180
Yahoo! Turbo (Yahoo!), 200
Yang, Jerry, 153, 158–159, 161, 178, 203
Yanowitch, Wendy, 181
Yost, John, 163, 165, 170

Zanca, Bruce, 58
ZDNet, 180
zero-margin sales, 253
Zoda, Marlo, 65

About the Author

Phil Carpenter is Director of Marketing for Critical Path, a global provider of Internet messaging and collaboration solutions. Prior to joining Critical Path, he served as Director of Corporate Marketing for RemarQ, which was acquired by Critical Path in January 2000. He has also held marketing management roles at PointCast, Intuit, and Mozart Systems and has served as Senior Consultant for the McKenna Group, the consulting practice founded by technology marketer Regis McKenna. Phil received an M.B.A. from the Harvard Business School and a B.A. from Stanford University.

A frequent contributor to management and technology journals, Carpenter has written articles for more than two dozen different publications in the United States, the United Kingdom, Canada, and Japan. From 1995 to 1997, Phil was a regular columnist for *Marketing Computers* magazine. He was also the coauthor of *Marketing Yourself to the Top Business Schools*, published in 1995 by John Wiley & Sons.

Carpenter lives in the San Francisco Bay Area with his wife, Carol, and daughter, Jessica.

You can reach him by email at philipcarpenter@hotmail.com.